THE RIVERMEN

THE OLD WEST

THE RIVERMEN

By the Editors of

TIME-LIFE BOOKS

with text by

Paul O'Neil

TIME-LIFE BOOKS / ALEXANDRIA, VIRGINIA

Time-Life Books Inc.
is a wholly owned subsidiary of

TIME INCORPORATED

Founder: Henry R. Luce 1898-1967

Editor-in-Chief: Henry Anatole Grunwald
President: J. Richard Munro
Chairman of the Board: Ralph P. Davidson
Executive Vice President: Clifford J. Grum
Chairman, Executive Committee: James R. Shepley
Editorial Director: Ralph Graves
Group Vice President, Books: Joan D. Manley
Vice Chairman: Arthur Temple

TIME-LIFE BOOKS INC.

Managing Editor: Jerry Korn
Text Director: George Constable
Board of Editors: Dale M. Brown, George G. Daniels,
Thomas H. Flaherty Jr., Martin Mann, Philip W. Payne,
Gerry Schremp, Gerald Simons
Planning Director: Edward Brash
Art Director: Tom Suzuki
  Assistant: Arnold C. Holeywell
Director of Administration: David L. Harrison
Director of Operations: Gennaro C. Esposito
Director of Research: Carolyn L. Sackett
  Assistant: Phyllis K. Wise
Director of Photography: Dolores A. Littles

Chairman: John D. McSweeney
President: Carl G. Jaeger
Executive Vice Presidents: John Steven Maxwell,
David J. Walsh
Vice Presidents: George Artandi, Stephen L. Bair, Peter G.
Barnes, Nicholas Benton, John L. Canova, Beatrice T. Dobie,
Carol Flaumenhaft, James L. Mercer, Herbert Sorkin,
Paul R. Stewart

THE OLD WEST

EDITORIAL STAFF FOR "THE RIVERMEN"
Editor: George Constable
Picture Editors: Jean Tennant, Mary Y. Steinbauer
Text Editor: Valerie Moolman
Designers: Herbert H. Quarmby, Bruce Blair
Staff Writers: Lee Greene, Kirk Landers,
Robert Tschirky, Eve Wengler
Chief Researcher: June O. Goldberg
Researchers: Jane Jordan, Nancy Miller, Loretta Britten,
Jane Coughran, Thomas Dickey, Denise Lynch,
Vivian Stephens, John Conrad Weiser
Design Assistant: Faye Eng
Copy Coordinators: Barbara H. Fuller, Gregory Weed
Picture Coordinators: Marianne Dowell, Susan Spiller
Editorial Assistant: Lisa Berger

EDITORIAL OPERATIONS
Production Director: Feliciano Madrid
  Assistants: Peter A. Inchauteguiz, Karen A. Meyerson
Copy Processing: Gordon E. Buck
Quality Control Director: Robert L. Young
  Assistant: James J. Cox
  Associates: Daniel J. McSweeney, Michael G. Wight
Art Coordinator: Anne B. Landry
Copy Room Director: Susan B. Galloway
  Assistants: Celia Beattie, Ricki Tarlow

THE AUTHOR: Paul O'Neil got a first-hand taste of steamboating in the 1930s when, as a collegian, he worked summers aboard Alaska Steamship Company vessels shuttling goods and passengers between Seattle and Alaskan ports. After spending more than a decade as a Seattle newspaperman, he moved to New York in 1944 where he was successively a staff writer for TIME, SPORTS ILLUSTRATED and LIFE before becoming a fulltime freelance in 1973. Since then, he has contributed to special issues of LIFE, to *Atlantic* magazine, and has devoted much time to the research and writing of this and other TIME-LIFE books.

THE COVER: The insouciant spirit that early became part of workaday life along the Missouri River was captured by George Caleb Bingham in his 1847 painting, *Lighter Relieving a Steamboat Aground.* One of a series of such idyllic scenes by the artist, who grew up in the river towns of central Missouri, it records a crew of bargemen at ease after removing cargo from the stranded steamer upstream. The frontispiece sketch of a buckskin-garbed riverman at the helm of a flat-bottomed boat was drawn by youthful New York artist William Cary during one of his two extended Missouri voyages, in 1861 and 1874. Cary brought back sketchbooks so crammed with rich detail that he used them during the rest of his 30-year career as a magazine illustrator.

CORRESPONDENTS: Elisabeth Kraemer (Bonn); Margot Hapgood, Dorothy Bacon, Lesley Coleman (London); Susan Jonas, Lucy T. Voulgaris (New York); Maria Vincenza Aloisi, Josephine du Brusle (Paris); Ann Natanson (Rome).

Other Publications:

PLANET EARTH
COLLECTOR'S LIBRARY OF THE CIVIL WAR
LIBRARY OF HEALTH
CLASSICS OF THE OLD WEST
THE EPIC OF FLIGHT
THE GOOD COOK
THE SEAFARERS
THE ENCYCLOPEDIA OF COLLECTIBLES
THE GREAT CITIES
WORLD WAR II
HOME REPAIR AND IMPROVEMENT
THE WORLD'S WILD PLACES
THE TIME-LIFE LIBRARY OF BOATING
HUMAN BEHAVIOR
THE ART OF SEWING
THE EMERGENCE OF MAN
THE AMERICAN WILDERNESS
THE TIME-LIFE ENCYCLOPEDIA OF GARDENING
LIFE LIBRARY OF PHOTOGRAPHY
THIS FABULOUS CENTURY
FOODS OF THE WORLD
TIME-LIFE LIBRARY OF AMERICA
TIME-LIFE LIBRARY OF ART
GREAT AGES OF MAN
LIFE SCIENCE LIBRARY
THE LIFE HISTORY OF THE UNITED STATES
TIME READING PROGRAM
LIFE NATURE LIBRARY
LIFE WORLD LIBRARY
FAMILY LIBRARY:
  HOW THINGS WORK IN YOUR HOME
  THE TIME-LIFE BOOK OF THE FAMILY CAR
  THE TIME-LIFE FAMILY LEGAL GUIDE
  THE TIME-LIFE BOOK OF FAMILY FINANCE

*This volume is one of a series that
chronicles the history of the American West
from the early 16th Century to the end of
the 19th Century.*

For information about any Time-Life book, please write:
Reader Information
Time-Life Books
541 North Fairbanks Court
Chicago, Illinois 60611

Library of Congress Cataloguing in Publication Data
Time-Life Books.
  The rivermen/by the editors of Time-Life Books; with text by
Paul O'Neil.—New York: Time-Life Books, c1975.
  240 p.: ill. (some col.); 28 cm.—(The Old west)
  Bibliography: p. 236-237.
  Includes index.
  1. Inland navigation—United States—History. 2. River boats—
United States—History. 3. The West—History.
I. O'Neil, Paul, 1909-   II. Title.
III. Series: The Old West (Alexandria, Va.)
HE627.T54   1975   386'.0973   75-7913
ISBN 0-8094-1498-8
ISBN 0-8094-1497-x lib. bdg.
ISBN 0-8094-1496-1 retail ed.

CONTENTS

High-chimneyed paddle wheelers crowd the St. Louis levee in the 1850s, when steamboating was beginning to hit its stride.

1 | A 3,000-mile waterway west

"A great spiral staircase to the Rockies" was one 19th Century traveler's memorable metaphor for the Missouri, whose tortuous bends led canoeists, keelboaters and eventually steamboatmen from the Mississippi all the way to Fort Benton, Montana—nearly half a mile above sea level and 3,000 miles from the river's mouth.

For generations of explorers and exploiters, the Missouri was the key to the West. It excited the imaginations of 16th Century geographers as a possible avenue to the Orient; later, it provided access to the fur riches that drew the first frontiersmen into the wilderness; and after the Civil War, it conveyed thousands of prospectors to Rocky Mountain gold.

The river's orneriness matched its promises. "The broad current," wrote journalist Albert Richardson in 1857, "is unpoetic and repulsive—a stream of flowing mud studded with dead tree trunks and broken by bars." Yet hundreds of steamboats ran this gauntlet to earn profits that might repay the vessel's entire cost in a single voyage.

Eventually technology overtook the rivermen. Beginning in 1859, railroads began to intersect the Missouri, siphoning off water-borne traffic. By 1890, when the last packet boat departed from the deserted levee at Fort Benton, the only reminders of the steamboat's glory days were river bends with names like Malta, Sultan, Diana and Kate Sweeney—each honoring one of the Big Muddy's paddle-wheeled victims.

The Missouri River constantly challenged pilots by shifting its course within the confines of steep bluffs. In this stretch east of Fort Benton, the river has retreated *(at right)* from the flank of the main trough to form a narrow channel — further constricted by the treacherous sand bar at the left.

Flat-bottomed Mackinaws—like the heavily laden *Last Chance,* about to leave Fort Benton in 1878—provided a cheap alternative to the steamboat for downriver-bound passengers and cargo. After the one-way journey, the makeshift craft were usually ripped apart and sold as lumber.

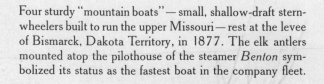

Four sturdy "mountain boats" — small, shallow-draft stern-wheelers built to run the upper Missouri — rest at the levee of Bismarck, Dakota Territory, in 1877. The elk antlers mounted atop the pilothouse of the steamer *Benton* symbolized its status as the fastest boat in the company fleet.

13

The ramshackle boomtown of Fort Benton, farthest navigable point on the Missouri, appears deceptively sleepy during a low-water spell in 1868. When the river was high, as many as seven steamboats a day might dock to unload cargo for overland conveyance to the Montana gold camps.

Beleaguered voyagers on the Big Muddy

"This night," wrote Nelson Green Edwards, bending by candlelight over a sheet of yellow foolscap, "early Squads of Indians are seen in the High Grass and on the Sides of the Big Hills . . . Lurking & Prowling in a very suspicious manner as if they meditated an attack before morning." Such displays of furtive hostility were not new to the unsettled West by this spring evening of 1869; but the writer had a vantage point far different from that of the wagoneers, cavalrymen, trappers and miners who had encountered the dangers earlier. Edwards, then just 19, was a riverman —the second (or mud) clerk of the Montana-bound Missouri River steamboat *Henry M. Shreve*—and his diary reflected the West as it looked to men who crossed the prairies on the waters of the Big Muddy rather than by land.

Indians seemed like pirates when seen from a boiler deck, and *Shreve*'s crew prepared to repel boarders after anchoring offshore for the night: "24 Musketts was loaded & Caped & Stacked in their Racks. The Brass Howitzer was got in readyness & Loaded with a Shell & Given in Command of John Dynan the Carpenter. Some 8 or 10 in the Cabin & as many more on Deck Stood Guard all night with their Armes all loaded & ready for an attack. Our Fource could have fired 100 guns in 5 minutes."

This communal belligerency had its effect. "There was considerable Stir & Commotion on Board all night but the thing passed off quietly," Edwards noted, "and no blood was spilt on either side." Still, the steamer had been in real danger; and she was only one of hundreds of vessels and Edwards only one of thousands of rivermen who ascended the Missouri—a 3,000-mile conduit linking St. Louis with the Rockies—during the era of western expansion. Most Americans have been left with the impression that the West was opened almost solely by 1) wagon trains and 2) the railroads, but a prairie schooner carried little cargo and the Iron Horse, for all its final dominance, did not reach the northern Continental Divide until the late 1880s. When weighed in conjunction with its network of westward-reaching tributaries, the Missouri River was, for almost a century, the most important single means of entree into the whole wild and empty subcontinent that lay between the Mississippi and the Pacific Ocean. It was a river that, more than most, meant different things to voyagers in different stratums of time. Men followed it in search of a water route to the Pacific Ocean, mythical kingdoms, furs, precious metals, homesteads, fortunes, adventure and glory.

The Missouri was not, by any means, the only stream that served as a road and channel of commerce for explorers and those who followed them. Rivermen penetrated Louisiana on the Red River of the South and into Oklahoma on the Arkansas; they moved into Iowa on the Des Moines River. The Army used Colorado River steamboats to supply posts in the burning southwestern desert; gold seekers traveled California's Sacramento and San Joaquin rivers in search of the mother lode and rode paddle steamers up the Columbia on their way to new diggings in Idaho and Montana. But none of these matched the Big Muddy in size or geographical import; no other watershed but that of the Mississippi remotely approached its vastness, its wildness and its strategic role in American history of the 19th Century. Early witnesses to its might believed, indeed, that *it* was truly The Father of Waters and that it remained the main stream, after flowing into the Mississippi, which ran south to the Gulf of Mexico. It was

In the hotly competitive Missouri River trade, steamboat lines circulated departure cards like these in public places, hoping to win customers away from their rivals.

Unable to ford the river, trappers and their Indian helpers use a bullboat as a ferry. Such crude, short-haul craft, invented by Indians, were constructed by lashing water-soaked buffalo hides over a frame of willow saplings. The scene was recorded by artist Alfred Jacob Miller in the 1830s.

so celebrated in the old emigrant song: *To the West! To the West!/ To the land of the free!/ Where the mighty Missouri rolls down to the sea.*

It was the great watercourse of the prairies — and the longest river on the North American continent: a broad if changeable and dangerous stream which swept from sources on the Continental Divide to a junction with the Mississippi 23 miles north of St. Louis. It led the upstream traveler almost due west across the state of Missouri and then, turning sharply right at the Kansas border, ran north and northwest for almost a thousand miles, dividing Kansas from Missouri and Nebraska from Iowa, bisecting South Dakota and most of North Dakota. After that it headed off due west, roughly parallel with the Canadian border, into the distant reaches of Montana and, finally, traveled west-southwest in a crude and enormous elliptical curve that fetched up under the eastern wall of the Rocky Mountains.

Recklessness was the hallmark of the traveler on the Big Muddy — and of men who invaded the vast wilderness it embraced. The Missouri Valley cradled some of the most warlike of American Indians: Osages, Pawnees, Arikaras, band after band of Sioux, and finally, nearer the Rockies, Assiniboins and the implacable Blackfeet. And the great stream itself demanded hardihood from men who used it. "I have seen nothing more frightful," wrote the French Jesuit Jacques Marquette when he and his fellow explorer Louis Jolliet approached the point at which the Missouri — then at the height of its June rise in 1673 — poured its yellow flood into the Mississippi. "A mass of large trees enters with branches interlocked — a floating island. We could not, without great danger, expose ourselves to pass across."

The river rose twice a year. The first period of high water began in April when the spring rains and prairie snowmelt raised the levels of its tributaries, often drowning the main valley under endless vistas of hurrying brown water. The second rise occurred in either May or June when the sun began melting the snow fields of the Rockies. Thousands and thousands of uprooted trees, hung up on bars in low water, were released like javelins when the water level rose, and the river became charged with floating logs. Thousands more of the trees grew waterlogged, sank at the heavy root end, and hung in the river, some motionless, some rising and falling in the current forming a great, hidden abatis upon

Boatable passages through the wilderness

Though the Missouri River was regarded with fear and awe by early French explorers, American rivermen turned it into a broad road to riches, the main artery in a 12,000-mile network of ready-made pathways to the densest concentration of fur-bearing animals in North America. Yet this vast watershed was only one of many portals to the West and its incredible wealth. In all, more than 20,000 miles of rivers and tributaries lay between the Mississippi and the Pacific Ocean, and in one fashion or another the rivermen found ways to exploit these corridors.

Light-draft vessels like dugout canoes and bullboats were useful on the Platte and other shallow channels; large freighters such as the keelboat, flatboat and Mackinaw, capable of hauling 10 tons or more, plied the Yellowstone, the Missouri and other major waterways.

The steamboat joined the flotilla in 1819 when the Mississippi side-wheeler, introduced eight years before, appeared on the Missouri. Drawing six feet of water and seriously underpowered, the first steamers were largely limited to the deep lower river. Changes widening the beam and lessening the draft gradually extended the vessels' range on the upper river in the 1850s. Finally, in 1859, a true Missouri riverboat came into being—a powerfully engined stern-wheeler that could carry up to 350 tons, while drawing only 31 inches of water over the shallow, ever-shifting bars.

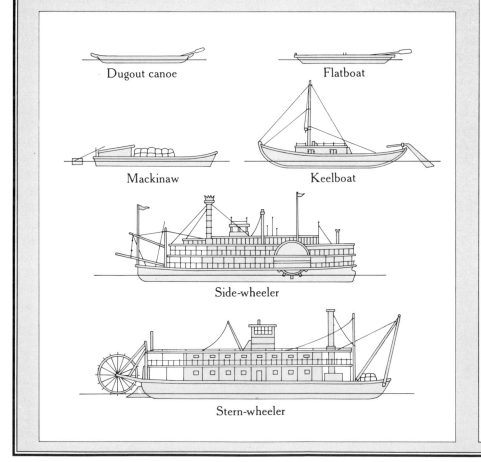

Dugout canoe

Flatboat

Mackinaw

Keelboat

Side-wheeler

Stern-wheeler

WASHINGTON TERRITORY

Columbia R.

Portland

The Dalles

OREGON

ID TER

Sacramento R.

San Joaquin R.

NEVADA

CALIFORNIA

A TER

PACIFIC OCEAN

MILES

0   100   200   300

LAKE
WINNIPEG

CANADA

Milk R.

Poplar R.

Fort Benton
Great Falls
Camp Cooke
DAUPHIN RAPIDS
Cow Island
MONTANA
TERRITORY
Fort Union
Fort Buford

Helena

Three Forks
BIG BELT MTS.
Musselshell R.
Yellowstone R.

POMPEYS
PILLAR

Fort Berthold
Fort Stevenson

Fort Abraham Lincoln
Bismarck
Fort Rice

ROCKY

Tongue R.
Powder R.
Grand R.

DAKOTA TERRITORY

MINNESOTA

LAKE SUPERIOR

MICHIGAN

LAKE MICHIGAN

BLACK HILLS
Cheyenne R.
Fort Pierre
Fort Sully
Fort
Thompson

WISCONSIN

Bighorn R.
BIG HORN MTS.

WYOMING
TERRITORY

Fort Randall
Yankton

Niobrara R.
Vermillion R.
Missouri R.

RY

Salt Lake City

North Platte R.

NEBRASKA

Sioux City

IOWA

Des Moines R.

UTAH
RITORY

Platte R.

Omaha
Council Bluffs

Nebraska City

ILLINOIS

INDIANA

Charlton R.

St. Joseph
Fort Leavenworth
Westport Landing

Independence
Lexington

St. Charles
St. Louis

Cincinnati

Louisville
FALLS OF THE OHIO

COLORADO
TERRITORY

Colorado R.

KANSAS

Jefferson City

Osage R.

MISSOURI

Ohio R.

KENTUCKY

TENNESSEE

RY

NEW MEXICO
TERRITORY

PUBLIC LAND

INDIAN
TERRITORY

ARKANSAS

MISS.

ALABAMA

Arkansas R.

Mississippi

Tennessee R.

Red R.

TEXAS

Natchez

MEXICO

Rio Grande

LOUISIANA

New Orleans

GULF OF MEXICO

which whole fleets of vessels might impale themselves.

Vast areas of the Missouri froze over in winter, and the first flood often littered itself with grinding floes. The open country through which the river passed was subject to tornadoes, violent thunderstorms, fierce gales and, along river bottoms, to sand storms as thick as those of the Sahara. Prairie fires could blister the paint of vessels that were forced close to the bank by the current. Dense clouds of mosquitoes, bred in the stagnant ponds of old meander channels, were a constant plague. And if a traveler happened to pitch camp ashore, he was likely to discover yet another peril; as one veteran riverman of the pre-steam era noted, "Travelers have often discovered that the bank was sinking, allowing little time to jump into the boat before the seemingly solid ground has vanished before their eyes."

The Missouri remained a critical route, nevertheless, for travelers going beyond the Mississippi. Its great northwestern arc not only led on to the Rockies, but enclosed an enormous system of tributaries; these streams — which watered more than half a million square miles of the Dakotas, Nebraska, Montana, Wyoming and Colorado — opened land routes to almost every other corner of the West. The longest and most usefully sited of the tributary trails lay along the Platte, which conducted the traveler 300 miles west across the grasslands of Nebraska and then, dividing, offered him a route to Colorado and another to the southern Wyoming plateau. It was followed by emigrants heading for the lush Pacific Northwest, by Mormons bound for the Valley of the Great Salt Lake, and by most of the fortyniners pursuing California's golden dream. Two hundred miles below the juncture of the Platte and the Missouri was the head of another major route across the wilderness — the Santa Fe Trail, traveled by throngs of traders and emigrants from 1821 onward. The way west, thus, really began on the Missouri.

Before the age of steam, men paid prodigious prices in physical energy to invade the Big Muddy. Cunning, luck and constant manhandling were needed to get the boats they used through the river's shifting, obstruction-infested bars and channels. Indians rode the Missouri in "bullboats" — circular, clumsy little craft made by stretching the hide of a buffalo bull (which tended to leak less than the hide of a female animal) over a framework of willow branches. But these little coracles could

only float small loads across streams or down short stretches of the big river, and they were far less useful than the sharp-prowed American Mackinaws later constructed by white settlers. The Mackinaws were flatboats up to 70 feet long, which could be quickly slapped together from whipsawed lumber and — given maneuverability by rowers and by a steersman with a big oar at the stern — could float tons of cargo downstream. However, Mackinaws could not be worked against the current, and the long upriver voyages were

negotiated in but two kinds of craft: dugout canoes and graceful keelboats.

Keelboats ran as much as 70 feet in length, were from 15 to 18 feet in beam, and boasted a roofed, midships cabin flanked, on either side, by a narrow, cleated walkway on which crewmen labored in poling the vessel upstream. There were seats for oarsmen—from six to 12 of them—forward of this enclosed storage space. A small brass cannon was usually mounted on the keelboat's bow and its captain stood atop the cabin, aft, to shout commands and handle a steering oar which was fixed at the stern. The keelboat also had a mast which not only took a sail but acted as the point of attachment for a long rope, or "cordelle." Since loaded craft of this type were often dragged when they could not be rowed, poled or sailed, crewmen used the cordelle to tow the keelboat as they waded up to their knees—or necks—in shallows or lurched through brush along the bank. The stalwarts who manned the boats were mostly of French extraction; except for one brief interim period of Spanish rule, the Missouri was a French stream from 1682—nine years after Marquette and Jolliet "discovered" it—until 1803, when it was ceded to the United States by the terms of the Louisiana Purchase. And these cheerful and hardy French keelboaters endured some of the most brutal toil and most dangerous voyages ever consummated on inland waters.

Keelboaters believed, and with some reason, that steamboats simply would not be able to endure the Missouri's snags and bars. The first paddle voyage on the river—by the little steamer *Independence,* which took a cargo of flour, sugar, whiskey and iron castings 250 hesitant miles to the village of Chariton in May 1819—was heralded as a miraculous feat not soon to be repeated. A great many heavy-hulled and underpowered early steamboats sank or broke down on following *Independence* into the river—as often because of their own deficiencies as because of the chilling problems of navigation all encountered. But the boats themselves improved, if gradually, and Missouri pilots—not a few of them St. Louis Frenchmen who had learned the river in keelboats—managed to surmount hazards that would have been insupportable on the Ohio or Mississippi. The American Fur Company got a little paddle-wheel boat all the way to Fort Union, in present-day North Dakota, in 1832, and company steamers went to the upper Missouri annually every spring thereafter. The smoke-plumed new vessels became the real key to exploitation and development of the northwest before the era of the railroad.

The Rockies, with their promise of furs and gold, were always the riverman's most challenging goal. Nevertheless, the great bulk of pre-Civil War paddle traffic was devoted to carrying passengers and freight to and from settlements on the lower Missouri, and to ferrying waves of Western emigrants to rude river camps (Westport Landing for the forty-niners, Council Bluffs for the Mormons) which became springboards for overland travel. This burgeoning trade, like the lesser traffic to the mountains, stemmed from St. Louis—the French town that became an American city and the gateway to the West for travelers who came down the Ohio from Pittsburgh and Cincinnati and up the Mississippi from the Gulf of Mexico. Boatloads of Irish and German immigrants bypassed New York and Boston, entered the U.S. at New Orleans and followed waterways north be-

fore fanning out into the part of middle America (Missouri included) that was becoming the staging area for the final Western assault. Brigades of Mormons came all the way from Liverpool to Iowa by water before heading west across the plains to Salt Lake.

In the 1860s, after decades as an occasional, if intrepid visitor to the Rocky Mountain West, the steamboat became a real force in the economic development and military occupation of this farthest wilderness. It was drawn into its new role for a multiplicity of reasons: gold was discovered in Montana and Idaho, the Sioux rebelled at invasion of their last hunting grounds along the upper river and the Yellowstone, and the Army began to respond in force. Scores of steamboats—many operated on a fleet basis by new business combines—churned upstream from new railheads at Sioux City, Yankton and, eventually, Bismarck, to Army posts in North Dakota and Montana and—at the head of navigation—to Fort Benton, a boomtown 200 miles from the Rockies.

These Missouri steamboats were ingeniously conceived: shallow-hulled, broad-beamed, multitiered craft (as they finally evolved) that would float in shoal water and could work their way, if laboriously, over sand bars. But the paddle boat was an imperfect tool for all that; it was cheaply constructed, propelled by crude though powerful engines and by cruder boilers, and remained a dangerous, unpredictable and flimsy contrivance until after the Civil War. Its failings were characteristic of all boats built west of the Appalachians, where streams were too shallow for the kind of deep-hulled, soundly built vessels used on the Hudson River and other Eastern waters. And the steamers that plied the Missouri were smaller, ruder and far less comfortable than the showy Mississippi packets that linger in American folklore as symbols of antebellum ostentation.

The noise of engine exhaust was constant on the Big Muddy's steamers, and this racket was accompanied by ceaseless vibration and by a stench of smoke and engine oil. Cabin passengers were subjected to corn husk mattresses in most cases and to towels whose absorbency, according to the uncharitable assessment of Mark Twain, was little greater than that of mosquito netting. Some boats provided deck passengers with barrels of river water for drinking and washing (prickly pears were added to "settle the mud") but there were other vessels

that simply offered the thirsty a bucket tied to the end of a long rope — a device that might yank the incautious man overboard when he lobbed it into the stream beside a moving hull.

Squalor — mitigated only slightly by river breezes and passing scenery — was the lot of that larger portion of the traveling public that bought cheap passage on the lower deck. Such unfortunates had to provide their own food, and were forced to jostle roustabouts and firemen for sleeping space amid stacks of cargo. These could include cages of complaining cats, which were crucial to life upriver since rats ate government grain faster than the horses at cavalry posts, and invaded new barns as if summoned by the Pied Piper of Hamelin.

It was seldom possible to go far on the Missouri without enduring exasperating delays. Every steamer carried two huge poles, or spars, which could be lowered to the bottom at a 45 degree angle when the vessel stuck on a sand bar. These long timbers were driven down and back, crutch-fashion — by cables attached to a capstan powered by a steam "nigger engine" — and forced the boat to slide a few yards ahead before they were robbed of their leverage by movement. This process — known as sparring or, more colorfully, as "grasshoppering" — was repeated until the steamer finally floated free in deeper water beyond the obstruction.

If sparring failed to conquer a bar at first, the captain might put part of the cargo ashore to lighten the boat, then reload once he was past the obstruction. And vessels that attempted to negotiate the upper reaches of the river in low-water periods sometimes resorted to "double tripping": they unloaded half the cargo at some con-

25

Paying the price of a risky upriver trip at low-water season, the 78-ton stern-wheeler *Expansion* lies grounded on a Yellowstone sand bar. The boat was freed by off-loading passengers and cargo. Once the craft was lightened the river's powerful current was able to wash away the silt beneath.

Steamboat lines furnished travelers with cards listing both distances between stops and cumulative mileage as a boat progressed upriver. The figures had to be periodically revised to reflect shifts in the channel.

DISTANCES ON MISSOURI RIVER
From SAINT LOUIS to

Mouth of Missouri	....	—	20	Mouth of Yellowstone	2	1996
St. Charles	25	45	Mouth Little Muddy	20	2016
Washington	44	89	Mouth Big Muddy	30	2046
Hermann	31	120	Mouth Poplar Creek	50	2096
Osage River	36	156	Spread Eagle	25	2121
Jefferson City	8	164	Wolf Creek Agency	26	2147
Glasgow	78	242	Porcupine Creek	30	2177
Lexington	95	337	Milk River	25	2202
Kansas City	68	405	Fort Copelin	10	2212
Leavenworth	33	438	Fort Peck	15	2227
Saint Joseph	63	501	Rouche's Grave	40	2267
Omaha	185	686	Round Bute	37	2304
Sioux City	175	861	Trover Point	40	2344
Vermillion	92	953	Muscleshell River	43	2387
Yankton	53	1006	Fort Hawley	37	2424
Fort Randall	96	1102	Carroll	22	2446
Brule City	90	1192	Little Rocky	15	2461
Brule Agency	31	1223	Harriett's Island	12	2473
Fort Thompson	7	1240	Two Calf Island	15	2488
Head of Big Bend	40	1280	Cow Island	20	2508
Old Fort Pierre } Black Hills Landing }	54	1334	Bud's Rapids	15	2523
			Dauphin's Rapids	15	2538
Fort Sully	25	1359	Fort Claggett	23	2561
Cheyenne Agency	12	1371	Drowned Man's Rapids	2	2563
Grand River Agency	108	1479	Arrow River	14	2577
Stand'g Rock Agency	56	1535	Steamboat Rock	4	2581
Fort Rice	34	1569	Hole in the Wall	6	2587
Fort Lincoln	40	1609	Citadel Rock	3	2590
Bismarck	5	1614	Eagle Creek	8	2598
Fort Stevenson	110	1724	Coal Banks	15	2613
Fort Berthold	25	1749	Mouth of Marias	24	2637
White Earth River	20	1869	FORT BENTON	26	2663
Fort Buford	125	1994			

OVERLAND DISTANCES
From FORT BENTON to

Sun River and Fort Shaw	60	Phillipsburg	285
Helena	140	Maria's Cros'g, Simmons F'y	75
Blackfoot	170	Fort Belknap	90
Diamond City	175	Blackfoot Agency	140
Deer Lodge	195	Fort Walsh } B. A.	160
Missoula	230	Cypress Mountain }	
Boseman	240	Fort McLeod "	225
Virginia City	265	Fort Edmondton "	475

Stages leave Benton for Helena Tri-Weekly.
"   "   Helena for all Inland Points Daily.

struggling up a rapids, she could be swept stern first into rocks below — as was the steamboat *Yellowstone* in 1870 — and could fill in a matter of minutes.

Female passengers seemed to bear these vicissitudes with less outward tribulation than males. Pilots and captains occasionally took their wives to the Rockies during the Montana gold rush of the late 1860s — even while sheathing their pilothouses with "boiler iron" against rifle fire by recalcitrant Indians. And the wives and children of many settlers rode the Missouri steamers as a matter of necessity. These pioneer women were treated like ladies and were expected to behave as such. They seemed to inure themselves against discomfort and danger in doing so: while they accepted a great deal of male folly as inevitable, they also assumed — perhaps with a kind of hopeful fatalism — that "the men" would also cope with any resultant difficulties. They seldom complained aloud; a tightening of the lips, a stiffening of the neck served to put men in their place — and on their mettle, too.

Mrs. Harriet Peck Fenn Sanders of Virginia City, Montana, seemed to find the more dramatic aspects of upper-river travel odd rather than frightening when she brought her two small sons, a nephew and her mother to Fort Benton on the steamboat *Abeona* in 1866. Her diary reflects an unswerving dedication to the mundane which apparently deadened other stimuli. "Alarm of Indians," she wrote in May. "They have attacked two boats and killed one man." But she is soon noting that she has "unpacked the fruit trunk (apples and lemons bought back in Omaha) to keep the boys happy."

She seemed more disturbed by the all but unnoticeable attendance at Sunday service — read by the captain during a layover — than by the fact that the place had been attacked only a few days before. "Mother, Mrs. Isaacs, Mrs. Houghton, Miss Hopkins and I went over onto *Trover,*" she reported, "and had a pleasant call." *Trover* was another steamboat that was engaging in a reckless if spasmodic race with *Abeona*. Both of the vessels kept hitting bottom, and when *Trover* hit twice and "got its guard rail broken" later on — necessitating repairs and a bout of grasshoppering — "three of her ladies" were able to cross in her yawl and return Mrs. Sanders' call.

Men were usually more restive. One R. M. Whitney, passenger on the steamer *Western,* grew so irri-

venient point along the shore, delivered the other half to its destination, then returned to pick up the rest.

Rapids were surmounted, if too swift for the engines, by "planting a dead man" — burying a big piece of timber in a ditch ashore, fastening a cable to it, and forcing the boat to inch ahead by winding this hawser back with the capstan. Roping could be dangerous, though not as dangerous as boiler explosions (which usually destroyed the whole vessel), fires (steamboats went up like bonfires, once ignited) or snags (hidden river obstructions could tear the bottom out of a hull in seconds). If the long cable snapped while a boat was tated at the constant clatter of sparring in 1872 that in his sleep he began to yell, "Stop that damned nigger!" A trader named Al Leighton "overturned his plate at breakfast" out of sheer irascibility at the same engine sound. Dan Scott, correspondent for the *Sioux City Journal*—who slyly reported these personal peculiarities—also offered his personal answer to river travel: sleep all day and drink all night. He was not the only one. Mates drank on duty, engineers drank on duty; roustabouts and firemen were often dosed with whiskey to keep them up to the mark, and most boats maintained bars—often as concessions operated by the bartender—that offered the passenger all the booze he could hold. Some drank simply because the steamboat had a nasty habit of blowing up. Still, danger did not diminish the drama of a steamer's gliding passage, nor the dreamy beauty of the wilderness vistas through which she passed.

Expectancy and bravado, boredom and suspense; these were the emotional by-products of the mountain voyage. Few travelers ever reflected them—or the backhanded humor with which they were tinctured—as well as mud clerk Edwards. Edwards, who went to Washington University on his return from the West, and who eventually practiced law in Missouri, was an impressionable (and cheeky) youngster when he boarded the steamer *Henry M. Shreve* in 1869 at the levee in St. Louis and began writing a log on his tablets of yellow paper.

Excerpts from this document make clear that Edwards was delighted with *Shreve,* "a very fast boat." He was fascinated at evidence of what lay ahead: "Met Steamer *Mary McDonald* with a Regiment of Troops & 1 Grisley Bear on Board." But Edwards soon became aware that *Shreve* was making her way through

an uncertain, even threatening, environment and that she was not completely proof against it. "The Boat Struck a Bluff Bar during the night. Leaked very badly for a time got ½ foot of water in the Hold & damaged Six Sacks Coffee." And, three days later: "One of the Boilers found to be leaking with a Split Seam 6 or 8 inches long. We lay here until 2 o'clock Sunday Morning thereby looseing 8 Hours." He soon saw survivors of a worse disaster: "Capt. Bill Massie of the Burnt Boat *Antelope* with his crew in 2 yawls lashed together making their way Home from the Burnt Wreck." And *Shreve* was forced to tie up and tie up again by high winds. "Blowing a perfect Hurrycane," Edwards wrote one day. "Lost 8 Hours."

Abruptly, the weather changed for the better. "Clear, Cool & delightfull with a bright & genial Sun Shining & the Senery is Grand & Picquereste & quite Varied with Ranges of Hills & High Roolling Prairies." But then *Shreve's* "Bow grounded & her Stearn came Swinging down Sweeping the entire main Shore until her Rudder Struck with Such force as to break it entirely off, which left us in a deplorable condition of a Vessel without a Rudder. We are now good to be detained a day or two at least. This misfortune of looseing the Rudder entire was bad management on Some one. The Carpenter, Mate & his Crew went down to the Bar & grappled & dragged for our lost rudder but could not find it. This Compelled the Carpenter to go to the nearest Woods to get Timber large enough to make an entire new Rudder." The second engineer then died of "Typhod Fever in his lungs" and the vessel "lay up again while poor Geo. Miller was interred on Pochahontas Island & followed to the Grave by many of the crew & Passengers—and with the flag

---

For Missouri River.

Independent Packet—For Leavenworth, Weston, and St. Joseph.
Steamer WM. H. RUSSELL................Kinny, master,
Will leave for the above and intermediate ports, THIS DAY April 13th at 4 P. M.
For freight or passage apply on board.
11ap   A. L RYLAND Advertising Ag't.

For Lexington, Kansas, Leavenworth, and St. Joseph.
Steamer MORNING STAR................H. McPherson, master,
Will leave for the above and intermediate ports, on THIS DAY April 13th at 4 P. M.
For freight or passage apply on board.
13ap   ALSTON L RYLAND Advertising Ag't.

For Boonville, Glasgow, Cambridge, and Brunswick.
Steamer C. W. SOMBART................H. McPherson, master,
Will leave for the above and intermediate ports on THURSDAY April 14th at 4 P. M.
For freight or passage apply on board.
7ap   A. L. RYLAND Advertising Ag't.

For Council Bluff, and Omaha.
Steamer SPREAD EAGLE................Labarge, master,
Will leave for the above and intermediate ports THIS DAY, April 13th at 4 P. M.
For freight or passage apply on board.
9ap   A. L RYLAND Advertising Ag't.

For Leavenworth, Weston, and St. Joseph.
Steamer DAVID TATUM................J. A. Williams, master,
Will leave for the above and intermediate ports on THIS DAY April, 13th at 10 A. M.
For freight or passage apply on board.
12ap   ALSTON L. RYLAND, Advertising Ag't

PacificRail road Packets—Connects at next days train—For Kansas, Leavenworth, Weston, Atchinson, and St. Joseph.
Steamer SOUTH WESTAR................John Porter, master,
Will leave for the above and intermediate ports WEDNESDAY, April, 13th at 10 A. M.
For freight or passage apply on board
11ap   ALSTON L. RYLAND, Advertising Ag't,

Pacific Railroad Packets—Connects at Jefferson City with next days train—For Kansas, Leavenworth, Weston, Atchinson, and St. Joseph.
Steamer ALONZO CHILD................D. D. Haven master,
Will leave for the above and intermediate ports, THURSDAY Aprıl 14th at 10 A. M.
For freight or passage apply on board.
13ap   A. L RYLAND Advertising Ag't.

Independent Packet—For Leavenworth, Weston, and St. Joseph.
Steamer METEOR................Draffen, master,
Will leave for the above and intermediate ports, THURSDAY April 14th at 4 P. M.
For freight or passage apply on board.
13ap   A. L RYLAND Advertising Ag't.

Pacific Railroad Packets—Connects at Jefferson City with next days train—For Kansas, Leavenworth, Weston, Atchinson, and St. Joseph.
Steamer NEW WAR EAGLE................White, master,
Will leave for the above and intermediate ports on FRIDAY, April, 15th at 10 A. M.
For freight or passage apply on board.
13ap   A. L. RYLAND, Advertising Ag't.

Independent Packet—For Nebraska City, Council Bluffs and Omaha.
Steamer EDITOR................Garrett, master,
Will leave for the above and intermediate ports, FRIDAY April. 15th at 4 P. M.
For freight or passage apply on board.
apl2   ALSTON L. RYLAND, Advertising Ag't.

For Sioux City, St. Helena, Niobrarah, and Fort Randall.
Steamer FLORILDA................Baldwin, master,
Will leave for the above and intermediate ports with dispatch.
For freight or passage apply on board.
1ap   ALSTON L. RYLAND, Advertising Ag't.

29

A daredevil steamboat duel en route to Montana

Almost as soon as steamboats invaded the Big Muddy, they began to engage in races, partly because fast boats won lucrative freight contracts and also because Missouri pilots were a hot-blooded breed who could not bear to find themselves in a vessel's wake. Usually the contest was brief and friendly, ending after a few miles. At times, however, a race became a no-holds-barred struggle imperiling steamboat hulls and passengers' lives.

One traveler who experienced such an all-out duel and never forgot it was Samuel Hauser, then a 29-year-old prospector heading for the Montana gold fields — and destined to become an enormously wealthy banker, rancher, railroad builder — and, in 1885, Montana's territorial governor.

The race that launched Sam Hauser into Montana took place on the upper Missouri on June 6, 1862, shortly after the steamboats *Emilie* and *Spread Eagle* cast off from their night moorings near Fort Berthold in present-day North Dakota. In his later account of the contest, Hauser, who was aboard *Emilie,* noted that passions for a showdown between the two boats had long been building. *Spread Eagle* had departed from St. Louis — 2,000 miles astern at this point — four days ahead of *Emilie.* But the trailing boat had poured on the steam all the way upriver and had finally caught up the night before. Now, in the first glimmerings of dawn and amid raucous shouts of challenge across the water, the stretch drive to Fort Benton began.

"Our boat waited until the other shoved off," Hauser recalled. "Gath-

Samuel Hauser in the 1870s

ering steam to the last notch, we followed, the boat trembling like a fig leaf at each puff. Accumulated steam soon carried us past them and such shouting you've never heard."

The rejoicing on *Emilie's* decks was short-lived, however, as *Spread Eagle* built a new head of steam and charged back into the lead.

"All turned imploringly to the pilot," Hauser went on. "He talked through the pipes to the engineer, and in a few minutes the distance between us was diminishing and faces began to brighten."

Emilie gradually drew abreast of her rival but was unable to surge out in front. For more than an hour the two paddle boats thrashed upstream in a bow-to-bow stalemate. Then they reached a point where the river was split by a towhead — an island submerged because of the high spring waters. *Spread Eagle* veered to star-

board to follow the wide-looping main channel. *Emilie's* pilot then took a seemingly desperate gamble, heading for a narrow chute nearby on the port side, in the hope that the swollen seasonal waters would make that shortcut passable.

As the steamers bore down on their chosen courses, *Spread Eagle's* pilot suddenly saw that the shorter route ahead of *Emilie* was indeed navigable. Rather than let the rival vessel take the lead, he threw the wheel over and rammed *Spread Eagle's* bow into *Emilie,* deliberately trying to disable her.

Although the point of impact was dangerously near *Emilie's* boilers, she suffered only light damage. The two boats were locked together, however, and *Emilie's* enraged pilot, according to Hauser, "let go the wheel, snatched his gun and would have shot the *Spread Eagle's* pilot but for his son holding him." Pandemonium swept both boats as officers, crews and passengers exchanged curses and threats while the vessels drifted aimlessly in the current together, without anyone at their helms.

"Fortunately," Samuel Hauser reported, "the two boats separated of their own accord and our engineer, without orders, turned on the last pound of steam causing us to glide by." That was the end of the competition. *Emilie* arrived at Fort Benton on June 17, four days ahead of her rival, and her demonstration of fleetness quickly earned her owner (none other than the intrepid pilot himself) a share of the river trade that more than compensated for the racing damage.

at Half Mast & with all the Interest & Solemnities of a funeral ceremoney in a more appropriate place. Capt. H. S. Carter to his credit be it Said attended the Grave in Person & directed the whole Burial Service in a manner that will long reflect credit to his Humain & Manly & Noble Hart & Character."

Edwards' primary duty involved the purchase of cordwood for the boilers. Wood meant power, and procuring it was every steamer's most continuous and exasperating problem, for long stretches of the upper Missouri valley were scantily timbered. The difficulty was exacerbated during the Indian troubles of the 1860s for few men dared operate woodyards in the occasional shoreside groves, and steamers were often reduced—as was *Shreve* on many occasions—to sending their crews ashore to log or to wrest snags and other drift from "racks" on sand bars. Edwards was grateful, on April 30, that he had managed to purchase eight and a half cords of hardwood and five cords of cottonwood at Hot Springs Wood Yard—24 days out of St. Louis—even though he had been forced to pay cash ($62.50) rather than trading flour, ax handles and other staples for it. But scarcity did not entirely blunt Edwards' critical view of the people with whom he dickered for fuel. The next day he wrote in his log: "Took 13 Cords Light & poor cotton wood at $5 a cord from ½ Breed Indian (½ Canadian French & ½ Dog or Some Such mixture.)"

Shreve took 67 days getting to Fort Benton and she did not achieve this goal without endless difficulty and exertion: breaking her rudder again, sparring continuously, smashing her "capstan wheel all to flinders," laboriously roping her way up a rapids, putting 60 cords of wood ashore to lighten draft (the fuel bill for the trip was $6,048.70) and finally hiring another smaller steamer to take some of her cargo upstream. But young Edwards was filled with exhilaration—as, apparently, were his shipmates—by "Clear & Bracing weather," by "the Sublime & Romantic river," and—best of all—by "the Sport & Glory of Buffaloe Slaughterings" as they approached their journey's end.

His log describes a "Buffaloe which came directly up to the Boat's Bow at which time 24 Loaded Musketts was brought in full Play besides the Numerous Henry Riffles, Sharps Shooters & Colt Revolvers used by Passengers & Crew. When he reached the Bank he could not get up as Some of the Shots had Broken his hind Leg. All continued to Shoot at him until he was down & Safe to get so we now have on board a Splendid young Buffaloe Bull 3 years old & in good order. Fresh meat enoughf to last ½ the trip down. We faired most Sumptiously on Prairie Chicken Pot Pie, Rost Hump of Buffaloe and other Smaller delicacies. We have had more fun & excitement than any day on the Trip. The Ladies all were equally Interested."

Steamboat travel was at its apogee on the Missouri when mud clerk Edwards wrote these lines. Fifty years had passed since *Independence*'s first incursion on the Big Muddy and paddle-wheel vessels had not only proliferated on its waters but, having gone through a long process of evolution in Ohio River builders' yards, had finally become reasonably dependable instruments of transportation. Still, shoals, rapids, snags—and greed —continued to bring them to grief.

Two types of steamboats had come into use on the Missouri—large vessels built to operate on the lower river and smaller boats constructed for "mountain" travel above the Yellowstone. In the late 1860s, however, the larger boats were sent off to Fort Benton by the dozen. They were dramatically unsuited for the dangerous water encountered on the mountain voyage, since they drew six or seven feet, loaded. But they could carry a great deal more cargo than the mountain boats and were lured to Benton by the Montana gold boom and the inflated prices it prompted: as high as $300 for a cabin passage and $15 a hundred pound for all cargo bound to the head of navigation. Daring, luck and good piloting got a surprising number of these lower-river boats through, but every traveler risked stranding when he bookcd passage on them to—or from—the Rockies. And no travelers in the long history of the river endured so thoroughly miserable a voyage—or were so victimized by rascality and ineptitude—as were the 275 unwary people who headed downstream for St. Louis on the big stern-wheeler *Imperial* in September of 1867.

Imperial's crew had been unable to coax her beyond Cow Island—198 miles below Fort Benton—on her trip upstream. But her captain remained determined that she should earn her way home; he sent emissaries to the town to sell as many passages to St. Louis (at $130 in gold dust per passage) as could be peddled among prospectors bound back to civilization. These agents proved wonderfully persuasive—for all the fact that three sounder steamers were about to depart from the levee at the town. They described *Imperial* as "a floating palace" which would make the Benton steamers look "like mud scows," offered free transportation (in open Mackinaws) down to Cow Island and the balked boat, and promised "a royal good time" with "a jolly good crowd" once their vessel was underway.

A young prospector named John Napton—who had come down to Fort Benton on a cayuse horse with $1,000 in dust from the diggings at Bear Gulch—was one of the 275 passengers who paid the price and eventually found themselves sleeping "thick as sardines in a box" on the overloaded *Imperial's* cabin floor. Napton wrote later of his experiences on the boat—which headed downstream without a pilot, went aground on 132 separate sand bars, and spent more than two months on the river before finally being abandoned a thousand miles from St. Louis.

Napton was not unduly disturbed by *Imperial's* lack of amenities—"I was faring much better than I had been when batching as a miner." But he soon began changing his mind. A deck hand's leg was broken by a cable, which snapped as *Imperial* was being sparred off a sand bar; the man eventually died for lack of medical attention. The captain grew more unpopular by the day—if only because he decided that he could not free *Imperial* from sand bars if passengers did not wade around in freezing water beside the boat and shift sand by dragging a long chain under her hull. And their plight was dramatized when the steamboat *Benton*—one of the three "mud scows"—tied up nearby after coming downriver "with full steam on and running like a race horse." *Imperial's* captain refused to return passage money to 15 passengers who decided, wisely, to transfer to the other vessel, and parsimoniously declined to pay the $1,000 fee for which *Benton's* second pilot offered to take *Imperial* to her destination. This last decision caused howls of criticism when the captain set out to follow in *Benton's* wake (and thus gain the benefit of her pilot's skill for nothing) but simply landed on another sand bar from which the passengers watched the "scow's" smoke fade away downstream.

"After *Benton* left us we passengers realized our situation and that some vigorous plan must be adopted. The last boat above us had passed; winter was coming on and provisions were getting low. We organized and had regular meetings—chairman chosen and committee appointed to see that our resolutions were enforced." One of them: "everyone—except the women and children of whom there were some six or eight—got off the boat in order to lighten it whenever we got stuck on a sand bar, and to also pull on a hawser stretched from the boat to land. It was wonderful the strength of 200 men when all pulled together. Notwithstanding these plans we were only making but little headway, some days four or five miles, sometimes forty eight hours on the same bar and as a last resort we concluded to cut away the upper deck of the boat and cache on shore all the freight which consisted of bales of furs and buffalo hides stowed in the hold of the boat. The captain then made us a speech and told us that if we would help a few more days we would reach Fort Buford at the mouth of the Yellowstone where we could get an ample supply of provisions, and—since the Yellowstone was almost as large a stream as the Missouri and would bring up the river level our troubles would be over."

The restiveness of those on board was assuaged at this point by a vast herd of buffalo which began crossing the river just below the vessel. "Everybody was eager for the chase. Both yawls were soon full of men and on their way down the river. Several who could find no place in the yawls concluded to go by land and among them were S-----, the boat's hunter, and his partner Arnold. The two men separated but S-----, on finding the trail brushy, concluded to return and found Arnold, lying in the path full of arrows, scalped and horribly mutilated. He hurried back to notify us that the Indians were upon us. All was confusion until the hunters safely returned with an abundance of buffalo meat. Twenty men went out in the morning to bring in the body. We could trace the exact way that Arnold had run by the arrows sticking in the ground. Most of the arrows had struck him in the back and one had gone through his body. He was from Georgia, but from what place no one knew."

Imperial, for all the captain's assurances, did not get past the Yellowstone until late in October, more than a month into her journey, and "made slower progress than ever with her whistle blowing constantly as a signal of distress, hoping that someone from somewhere would come to our relief. We now landed each day at

some bull berry patch to give us all a full feed since the last food cooked on the boat in these starvation days was a barrel of currants with very small white worms in them. They were served as long as they lasted and no remarks made. An old Mormon who generally sat at the head of the long dining table would give us a discourse on hard times in about the following style: 'Well, boys, this looks a little bad but it might be worse. I landed in Salt Lake Basin in '46 and lived without flour for six months and it never worried me. This river is lined with bull berries and rose bush balls and they are both good — and you must remember our friend on the lower deck has two horses, a little thin I must confess, but there is no better meat than horse flesh, and I have also noticed several dogs aboard.'"

But writer Napton found a fellow with better advice than this leathery patriarch — "a man named Pitcher from St. Louis who always came out in the morning with a broad smile and apparently satisfied with the situation and with everybody. I said to him one day, 'Pitcher, how is it you seem so well contented? I never hear any complaint from you.' He answered, 'To tell you the truth, Jack, I have had bread all the time, and if you will properly approach the steward and at the right time, you can get bread too but it will cost you something.' This I immediately did. The steward, realizing whither we were drifting, had cooked up a lot of bread, how much I never found out. He had taken off some of the weather boarding and stowed the bread away in the side of the cook room and was selling it to passengers. He handed me a loaf that in any bakery could be bought for five cents and would only charge me five dollars for it. Where could I eat it? My cousin, Lewis Miller, suggested that we go to bed, and if anyone came upon us we could hide it under the blankets and we finally did, although it was only about 4 p.m. After this

Overlooking no ploy to attract new business, steamboat owners made sure that the mail they carried bore their vessel's name. Special stationery was supplied to passengers, and the purser hand-stamped all letters that came aboard.

SOURI RIVER & Ft. BENTON PACKET

STEAMER

NELLIE PECK

DURFEE & PECK, Owners,

LEAVENWORTH, KANSAS.

Frank Wegner. Esqr.

Half way House. Rock Creek.

Benton Road.

Montana Territory.

MISSOURI RIVER PACKET POLAR STAR

THREE CENTS

PACKET POS PAY

B/

Miss A & I Denniston Ho.

Northwest Transportation Co. Peck Line.

STEAMER FAR WEST,

J. M. BELK, Master. E. WOOD, Clerk.

J. C. O'CONNOR, Gen. Agt.

BISMARCK, D. T.

BISMARCK JUL 11 1882 DAK.

E. B. Vincent. Esq

Fort Sully

Dakota

I was satisfied in my own mind that it was a fight to the finish and 'the Devil take the hindmost.'

"On the first of November we were about where the city of Bismarck is now located and where Lewis and Clark wintered with the Mandans. It was a cold disagreeable day. The boat tied up and some of us walked to the top of the adjoining bluffs to take a look at the surrounding country. It was one vast, boundless plain extending in every direction. The want of all animal life, its silence and utter desolation were oppressive. One of the men said, 'Look at the ice floating in the river. I tell you right now, fellows, we are in a hell of a fix.' No one made any answer to this remark, but it made a deep impression on me."

Not long afterward, Napton spotted a derelict Mackinaw on a small island in the middle of the river. Clutching at any hope of escape, he asked the captain to halt the steamer so that he could examine the Mackinaw's condition. The captain refused, and the *Imperial* made another 10 miles before mooring for the night.

But Napton was not so easily deterred. Early the next morning, he and five other men went ashore and walked back toward the abandoned boat, carrying an ax, two oars and some rope. They passed the island and continued on another mile until they reached a grove of trees. There they put together a small raft. Two of the men boarded it and set out to discover whether the Mackinaw could be floated.

"The river was three quarters of a mile wide and to us left on the bank it seemed that they would miss it, but they found it, buried in four or five feet of sand, mud and driftwood, and dug with the oars and the axe. While they were working at the boat we saw Indians coming over the bluff on the opposite side from us until there must have been three hundred of them. They shouted and made all manner of signs with their blankets but would not venture in the river, and I was never more relieved in my life than when one of the men on the island waved his hat to let us know the boat was all right. They brought it to shore to let us in and we went down to *Imperial* and bade our friends goodbye.

"Sometime during the first night after we left her two more boats came down upon us at full speed in the moonlight. These were passengers who had stolen both

yawls of *Imperial,* leaving her crew in a helpless condition as these boats were needed every day in hunting for the channel of the river. They could make better time than we could and soon disappeared downstream. There were twelve of us in the Mackinaw and four of us worked the oars all the time. We traveled all day and all night when not too dark and one day when the wind was favorable we hoisted our blankets for sails and we thought made fully a hundred miles. We hired horse wagons at Yankton to take us to Sioux City, took a stage to St. Jo, and arrived at Booneville, Missouri, where my cousin lived, exactly three months after leaving Bear Gulch, Montana."

Imperial eventually reached a point 150 miles from Sioux City where the passengers were put ashore (without refunds); the boat was later sold at public auction.

John Napton and his cousin Lewis Miller were not the only steamboat passengers who fretted at interminable delays during river travel, or found themselves left to their own devices in a hostile wilderness. But the ineptitude, cynicism and indifference evinced by *Impe-*

rial's captain were rare. While other captains, engineers and pilots often erred, they usually did so out of an excess, rather than a lack, of pride, enthusiasm and daring. It is fascinating, for instance, to note how pilots reacted — since they were among the earliest humans to savor the delights and temptations of modern motive power — to the progress they could induce by jangling a bell or yelling down a speaking tube. Steamboatmen were denied the kind of open water enjoyed by ocean seamen and could only envy the comforting rails that guided the early railroad engineer to his destination. But if a pilot was resigned to the endless delays of roping or sparring, he seldom gave in, when facing difficult water or even sand bars, without trying something more satisfying to the soul: calling for boiler pressure and more boiler pressure and hoping for the best.

Steamboat engineers had no way of telling how much horsepower they had at hand and no way — for decades — of gauging steam pressure or even the limits imposed by their crude safety valves. In times of stress they simply ordered extra fuel into the fireboxes, tuned their senses to the resultant vibration and, with their ears,

37

At the Great Falls, 35 miles above Fort Benton, the Missouri plunges 80 vertical feet and pours its torrent into a series of lesser cataracts. From here on, travelers bound for the Rockies had to go overland.

estimated both power output and strain on the boilers —as did the man in the wheelhouse above. The single cylinder, high-pressure engines of the day exhausted steam with a sound like slow cannonading—a cacophony that could be heard for miles under even normal operating conditions, and this attained a howitzer-like intensity as pressure mounted. The racket would sometimes culminate in the hideous roar of exploding boilers, but passengers seemed as exhilarated as the steersman and engineer when a boat labored noisily up through fast water with the safety valve tied down. The public, in fact, boycotted the Cincinnati & Louisville Packet Line steamer *Jacob Strader*—built in 1853 with "safe" low-pressure engines—because she could not be heard coming upstream.

At the same time that Missouri River steamboatmen were catalyzing America's posture toward engine power and speed, they were magnifying other American attitudes. Steamer officers, for example, were certainly not alone in a kind of cheerful contempt for ethnic minorities, but they were in a position to augment their bias more dramatically than most. Slaves were used as roustabouts (their owners charged wages for them and allowed them to keep what they earned on Sunday) and they were treated with some care since the boat was always billed by the owner if they were crippled or lost. But the European immigrant was another matter altogether. "Oh, hell!" cried one pilot, steaming on after being informed that a deck hand had fallen overboard; "it's only an Irishman!"

The roustabouts—or roosters as they were called in river slang—led an exhausting and thankless life. Firemen stood four-hour watches but the deck hands remained on call day and night, slept when they could in crannies amid the freight, and were expected to carry cordwood, bales and crates at a run over narrow, limber gangplanks that were often slippery with rain or ice. The crew's food was frequently execrable—though bigger packets served them pans that were full of passengers' leavings into which they groped with their hands when summoned by the cry, "Grubpile!" and upper-river boats sent hunters ashore for game, which was usually shared by everybody aboard. Negro roosters were considered the most amenable to toil. German immi-

grants rated next in dependability. Missouri farm boys, many of whom joined steamers to escape the plow, were thought to be a shade too independent (but were forgiven for it since they were American). Irishmen were considered to be the most rebellious and unreliable of all.

Steamboat mates—bully boys who played little or no part in the actual operation of the vessel—were charged with the task of driving the roustabouts. Some managed with their fists and a continuous administration of profanity. But most of them used clubs (and carried pistols since the roosters carried knives) and there were a brutal few who were not above shooting a recalcitrant deck hand and heaving the corpse overboard. Roustabouts exerted a certain leverage, nevertheless; they could always desert a boat when she needed them most. The practice was actively discouraged; the mate of the steamboat *Mountaineer* ordered Negro roosters to chase four white deck hands who left the boat at Sioux City in 1867, thus prompting a street fight in which the combatants belabored each other with stones and clubs, and in which one hapless deserter was "kicked in the face and head" and dragged back aboard.

Still, deck crews could win higher wages and better working conditions—for one voyage at least—if they went on strike during the harvest season, when alternative employment abounded. Moreover, roustabouts were not as discontented with their life as some of these episodes would suggest—and since they were paid (though badly) in actual cash, most of them skipped every third or fourth trip to heal their bruises and blow their money in riverbank bars and brothels.

But if life on a steamer was rude, and if the vessel herself was a dangerous contraption engaged in a frustrating and unpredictable contest with nature, she was also a mirror of the frontiers she served and was received uncritically—and usually, indeed, with admiration—by people for whom risk and hardship were the warp and woof of existence. Captains, pilots and owners were not only adventurers but men of dignity and a certain sentiment. Listen to the names of some Missouri steamboats: *Arabia, Andrew Jackson, Daniel Boone, Emerald, Highland Mary, Kit Carson, Star of the West, War Eagle.* Such vessels were serious in-

Running low on fuel for her fireboxes, the side-wheeler *De Smet* halts to pick up enough fallen timber to get her to the next woodyard. Such unscheduled stops were almost welcome on monotonous voyages that often lasted two months.

struments of a serious commerce; they invaded the Missouri valley wilderness, in the main, by inching a little farther up the endless stream every year, covering regular beats or "trades" in the process, and stopping every mile or so to pick up goods and passengers in places like Bellefontaine's Bend, Overall's Wood Yard, Cattleville Landing, Booneville and Arrow Rock.

Steamboat stops like these were closer to the frontier before the Civil War than later maps suggest; most of them were muddy and semilawless settlements of hard pressed people betting on fate and the future. And there was savage guerrilla fighting along the lower river after the war began; steamboats were considered fair game by jayhawkers, redlegs and bushwhackers, and it was the incautious pilot who tied up for a night at a landing rather than mooring in midstream. Guerrillas waylaid them anyhow, usually — as was the case with the steamboat *Mollie Dozier* — by hiding at some isolated woodyard the vessel was known to utilize, and swarming aboard before the boat's crew could be armed. A gang of rebel bushwhackers cleaned out *Mollie Dozier's* safe, sacked up the whiskey in her bar, raided her galley and, on finding a Union officer in one of her staterooms, took him ashore and killed him by dragging him behind a horse at the end of a rope.

But no pilot or captain could be as concerned with human eccentricity, over the long haul, as with the eccentricity of the Missouri itself. Some 700 different steamboats plied the Missouri between 1819 and the final disappearance of paddle-wheel traffic after 1900; of these about 300 were destroyed in service and left their bones in the river — the great majority after being holed by submerged hidden trees. Scores and scores of them sank in the narrow channels at river bends and became impediments to navigation themselves. Wrecks were so much a part of river life that they were sometimes received with a certain ennui: a report on the sinking of the steamer *Washington* stated, "Two sisters, large and fat, floated and were picked up by a skiff . . . another woman, thin and lean, sank and drowned." The river not only sent steamers to the bottom, but filled their hulks with mud and sand so rapidly that efforts to raise them or retrieve machinery and cargo were always difficult. Speed was vital: wreckers who built a cofferdam around the hull of the sunken side-wheeler *Twilight* got so drunk, alas, on a barrel of whiskey re-

covered from her hold that rising water filled her up again before they could recover.

And no pilot or captain could let himself forget the tribes of Indians that lived in the Missouri watershed. Most of these people were amenable to trading and to intrusion by rivermen; one E. W. Carpenter, writing of a trip to Benton in 1865, described groups of Indians that thronged about his boat at wood stops on the upper river: "Precious sets of bucks, ringed, streaked and striped in visage and equally in morals; talented in stealing and duplicity, in begging and loafing." But the Sioux remained incorrigibly resentful. They seem admirable, in retrospect, for their foresight, fierceness and sense of worth, but steamer crews considered them — to quote a report to Congress by Meriwether Lewis — the "vilest miscreants of the savage race who must…remain the pirates of the Missouri . . . until our government reduces them to order by coercive measures."

Yet, the Missouri had a richness and a grandeur, too; when the sun shone and the sky was blue it led the traveler through a wilderness so vast, so wild, so lovely, along many leagues of its valley, as to touch and inspire the most hard-bitten of them. Pelicans fed in its shallows. Enormous rafts of ducks floated on its eddies and backwaters during the seasons of flight, and countless deer, elk and buffalo drank at its edges. Fantastic towers and battlements — home of the mountain sheep — rose above the stream as it penetrated the approaches to the Rocky Mountains.

The river itself grew increasingly threatening in the 198-mile stretch between Cow Island and Fort Benton. There its bottom changed from soft sand to hard rock and steamers entered a succession of 15 stretches of white water in which hulls were in continuous danger from sharp reefs and outcroppings. But the Missouri pilot's Mecca was the Rockies and, particularly, Fort Benton. And the boat that won through to discharge a cargo at the Benton levee usually made more money than she herself had cost — vessels earned $20,000 to $40,000 almost as a matter of routine. The steamboat *Peter Balen,* "an old tub worth not over $15,000," made a profit of $80,000 — a small fortune in 1866 — on one voyage to the mountains. Steamboat men kept heading upstream. Few of earth's institutions ever offered such an amalgam of danger, beauty and chance of gain as did the Missouri when the West was young.

2 | The great fur rush upriver

In 1806, when pathfinders Meriwether Lewis and William Clark returned to St. Louis after their epic exploration of the Missouri and points west, they reported exultantly: "We view this passage across the continent as affording immence advantages to the fir trade."

Their glowing tales of the beaver supply on the upper Missouri and in the Rockies instantly set off a frenzied fur rush up the Big Muddy. Entrepreneurs and adventurers of every description attempted the river in keelboats or in dugouts made from giant cottonwood logs. Rowing, sailing and—more often than not—hauling their clumsy craft against the current, they generally expended an entire summer in attaining the upper reaches of the stream. But once a trapper arrived in beaver country he could expect to harvest about 120 pelts per year—worth the then-tidy sum of $1,000 or so back East.

There was no artist on hand to record the beauties and hazards of their first journeys. But in 1833, a peripatetic German naturalist, Prince Maximilian, boarded the keelboat *Flora* to explore the upper river, unchanged since the early days of the fur trade. With him was a Swiss artist, Karl Bodmer, who faithfully recreated life on the Missouri as it was before the age of steam.

The keelboat *Flora,* anchored near a Gros Ventre camp on the Missouri, is besieged by Indians eager to barter beaver pelts for brandy.

On the way downstream with a load of furs, traders ground
their craft on a bank and disembark for the evening meal.
Before settling in for the night, wilderness veterans usually
sent scouts into the woods to check for hostile Indians.

47

A cavalcade of Mandan Indians crosses the frozen Missouri after a midwinter visit to Fort Clark, a major trading post sited on a bluff near present-day Bismarck. The ice could easily support them: it formed early in November, reached a thickness of four feet, and did not break up until April.

In artist Bodmer's dramatic masterpiece, trappers receive an unpleasant — but not uncommon — surprise: a pair of ravenous grizzlies has discovered the meat cache left by an advance contingent of hunters, leaving little but bones for the landing party to take back with them to their keelboat.

Manuel Lisa: merchant prince of the trappers' domain

Common honey bees (*Apes melliferae*) did not exist in North America before the Europeans brought them across the Atlantic in the 17th Century, but they proliferated in the New World and were received as omens when they materialized, after more than a hundred years of travel, among the Indians of the Missouri Valley. The bees moved upstream just ahead of river-borne traders, and tribe after tribe assumed that nature had sent them as harbingers of the white invaders. The assumption hardened because the intruding humans seemed to share behavioral traits with the intruding insects: unnatural industry, boldness, a passion for acquisition and a reflexive use of weaponry. Few of the newcomers demonstrated these qualities as dramatically, however, as Manuel Lisa—a black-browed bravo of Spanish blood who swims back to us through history as the most egotistic, the most controversial and the most farseeing of the adventurers who sought wealth and personal dominance on the Big Muddy before the age of steam.

Beaver pelts were the riches that drew men like Lisa up the Missouri, and the capricious Indian tribes of its valley were the implacable croupiers of success or failure, life or death, with whom every fur trader was compelled to gamble. No one diced with them more skillfully—or recklessly—than Lisa. And no one made more enemies among his own kind in doing so: he was not only arrogant, headstrong and a foreigner (to both the French and Americans in St. Louis) but also—more galling yet—was seldom wrong in his larger schemes and assumptions.

It was Manuel Lisa who first deduced, partly on the strength of discoveries by Lewis and Clark, that a fortune awaited the man who could tap the untouched fur sources on the flanks of the Rockies. And it was he who first employed white trappers—soon renowned as "mountain men"—to free himself from uncertain reliance on Indians as the sole source of his bales of pelts. Beyond all this, in winning through to those distant regions that were the arena for his dreams, he proved himself the riverman supreme.

In his day, keelboats were the principal cargo craft used to ascend the Missouri, and Lisa rode one of these vessels into legend in an incredible chase in 1811. That year, John Jacob Astor, the reigning power of the American fur business, dispatched a large expedition overland to begin trading in pelts in the Pacific Northwest. His agents traveled up the Missouri on the first leg of their journey across the West. Since Lisa planned to go upstream on the affairs of his own fur company and was wary of attack by the Sioux and other dangerous river tribes, he set out to catch Astor's fleet and to use it as protective cover beyond the Platte. It was a mad idea. His rivals were 19 days ahead of him when he started and, thanks to his bitter enemies among them, did their best to stay ahead of him once they became aware of his pursuit. But his men caught them anyhow, rowing, poling and towing their heavily laden craft some 1,200 awful miles upstream in just 61 days. This feat of speed, endurance and leadership was never matched on an American river.

History has encapsulated Lisa as a man who was motivated by that most American of ambitions, hope of riches gained through success in trade. But this is too narrow a view of him, and one that presents too constricted an understanding of the great river he utilized. If Lisa was the first entrepreneur of the Rocky Mountain fur trade, he was also—in his conquistador's dreams, his black temper and his love of chance—the last of another

To his detractors a ruthless scoundrel, to his admirers a courageous captain of risky enterprises, Manuel Lisa led the first commercial trapping party up the Missouri.

breed: the hot-blooded soldiers of fortune who, for 250 years, had probed North America for precious metals, furs, imperial territories and — most coveted of all — a water corridor through the continent that might give European ships easy access to the spices, silk, gemstones and tea of the Orient.

Lisa shared more than Spanish blood and Spanish pride with Francisco Vasquez de Coronado, the explorer of the Southwest, and more than hardihood and recklessness with those agents of the French crown who entered middle America and the plains from the north. All of them were thralls of the Missouri River, the great watercourse of the West, though many knew it only as a rumor.

The Missouri was not, simply, discovered. It flickered in the consciousness of men like a mirage — a mirage distorted by ignorance and by self-serving hope — for more than a century before Marquette and Jolliet laid eyes on its juncture with the Mississippi in 1673 and thus verified its existence. The first white men to hear of it had been the Spanish explorers who entered North America from the south. In 1541, Coronado led an expedition out of Mexico, across the Texas Panhandle and into Kansas where, according to myth, there was a land called Quivira that harbored such fabulous wealth that ordinary citizens ate from bowls made of gold. Coronado and his men found no such riches, much less a ruler who — said legend — took afternoon naps under a tree hung with innumerable little gold bells that put him to sleep as they swung in the air. But they did meet Indians who told them about the Missouri, a "great river" to the north.

Hernando de Soto discovered the Mississippi River almost simultaneously, having advanced upon it from Florida. Spanish geographers were quick to assume that his river and Coronado's were one and the same — a single mighty stream that began somewhere in the West, passed through lands to the north of Quivira and emptied into the Gulf of Mexico.

This theory was funneled to the world through one Pedro de Castañeda, a soldier who participated in Coronado's exploration of North America and who, in or around the year 1555, produced a detailed history of the expedition. "According to information that was considered reliable," Castañeda wrote, the great river "comes from very far, from the land of the southern cordillera" — the southern mountains. Although Castañeda's information — presumably from Indians — had positioned these mountains north of Kansas, he called them the "southern cordillera" because he believed they existed in the vicinity of the "South Sea," which was the name his countryman Balboa had given to the Pacific Ocean upon discovering it in 1513.

Spanish empire builders knew that South America narrowed at Panama and widened again only moderately in Mexico; many of them had hoped that the country north of Mexico might continue in proportion, or perhaps even narrow again into another isthmus. Although Coronado proved otherwise, Castañeda salvaged something of the dreams for easy intercourse with the Orient by postulating the existence of a stream that ran to the Gulf of Mexico from mountains in the vicinity of the Pacific.

The Spaniards stayed in the Southwest thereafter, save for a few tentative probes of the plains and one overland expedition as far as the Platte conducted 53 years after Coronado's trek. Meanwhile, the early French explorers of Canada also heard of a "great river" from northern Indians. Officials in Paris and Versailles, having suffered grave disappointment when the St. Lawrence River failed to offer a way to India and China, nursed high hopes of bending the rumored stream (which the Indians called the Minanghenachequeke or Pekitanoui, for Muddy Water) to the designs of empire. At one point, French scholars assumed that the river ran west rather than east, an idea that stemmed, in part, from simple wishfulness.

Certain adjustments of concept were made after Marquette and Jolliet found that the river flowed east after all. The French then decided that the Big Muddy's sources lay close to a great inland sea that either opened directly onto the Pacific or ultimately "discharged" into that ocean through a broad, navigable stream. The route to the Orient thus remained reasonably clear, though the traveler faced a regrettable inconvenience in getting there: he would have to paddle upstream rather than coast down.

Such assumptions were often honestly conceived. Indians had told the French about an "ill-smelling inland sea" — which suggested salt water — and had given it a location near the Muddy Water. The French, like the Spanish before them, listened raptly to Indian reports

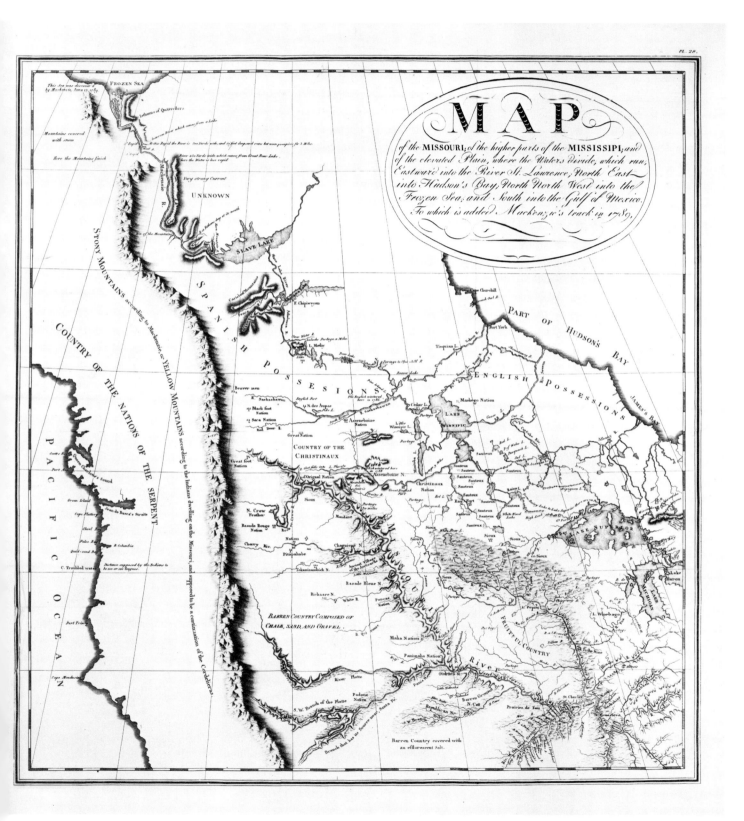

Having come 1,000 miles up the Mississippi from New Orleans in 1763, fur trader Pierre La Clede extends his hand in friendship to an Osage

chief at the spot where St. Louis would rise. This re-creation of the city's founding was painted by German artist Charles Wimar a century later.

The fur rush was at its peak in the early 1830s when Karl Bodmer made this study of a beaver den on the Missouri. Factories in England and Germany turned the pelts into top hats that sold for about $10 each.

without realizing that these were usually passed from tribe to tribe. The process of transmission not only produced a gradual alteration of substance, but — since each proclaimant gave his tale an immediacy it did not usually deserve and assumed it had sprung into being not far from where he had heard it — also produced a foreshortened idea of time and distance. Frenchmen, therefore, had no way of knowing that the "ill-smelling inland sea" was probably Lake Winnipeg, a large body of water, edged by mud flats and marshes, in what is now Manitoba. It lay nowhere near the Pacific Ocean, and the nearest point of the Missouri was 300 miles to the southwest of the lake.

Indians tended, while reworking geography, to endow the wilderness with all sorts of wondrous civilizations akin to the one that had lured Coronado to Kansas. In the early 18th Century, for instance, the French explorer Étienne Venyard, Sieur de Bourgmont, ventured a few hundred miles up the lower Missouri in

full expectation of verifying Indian reports of white dwarfs who had eyes set out an inch from their noses, lived on the inland sea, trafficked in rubies and wore boots studded with gold. Although Bourgmont failed to meet them, he remained convinced that they retreated deeper into the West on hearing of his approach and that they would be found in due course.

White men sometimes started such rumors themselves — although their imaginings usually met with much greater suspicion. Such was the fate of one Mathew Sagean, a French marine who delivered himself of a wild flight of fancy while serving at Brest on the Brittany peninsula in 1701. Sagean's tale was admittedly somewhat dated; he swore that he had been captured by English pirates after service with Robert Cavelier, Sieur de la Salle — an explorer who came upon the mouth of the Missouri nine years after Marquette and Jolliet. But now he felt duty-bound to reveal secrets that he had kept locked in his breast during 20 years among "heretical foreigners," as he called the English.

He and some French companions, Sagean said, had paddled upstream for about 500 miles and then carried their canoes overland an unspecified distance —meeting lions and tigers en route. Finally they entered the great nation of the Acanibas, whose king lived inside walls of solid gold. Sagean was not fond of the Acanibas: their heads had been made narrow and hideous as the result of being pressed between boards in infancy; their women had huge ears; and their taste in music, in his opinion, left a good deal to be desired. Still, they sent caravans of gold to Japan and received iron and steel in payment. They were hospitable: girls who refused to bed down with the Frenchmen were dispatched with daggers. They had many parrots and monkeys. And they gave away gold bars; Sagean claimed he had carried off 60 of these bars when he left (amid "terrific howlings" by his hosts) but had, alas, lost them all to his monstrous English captors.

No one in the New World was inclined to act on Sagean's inventive report, even though the Comte de Ponchartrain —one of Louis XIV's ministers and a more credulous man than most — shipped Sagean all the way to Louisiana to circulate his tale. But the desire to find a water route to the Pacific —hopefully one less strenuous than the eastward-flowing Missouri —remained as keen as ever. Ironically, it was the search for an alternative stream that finally led white men to the upper Missouri at last.

In 1727, a Quebec-born fur trader, Pierre Gaultier de Varennes, Sieur de la Vérendrye, heard the old story of a west-flowing connection with the Pacific from a new source — from Indians at Lake Nipigon, 35 miles north of Lake Superior. He pursued it so doggedly as to become one of Canada's greatest explorers. La Vérendrye was a blunt, purposeful patriot who served in the French Army (incurring nine wounds) during the War of the Spanish Succession and who devoted himself wholeheartedly to the fortunes of the government's fur operations after returning to his native Quebec. He spent seven years cultivating the Crees and Assiniboins, and building a series of trading posts (Fort St. Pierre, Fort St. Charles, Fort Maurepas) north of the border of present-day Minnesota.

La Vérendrye sent 30,000 beaver pelts back to Montreal each year, but he paid a tragic personal price for unsealing the riches of the wilderness. In 1736, his oldest son, with 20 other men, was murdered by Sioux on an island in Lake of the Woods. The Indians decapitated their victims and, in an eerie gesture of contempt, wrapped their heads in beaver skins. La Vérendrye nevertheless pressed on, determined to find the river described by Indian informants.

He built Fort Rouge at the site of Winnipeg in 1738 and that November —properly positioned at last and with an escort of 400 friendly Assiniboins —marched across the frozen prairies and came upon the upper Missouri at the Mandan villages near present-day Bismarck, North Dakota. Just as he had hoped, the stream flowed southwest (though only because of a vast local bend). Unfortunately, his interpreter decamped before he could wring any detailed geographical information from the Mandans. He was not impressed by what he learned from that tribe's use of sign language: they told him they lived at the center of the world. But it was clear enough that the Pacific lay much farther away than he thought. He retreated to Canada in discouragement and declining health prevented him from resuming the search.

However, the upper Missouri had at last been seen by a white man, and others soon drifted toward its waters — Gallic canoemen coming from the trading posts that La Vérendrye had established to the north. No white men ever blended so successfully with the tribal cultures of the Missouri Valley as did these *"coureurs de bois"*—literally, "runners of the woods" — who rode the Missouri in wooden dugouts to seek furs, savor the wilderness and take wives among the *sauvages* (a term that, for all their acceptance of Indian ways, they stubbornly refused to abandon). There is no way of knowing how far upstream they went; these adventurers were illiterates who kept no records. But it is known that two of La Vérendrye's surviving sons returned to the river in the spring of 1742 and traveled to the west of it for months, encountering various Plains Tribes. The two wanderers probably saw the Black Hills and, quite possibly, a front range of the Rockies.

The world paid them little heed. England soon swallowed French Canada, and the Dakota prairies swallowed the lead tablet the brothers left behind to claim for France all that they had seen. (The tablet was rediscovered in 1913 by a 14-year-old Fort Pierre,

South Dakota, schoolgirl.) Their father's work, however, did not have to wait that long for a degree of vindication. When Lewis and Clark headed across the continent to the Pacific in 1804, they traveled much of the way on the Missouri. And even though the great waterway failed to breach the barrier of the Rockies, it instantly became an artery of commerce, largely because of the labors of a worthy heir to generations of empire builders — Manuel Lisa.

In trying to take the measure of Manuel Lisa, one must grapple with sketchy records and peer through mists of enigma. Clues to his beginnings are almost nonexistent: old records simply show that he was born in New Orleans to Cristóbal and Maria Ignacia Rodriguez de Lisa, that his father served the Spanish crown, and that Manuel went by boat to the Wabash River as a trader when he was very young. His need for ascendancy — and a knack for stepping on the toes of others — were well developed by the time he arrived in St. Louis in 1798 at the age of 26. And so was a gift for political maneuvering.

St. Louis and the Missouri River valley were then under Spanish rule, the result of a 1762 treaty by which France had ceded to Spain all of its territory west of the Mississippi River. Lisa—being Spanish—had something of an advantage over French merchants in dealing with officialdom, and he was not the slightest bit reticent in exploiting it. He set his sights on a particular plum of privilege: the rights to trade with the Osage tribe. The trading license had been held for at least a decade by the Chouteaus, a founding French family of St. Louis; but Lisa, after recruiting three French partners to raise capital, suggested to authorities that he, as a fervent Spanish patriot, was a more deserving beneficiary. In his petition, he further proposed to demonstrate his loyalty to the crown by making a $1,000 "gift" to the royal treasury.

These persuasions had the desired effect. Lisa, however, soon found that the Spanish Lieutenant Governor was less than attentive to his complaints in the matter of a sneak trader who was attempting to barter with the Osages, offering them brandy for pelts. He sent the official a wrathful and impudent letter: "Your intention at all times has been to ignore us and give us sufficient proofs of the antagonism which you have toward us in

matters pertaining to the trade of the Missouri." The Lieutenant Governor instantly threw his intemperate countryman in jail to cool off, and Lisa was forced to write an abject letter of apology for his outburst. "It is not right," he admitted, "that a subject like I should criticize or conceive any wrong idea of the actions of a superior person, who at all times has shown his good heart." This recantation, along with a promise to show proper respect in the future, won his release.

Meanwhile the Chouteaus, who had been seething with resentment and ill will ever since the Spanish ruling clique turned their monopoly over to the young interloper, taught Lisa something about the deviousness of the fur trade. The official agreement allowed him the sole right to deal with the "Osages of the Missouri" — a redundant wording, since the Indians had dwelled only in the Missouri Valley from time out of mind and had no tribal divisions elsewhere. Yet the Chouteaus somehow talked almost half of the tribe into moving to the valley of the Arkansas River; and there the French entrepreneurs went on trading with the Osages as usual.

Lisa nevertheless continued to do well in St. Louis and the outlying area by dealing in real estate, buying and selling slaves, operating general stores and outfitting fur-trading expeditions to various tribes in the lower reaches of the Missouri Valley. Many of his customers bought on credit and then found themselves unable to pay, hence Lisa was constantly embroiled in lawsuits to recover debts. Justice was usually on his side, but he earned himself a reputation for litigiousness and a good many confirmed enemies.

International maneuvering, meanwhile, wrought some drastic changes in his theater of operations. In 1800, Spain secretly ceded much of its territory west of the Mississippi to France, although continuing to maintain control; then, in 1803, Napoleon sold these holdings —800,000 square miles—to the United States for $15 million. President Thomas Jefferson immediately dispatched Meriwether Lewis—his private secretary—and fellow Virginian William Clark to investigate the region's inhabitants, its natural resources and its potential avenues of commerce. During the winter of 1803-1804, the explorers began to assemble men and equipment outside of St. Louis. They purchased some of their supplies from Manuel Lisa and a partner, François Benoît. Somehow the two merchants managed to incur

Solid St. Louis citizens in a cutthroat business

In the 1820s, Manuel Lisa faced fearsome competition on the Missouri from two quarters—the wealthy fur-trading Chouteau clan of St. Louis and John Jacob Astor, head of the nation's biggest fur company. Things were simpler for the generation of fur entrepreneurs that followed Lisa; they only had to fear the Chouteaus.

The Chouteau family's rise to supremacy on the Missouri River began in 1834, when Pierre Chouteau Jr. purchased the western division of Astor's American Fur Company for an estimated $250,000. Although Chouteau was a model of gentility in St. Louis—a city his grandfather had helped to found—he wasted no time

on good manners doing business away from home; and neither did his son Charles, who eventually took over the million-square-mile fur empire. They instructed their men to scare off rival traders with threats of gunplay; they sold illegal whiskey to Indians; and they regularly bribed Indian agents to divert annuities—free provisions owed to the tribes by treaty—to their company, which then sold the goods at a near-total profit.

When the Chouteau company was felled by a dying fur market in 1865, it was little mourned. One of the few Indian agents to turn down its bribes called it "the most corrupt institution ever tolerated in our country."

Pierre Chouteau Jr. in the 1820s

This St. Louis warehouse served as Pierre Chouteau's first headquarters: heady profits soon built a bigger main office—plus one in New York.

Lewis' ire: "Damn Manuel and triply damn Mr. B.," he wrote. "They give me more vexation than their lives are worth. I think them both great scoundrels."

Lisa seemed more contentious than ever after the departure of Lewis and Clark upriver that spring. He sued more than 20 people for debts that totaled several hundred dollars. At the same time, hungering for new fields to conquer, he conceived a grand scheme to open up trade between St. Louis and the silver-rich city of Santa Fe, 900 miles distant. Unfortunately, the new governor of the Louisiana Territory, U.S. General James Wilkinson, decided — as he wrote to a colleague — that "no good can be derived to the United States from such a project, because the prosecution of it will depend entirely upon the Spaniards, and they will not permit it, unless to serve their political, as well as their personal interests."

The hot-tempered trader brought down on his own head some of the general's suspicion. Wilkinson had ordered Lieutenant Zebulon Pike to make a journey of exploration into the country that lay athwart Lisa's proposed route to the Southwest, and Lisa detained the

expedition by having Pike's interpreter arrested for debt. Whether or not this action had an ulterior motive remains unknown. In any case, Lisa dropped the Santa Fe plan — and it would not be revived until 1821, when another Missouri trader, William Becknell, opened the Santa Fe Trail.

But Lisa did not have to look far for a suitably promising alternative. Lewis and Clark arrived back in St. Louis on September 23, 1806, and reported that the headwaters of the Missouri and the streams of the Rockies were immeasurably rich in beaver, verifying rumors that for years had been filtering downriver from Indians. Lisa instantly made ready to travel this road to fortune. He bought two keelboats and hired 50 men, many of them veterans of the Lewis and Clark expedition, to serve as crew. Once they had reached their destination these men, according to Lisa's plan of operations, would slip into the role of trappers. This was a radical departure from normal fur business practices: ordinarily, Indians harvested the pelts, which were then obtained by the whites through trade. But Lisa realized that, to build a viable business, he must employ white trappers to bear the brunt of menial work on the upper Missouri River; Lewis and Clark had reported that the Indians of the region were war-loving horsemen with minimal interest in pursuing such an odd little beast as the beaver.

For all his careful preparations, Lisa found no backers among his fellow merchants in St. Louis; they felt that an expedition to such a distant and little-known region was hopelessly risky. Undaunted, Lisa and his small party set off up the river on April 19, 1807. At the mouth of the Platte, he met and recruited John Colter, who had gone to the Rockies with Lewis and Clark and become so enamored of the wilderness that he declined to come back. Colter proved an invaluable guide to the waters ahead. But it was Lisa's own brash insouciance — and perhaps something more — that got the expedition past its first crisis.

Near the mouth of the Grand River in present-day South Dakota, Lisa's party saw 300 Arikaras crowded on shore. The Indians, some of them equipped with guns procured from British and French traders to the north, fired a warning volley across the bows of boats and indicated that they should land. Lisa acceded, but when he reached shore, he commanded the Indians not to set foot on his vessels. When he sensed that they were preparing to attack, he pointed his keelboat's bow-mounted swivel cannon directly at the crowd. The Indians scattered in terror, and finally a few Arikara chiefs came forward to smoke peace pipes, stroke Lisa's shoulders as a gesture of friendship, and speak of trade.

That, at least, was Lisa's account of the incident. But some voyagers who came upstream behind him had reason to believe that it was only half the story of a monstrous plot by which he had traded the lives of others for his own. Chief among these detractors was Ensign Nathaniel Pryor, a veteran of the Lewis and Clark mission to whom the government had entrusted a bit of business left over from the transcontinental reconnaissance; the explorers had brought a Mandan chieftain downstream to meet with President Jefferson, and — not long after Lisa left St. Louis — Pryor was given the task of returning the chief to his tribal homeland. He traveled upstream in company with a trading party, led by Pierre Chouteau Jr. and bound for the Mandan villages. But the Arikaras, whom Lisa had bypassed so easily, attacked the Pryor-Chouteau fleet, killed three men and chased the lot of them back downstream in confusion.

Pryor picked up an Indian woman along the river and, after interrogating her, arrived at the conclusion that the attack stemmed straight from the treachery of Manuel Lisa. The Spaniard, said Pryor, had bribed the Indians with arms and confided to them that boats bearing a chief of the Mandans — old enemies — would soon follow him into view, whereupon the Arikaras permitted Lisa's party to pass and waited to ambush the next vessels. These charges remained unverified, but whispered rumors of Lisa's perfidy never died out.

Still, there was no denying Lisa's personal bravery. He got his precious trade goods past the Mandans farther upstream by walking through 20 miles of scattered Indian villages, handing out presents to such chiefs as he met to distract them while his boat proceeded past the trouble spot. Sterner methods were necessary when a great mass of Assiniboins — apprised of his approach by scouts — painted themselves for war and gathered where the channel ran close to the shore ("The prairie," Lisa later told people in St. Louis, "was red with them"). He loaded his swivel gun, headed directly for the gesticulating mob and sent the warriors "tumbling over each other" by loosing a volley over their heads.

It took Lisa until November to run the gauntlet of river tribes, ascend the Yellowstone to the entrance of the Bighorn River (a turn he made at John Colter's suggestion) and to prepare there, with such patience as he could summon, for the long mountain winter.

His luck turned at last, however, under the warm sun of spring. The Yellowstone country was alive with beaver; the Crow Indians (whose lands he had invaded) were friendly; and his new system of using white trappers rather than relying entirely on trade proved more productive than he had dared to imagine. He was back in St. Louis by August of 1808 with a small fortune in pelts and was received as a conqueror by the leading citizens of the town. Old rivals lined up to help finance his expansion as the Missouri Fur Company. Pierre and Auguste Chouteau joined up; so did Governor Wilkinson's brother, Benjamin.

All the new investors anticipated vast and almost instant wealth on joining forces with Lisa. In the spring of 1809 the firm sent no fewer than 350 men upstream in a fleet of 13 keelboats and barges. Some of the men stayed on Cedar Island, 550 miles above the Platte, charged with building a fortified post in Sioux country; others — including Lisa himself — went up the Yellowstone as far as the Bighorn River; but the majority followed the Big Muddy to the mountains. The company had grandiose plans: it proposed to build a new post where the Jefferson, Madison and Gallatin rivers meet to form the Missouri; this fort would add the fur resources of the virgin Blackfoot territory to those of the Crow lands that had proved so fruitful the year before.

Lisa returned to St. Louis in November 1809 to procure supplies that would be needed the following year. The expedition to the "Three Forks" proceeded smoothly enough with Andrew Henry, a partner and a brave and able man, in command. But disaster after disaster befell it — and the company — in 1810. The Blackfeet would not tolerate trappers in their land and began to stalk and murder them with horrifying regularity. George Drouillard, an old associate of Lisa's, ventured only two miles from the trappers' fort and was later found — as a comrade reported — "mangled in a horrible manner, his head cut off, his entrails torn out and his body hacked to pieces." Between 20 and 30 trappers were slaughtered in all. Henry led the survivors across the Continental Divide and set up winter quarters on the Snake River; fierce blizzards besieged them, and they subsisted — barely — on horse meat. The new post at Cedar Island caught fire, meanwhile, and burned to the ground — destroying about $15,000 worth of furs being held there while on the way to market.

The company was threatened on other fronts as well. War with England appeared imminent, and St. Louis merchants feared that conflict might lead British agents to rouse the river tribes against the United States — or, more specifically, against American fur traders. John Jacob Astor, long the dominant force in fur trading in the Great Lakes region, had decided, moreover, to extend his business westward and had formed the Pacific Fur Company for the purpose. His Western venture, led by New Jersey merchant Wilson Price Hunt, was supposedly aimed solely at reaping the fur resources of the Oregon country. Astor indeed had sent a ship around the Horn with matériel to erect a trading post — which would be called Astoria — at the mouth of the Columbia River. But Lisa and the other owners of the

A distinctly pedestrian mode of navigation

Moving a ten-ton keelboat up the Missouri called for a variety of propulsive methods — all but one of them testing the limits of human brawn. The exception was windpower, and it was only intermittently practicable because of the river's meanderings. Where the current was slow the crew used oars, and where the bottom was firm they could pole the boat. But since the current was swift for long stretches and the bottom was usually soft alluvium, most days were spent cordelling — a technique more akin to mule-skinning than boatmanship.

In cordelling, as many as 20 men stepped ashore and pulled the vessel upstream with a towline — the "cordelle." The line was tied to the top of the mast to lift it clear of bushes along the bank, and it passed through a ring at the end of a "bridle": a short auxiliary rope attached to the bow. This arrangement helped to prevent the boat from swinging about as it was hauled forward.

The men laboring on shore did not have the benefit of paths; they crashed through underbrush, scrambled across steep bluffs and sloshed through muddy shallows. When both banks of the river were impassable, the keelboaters resorted to "warping," a variation of cordelling in which a skiff and capstan were used in lieu of straining pedestrians. The skiff was rowed several hundred feet upstream to anchor the cordelle to a snag or tree; crewmen on the keelboat then pulled their vessel forward by reeling in the towline on a capstan. Continuous progress could be made by anchoring a second towline while the first was being hauled in.

Warping might gain a keelboat six miles a day, and cordelling covered 15 miles a day if the boat was manned by a strong-backed crew. Yet Manuel Lisa, using both techniques during his keelboat sprint upriver in 1811, somehow averaged 18 miles a day — a record that was never equaled.

Missouri Fur Company were compelled to wonder if the fur magnate might not also have his eye on their own upper-river trapping grounds.

The prospect of war and possibility of ruinous competition led the St. Louis investors in the Missouri Fur Company to decide that any further expenditures would merely send good money after bad. They therefore refused to give Lisa sufficient funds to resupply the beleaguered Andrew Henry. They turned over virtually all control of the firm to Lisa in the process — thus, in effect, washing their hands of the whole enterprise until such time as he should rescue it from disaster. None of them felt this likely without a new infusion of capital; they assumed that the company would very probably cease to exist by the following winter.

Lisa, a realist, certainly understood the precariousness of the situation; yet he began planning another journey to the mountains. He could afford only one keelboat by this time, and only 20 men to work its oars and poles on the toilsome upstream trip; but he felt dutybound to find Henry and his trappers if they still lived. He was loath, beyond that, to abandon so rich a project

as the upper-river trade without discovering for himself whether it could not be restored. Lisa was a man who liked to say, quoting Don Quixote, "A good heart breaks bad fortune," and he seems to have been stimulated by the hair-raising role in which he had been cast and uplifted by a kind of warrior's condescension for those who proposed to stay behind. Thus, in the spring of 1811, he made ready for the expedition that lives in history as the "great keelboat race."

It was never really a race, in the accepted sense, at all. Lisa simply wanted to travel beside Wilson Hunt, his opponent, rather than beat him to any mark. Lisa was motivated by a simple desire for survival: with one lone boat, he would have become an easy target for the warlike tribes that roamed the banks of the river above the Platte; but if he could attach himself to Hunt's fleet of four keelboats, he was far less likely to lose his scalp. Hunt, having managed a 240-mile head start, wanted to stay in front for a kindred reason: he had heard Ensign Nathaniel Pryor's story that Lisa had bought safety from the Arikaras by sacrificing boats in his wake,

By cordelling, poling and sailing all at once — an unusual combination — lower Missouri keelboatmen of the 18th Century make excellent progress.

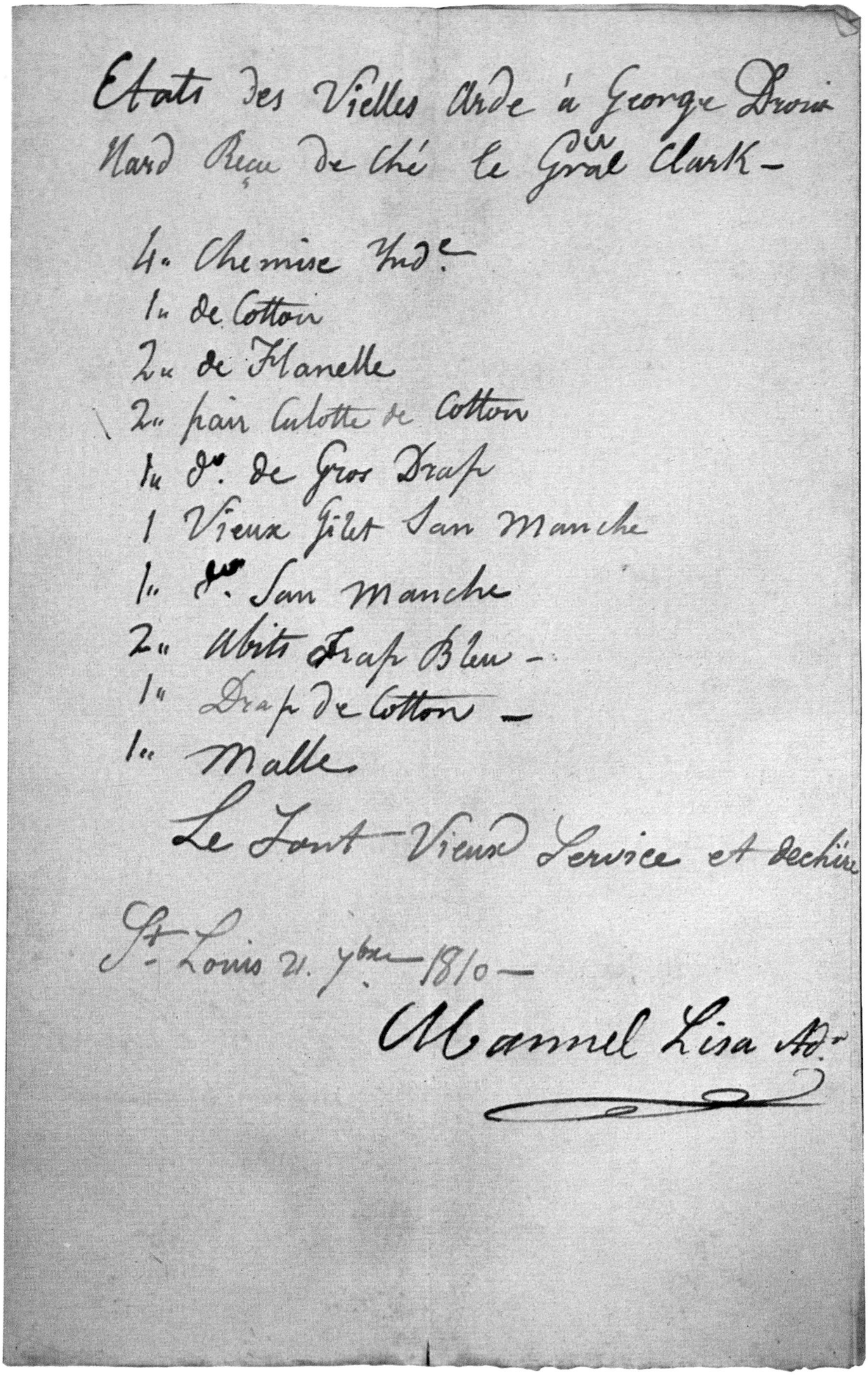

Etats des Vielles Arde à George Drois
Nard Reçu de ché le Gñãl Clark —

4" Chemise Ynd?
1" de Cotton
2" de Flanelle
2" pair Culotte de Cotton
1" d°. de Gros Drap
1 Vieux Gilet San Manche
1" d°. San Manche
2" Abits Drap Bleu —
1" Drap de Cotton —
1" Malle
Le Tout — Vieux Service et dechire

St Louis 21. 7bre — 1810 —

Manuel Lisa A°r

and he had no intention of exposing himself to such a murderous maneuver.

Hunt headed upstream on March 14, despite Lisa's best efforts to detain him by salting away a key member of his expedition. Hunt had employed as interpreter a certain Pierre Dorion, a half-breed who had worked for the Missouri Fur Company; Dorion had gone into debt with the firm—mostly for whiskey costing $10 a quart upriver—and Lisa now attempted to have him arrested for defaulting. However, the half-breed was warned that the law was after him; he hastened upriver and waited on the bank until Hunt came by to pick him up.

Lisa spent the next three weeks readying his single craft for the catch-up voyage. His keelboat was loaded to 20 tons; one can calculate thus—by a rule of thumb that relates size to burden—that it was about 50 feet in length, eight feet in beam, and that it drew two feet of water. Its bow was decked to leave room for oarsmen up forward; but the rest of the hull, except for the cleated boards along the gunwales, boasted a raised cabin with six feet of interior headroom. The mast stood just ahead of this house, and the steersman—normally Lisa's *patron* or first lieutenant, but often Lisa himself—perched on its roof to work the long oar pivoted at the pointed stern. The expedition's trade goods—blankets, tobacco, knives, guns and beads—were concealed in a crude enclosure made of shingles. Immediately aft was a bunkroom in which Lisa slept and in which were racked two big brass blunderbusses as well as muzzle-loaders for the crew. A brass swivel cannon on the bow added a more noticeable note of warning.

On April 2, 1811, the boat set off from the village of St. Charles—a muddy hamlet, situated 28 miles above the river's mouth, from which most expeditions took their departure from civilization. The water was high (the ice only recently having broken) and the weather cool but pleasant. Lisa, however, was tense with exasperation. His crewmen had spent the previous night in a tavern and were drunk, obstreperous and hard-

A scrawled document in imperfect French records the belongings of one of Manuel Lisa's trappers—George Drouillard—who was ambushed and mutilated by a party of Blackfeet in the spring of 1810. The man's estate consisted of a few shirts, coarse sheets and a sleeveless sweater—"all well-used and worn," Lisa noted at the end of the list.

ly able to set their oars in the water. He put the boat against the shore after a few miles and kept it there for a day so that the men could recover. But once he was fairly underway and at grips with the awful river, he became a different man—cheerful, tireless, sensitive to every change of water, wind and weather, and the personification of boundless confidence.

His moods, and the events of the days ahead, were carefully noted in the journal of Henry Brackenridge, a footloose and inquisitive young man who had signed on as a hunter, mainly because the job offered a matchless opportunity to study the flora and fauna of the West. (Wilson Hunt, for his part, had brought along two naturalists, Thomas Nuttall and John Bradbury.)

Brackenridge admired Lisa and added balance to the accounts of his character that accrued from the pens of his enemies. "Mr. Lisa," he began, "hopes to retrieve the affairs of his company, carry assistance to the remnant of men under Mr. Henry, and privately entertains the hope of making peace with the Blackfoot Indians. A person better qualified for this arduous undertaking could not have been chosen. He is at one moment at

Trappers unload pelts to be exchanged for gunpowder, whiskey and other staples at Bellevue, a compound of traders' cabins and storehouses near

present-day Council Bluffs, Iowa. The post, given a pastoral air by artist Karl Bodmer, was built in 1810 by St. Louis-based fur merchants.

the helm, at another with a pole in impelling the barge through the rapid current. His voice, his orders, his cheering exclamations infuse new energy. I believe there are few persons so completely master of doing much in a short time." Lisa, for all his imperiousness, was often conciliatory toward those he commanded. He was that anomaly, the fiery and demanding leader who could be one with those he led. And he now drove his *engagés* by force of example.

It would be hard to conceive of labor more brutal than was entailed in dragging, poling and rowing the dead weight of a loaded keelboat against the Missouri's spring flood—labor made more arduous yet by the violent thunder and rainstorms that assaulted the laborers. The Gallic crew was able to row on occasional stretches where the current slowed, but mostly the men fought the river yard by hard-won yard—pushing with their poles from the running boards or hauling from the bank on the long cable, or cordelle, that was attached to the keelboat's mast.

Miseries and hazards abounded. Submerged waterlogged trees threatened the vessel as they would later threaten steamers. Drifting trees washed down on the boat, and at sharp bends caving banks imperiled craft and crew. The weather stayed cold and the French boatmen stayed wet at night under little tents made by raising their blankets on branches jammed into the sodden ground ashore.

"I do not believe," wrote Brackenridge, "an American could be brought to support the fatiguing labors which these men endure." He marveled at how they were able to sustain their exertions on a diet consisting of "fried corn hominy for breakfast, fat pork and biscuit for dinner, and a pot of mush containing a pound of tallow for supper."

Lisa was able to raise his sail—unspeakable luxury—after 10 days of slow struggle and made 28 miles before a following wind. But then, sensitive to his crew's sense of omen and of debt to fortune, he patiently wasted time to let them perform the good deed of rescuing an ox that, having wandered from some distant settler's clearing, had sunk to its shoulders in wet sand and was being eyed by an assemblage of buzzards. And he yelled as loudly as the rest, two days later, when the towing crew treed a bear. Guns were broken out, "amidst"—as Brackenridge put it—"the shouts of 15 or 20 barbar-

ians," and the bear, brought to ground with wounds, was dispatched with an ax. The barbarians were as invigorated by braining a bear as by saving an ox and pressed on with renewed spirits.

Lisa had fully hoped to catch Hunt by the time the Astorians reached the Platte River, above which lived the Sioux and other dangerous tribes. His worn crew had toiled past the mouths of the Gasconade, the Osage, the Chariton and the Kansas. They had covered almost 600 miles in five weeks of unremitting labor. But the Astorians, as Lisa learned by talking to two deserters coming downstream, were still more than 100 miles ahead and were now moving faster than in earlier stages of their voyage.

Lisa attained the mouth of the Platte on May 10. "The river," commented Brackenridge, "is regarded by the navigators of the Missouri as a point of much importance, as the equinoctial line amongst mariners." The crew celebrated by a boisterous ritual: they seized anyone who had not passed the Platte and shaved his head. "Much merriment was indulged on the occasion," noted Brackenridge, but Lisa himself grew steadily more grim. The keelboat was detained there for the better part of two days by "dreadful storms" that drove him to shelter at the bank.

Lisa swallowed his pride after proceeding a few days beyond the Platte and sent a messenger overland —shortcutting innumerable bends in the river—to ask the Astorians to wait for him. Hunt sent back agreement to a rendezvous at the mouth of the Niobrara River, but actually pressed on harder than ever. And Lisa's crewmen, now in open prairie country and aware of approaching peril from Indians, began exhibiting the subtle debilitation of fear as well as the signs of awful physical weariness.

The weather improved; on occasion, in fact, it grew insufferably hot. The food improved, too. The crew members gathered duck eggs along sand bars and augmented their mush with venison and wild fowl. But they endured blinding sandstorms and rapids "agitated as by violent wind."

Brackenridge stood in continual awe of the Missouri's power. "A delightful day," began one entry. "The water has risen to its utmost height, and presents a vast expanse—the current uniformly rapid, in some places rolling with the most furious and terrific violence.

The unsaintly hero who called himself Miche Phinck

Of all the folk heroes of the American frontier, none bragged louder, brawled meaner, shot straighter or drank harder than Mike Fink, the storied king of the keelboaters. Unlike many of his peers in Old West mythology, the man behind the swashbuckling picture at right (from an 1838 magazine) was a flesh-and-blood mortal who actually performed many of the deeds—and misdeeds—on which his legend is based.

Mike Fink—he insisted on spelling it Miche Phinck—was born around 1770 on the Pennsylvania frontier and in his teens served as an Indian scout. Even then he was an unbeatable marksman, and he earned the name "Bangall" among militiamen at Fort Pitt. When the Indian wars of the region ended in the early 1790s, Fink, like many other scouts, spurned a sedentary life as a farmer. Instead, he drifted into the transport business on the Ohio and the Mississippi—and quickly picked up a new nickname: "the Snapping Turtle." It was said that he could drink a gallon of whiskey and still shoot the tail off a pig at 90 paces; and Fink himself proclaimed on every possible occasion that he could "out-run, out-hop, out-jump, throw-down, drag out and lick any man in the country."

To the roughhewn keelboatmen, licking a man usually meant stopping just short of killing him. When fighting "rough and tumble"—as it was called—they tried to gouge out each other's eyes and used their teeth to tear off pieces of an opponent's lips, nose or ears. A combatant could halt the carnage by yelling "Enough!" but

Fabled keelboater Mike Fink

the keelboaters' code of honor suggested that a real man would not cease fighting after the mere loss of an eye or ear but would try to maim his adversary in return. In this violent world, Mike Fink had a reputation as an oft-bloodied but unbeaten champion.

For reasons perhaps unclear to his women, Fink also won fame among keelboaters as a lady's man. While most of his fellows boasted of having a woman in every port, Fink customarily kept one aboard as well. His methods of ensuring their fidelity were unique. Once when a Fink damsel was foolish enough to wink at another man, he set her clothes on fire; she saved herself by jumping into the river. To reinforce an attitude of respect

in his women, Fink regularly used them for target practice by shooting small objects off their heads.

An unusually cruel sense of humor—often expressed with a gun—was Mike Fink's hallmark. Perhaps its nadir was reached when, on the levee in Louisville, he spotted a slave with a protruding heel. Without a word, Fink raised his rifle and shot off the back of the man's foot. Hauled into court, he pointed out to a judge that his victim would never have been able to wear a fashionable boot if a good Samaritan, namely himself, had not intervened on the man's behalf.

Although Fink's sadistic wit merely cost him a few weeks in jail in that incident, it ultimately resulted in his death. In 1822, he and two long-time cronies named Carpenter and Talbot joined a fur-trading expedition to the upper Missouri valley. All through a long, dreary winter on the Musselshell River, Fink and Carpenter vied—sometimes venomously—for the affections of an Indian woman. The resolution of their quarrel came during a drunken spree, when Fink proposed they take turns shooting cups of whiskey off each other's heads—a trial of marksmanship they had staged in nearly every port on the Mississippi. Carpenter agreed and, after losing the coin toss, blithely walked into the open, balanced his cup carefully on his head, then signaled Fink to proceed. Fink promptly blew his brains out. "Carpenter," mourned Fink, "you have spilled the whiskey." This eulogy proved too much for Talbot, who hauled out his pistol and shot Fink through the heart.

One of these places, below Vermilion creek, was sufficient to appall the stoutest heart: the river forms an elbow at the termination of some bluffs; the water, compressed between them and the sand bar, dashes against the opposite rocks. The middle of the river appeared several feet higher than the sides. The distance to cross, before we could reach the opposite eddy, was not more than twice the length of the boat. We were not able completely to effect it, being swept down with the rapidity of flight, but we fell into the current of the opposite side before it had gained full force, and were able, with great difficulty, to gain the eddy. Great quantities of drift wood descend, and thirty or forty drowned buffaloes pass by every day."

Some among the crew developed fevers and a kind of pleurisy, and they complained bitterly to Brackenridge that "it was impossible to stand it for so long . . . that they had never so severe a voyage." They found it

impossible, however, to complain face to face to Lisa —and impossible not to respond to his outward ebullience as he stood at the steering oar and led them in the curiously innocent songs with which they set the cadence of their toil:

Behind our house there is a pond, fal la de ra.
There came three ducks to swim thereon:
All along the river clear,
Lightly, my shepherdess dear.

But Lisa, too, had doubts, although he expressed them only to Brackenridge. He had become certain that Hunt was getting past the Sioux through recourse to the very ruse that Ensign Pryor had charged Lisa himself of using with the Arikaras: "telling them that a second trader is coming on with goods."

Lisa sometimes expressed indignation toward those who accused him of rascality: "I go a great distance while some are considering whether they will start today or tomorrow. I impose upon myself great privations. Ten months of the year I am buried in the depths of the forests. Cheat? The Indians call me *Father!*" Yet he knew, as well as any man, that the fur trade was conducted amidst an atmosphere of suspicion and skullduggery — which included theft, murder and the use of Indians against competitors.

But luck now favored their boat. It brought good weather, following winds and moonlight. Lisa, able to use his sail rather than the backs of his crew for long periods — and bent on traveling when the Sioux were sleeping maintained his chase far into the night whenever the soft lunar illumination was not shut off by clouds. Under such favorable circumstances, the boat covered 75 miles in one period of 24 hours.

On June 1, after two weeks of steady good fortune, all on deck heard gunfire, spotted Indians waving rifles, and "concluded that we should be robbed and killed." Lisa seemed exhilarated. He ordered every rower armed, headed the keelboat directly at the Sioux band on shore and leaped out (followed instantly by the intrepid Brackenridge) to grab and shake the hands of the startled warriors. Then he commenced, in sign language, a pitiful hard luck story, maintaining "that he had been unfortunate, that his young men had been attacked by Indians at the head of the Missouri who were bad people, and that he was now poor and much to be pitied." He handed out presents to the Indians after this spiel and was told that Hunt, who once had been 19 days in the lead, had passed by only two days before. Lisa climbed back into the boat while the Sioux examined their baubles and ordered it pulled into the current and safely away upstream.

The crew revived after their deliverance from this first Indian threat — and with the knowledge that the surer shield of Hunt's flotilla was not far ahead. The next morning — at a point somewhere between present-day Yankton and Pierre, South Dakota — they pulled alongside Hunt's flotilla of four keelboats. Then, relaxing, they "continued under sail in company the rest of the day. We encamped in the evening twelve hundred miles from the mouth of the Missouri."

The great race was over, after such extended paroxysms of labor and — one is impelled to conclude — such moral ascendancy by a leader as had never before and

would never again be seen on an American river.

The satisfactions of accomplishment did not inhibit Lisa's rashness or instinct for making trouble. He had hardly intruded on Hunt's expedition before he attempted to force the other leader's interpreter, Pierre Dorion, into his own party, using as leverage the debt for which he had attempted to have the man jailed months earlier. Dorion was outraged. Reported Brackenridge, "He grossly insulted Mr. Lisa and struck him several times." Lisa ran to his boat, blind with fury, and came running back with his knife. Dorion armed himself with two of Hunt's pistols. Their exchange of invective soon drew Hunt into the quarrel, and he challenged Lisa to a duel. Naturalist Bradbury managed, however, to lead Hunt away; Brackenridge took Lisa off in another direction.

There, happily enough, the matter ended. Although the two leaders remained sullenly suspicious of each other for several days more, they continued to move upstream in concert, keeping to opposite sides of the river and abstaining from any contact. But they became more appreciative of each other when the Arikaras, whom each believed the other might incite to treachery, were moved to discretion by the size and strength of the keelboat fleet and welcomed it and its men with assurances of friendship. Arikara chieftains went so far, in fact, as to apologize for the bloody affair of Ensign Pryor and to blame it, in tones of bland regret, upon "bad people whom we could not restrain."

Hunt decided to leave the river at this point and head overland toward his planned rendezvous at the mouth of the Columbia with the ship John Jacob Astor had sent around the tip of South America. He sold Lisa his boats, since he had no intention of soon returning this way, and Lisa traveled to the Mandan villages to procure horses that the Astorians wanted in payment. Hunt's party struggled through the Rockies on these mounts — and later in crude canoes — reaching their destination in midwinter. But their great trek was in vain. Astor's plans for a fur empire along the Pacific were upset when the British seized his new post in the War of 1812 and used it as a fort; he retreated from the Northwest thereafter.

Lisa thought better of his outlandish idea of pacifying the Blackfeet and stayed on with the Arikaras. There, in September, his friend Andrew Henry rejoined him; Henry had left his Snake River refuge and recrossed

An Easterner's rude introduction to wild Western ways

To boatmen of the period, the upper Missouri meant hundreds of miles of treacherous water; to St. Louis capitalists it meant riches. But to the traders who lived there it was a land where men competed with maggots for buffalo meat, and the only dog not fit for eating was one that had fed on human bodies—a not infrequent circumstance. These traders were pivotal in the fur industry's invasion of the wilderness, occupying outposts along each newly conquered stretch of river and bartering goods for pelts with Indians or white trappers.

One of the most lucid—and gritty—accounts of the trader's life was the work of an unlikely chronicler, Henry Boller, scion of an aristocratic family from Philadelphia. In 1858, lusting for adventure and romance, Boller dropped out of college to take a $300-a-year job as a storekeeper at Fort Atkinson, a tiny trading post that lay 250 miles below the mouth of the Yellowstone River. His new life palled quickly enough.

He found his sleeping accommodations infested with bedbugs and noted in one of many letters home: "After several weeks my body was covered with red spots that itched intolerably." Nor was he pleased by a diet of "biscuit, beans or rice, and dried buffalo meat that smelled disgustingly." In a few weeks the menu changed: "I have spoken, I believe, of our stinking dried meat—it stinks no more—it is alive with maggots, nice fat ones that squirm and wriggle beneath the teeth like troopers."

As storekeeper, Boller spent most days keeping track of inventory, recording the transactions of the traders who worked out of his store, and drinking coffee with local Indians. His most frequent companion was Four Bears, a Gros Ventre chief. Boller described him as "a great friend" and also as the father of an eight-year-old boy "who was only five when he killed his mother with a pistol."

To break the monotony of his daily routine, Boller sometimes accompanied traders on their treks to distant Indian camps. He soon discovered that not all these grizzled frontiersmen had preternatural skill at backwoods travel: "Pete took the lead, but before his horse made 20 steps it got into quicksand, fell and rolled its rider off." Undaunted, Boller and the trader pressed on, but "after going a mile, Pete mistook the faint trail and we got lost in the timber."

August on the upper river brought a bit of rain—and also a cholera scare and an epidemic of boils. Frosts came in September, snow in October, and the Missouri froze over in November. In January, Boller wrote, "some days are so stormy and cold that even the Indians cannot venture out of their lodges . . . and water has frozen within four feet of our blazing fireplace."

But winter was not an altogether unpleasant season. Hunters in the area brought in loads of buffalo hides—thicker because of the cold, and hence more valuable—and they also supplied the fort with plenty of fresh meat. Boller often went after buffalo himself, and one expedition provided him with an incredible display of veterinary surgery, Indian style. During the hunt, a horse was gored so badly that its entrails were dragging on the ground as it walked. "Some Assiniboines caught the horse," Boller recalled, "threw him down, replaced the guts and sewed up the rent with an awl and sinew. The horse was able to walk back to camp, eat well, and entirely recover, bearing no trace of the injury save a slight lump on his side."

The country bred hardiness in men, too. When the river ice began to break in the spring, Boller watched with astonishment as young Indians took part in a chilling celebration. "The ice," he wrote, "rushed down the swollen river with incredible velocity, fully 10 miles an hour, grinding and crushing. For bravado, some of the young men would jump from piece to piece—others would swim."

Though Boller declined this challenge, he found many other aspects of the wilderness life style contagious. Toward the end of his second winter he wrote: "I have not changed my shirt and clothes for two months and wash my hands and face about once a week. When I voyage, I go it Indian style—leggings, breech-clout and blanket." About two months later he added. "My language and manners are ill-suited to a refined society."

But he did not miss society's polished ways. Although he later returned to Philadelphia for brief visits, the West always drew him back. In the mid-1860s, he followed a gold rush to Montana and, a decade later, tried cattle ranching in Kansas. Finally, as the frontier became settled, he moved to rambunctious, silver-rich Denver and operated a diversity of businesses until his death in 1902.

Wilderness convert Henry Boller models his Indian garb in the 1860s.

the Divide after most of his men straggled off on their own, and had followed the Yellowstone valley back to the Missouri. With his help, Lisa built a new trading post a few miles above the site of present-day Omaha and modestly named it Fort Lisa.

He acted as a government agent during the War of 1812, keeping various segments of the Sioux nation so close to a kind of civil war that English hopes of their stirring havoc in U.S. territory never materialized. The Santee Sioux, whom the British had befriended, stayed stolidly in their villages for fear of attack by the Teton Sioux—whom Lisa won over by handing out presents, buying furs at a fair price and even taking chiefs on a jaunt to St. Louis. Lisa's way with Indians also stood him in good stead after the war was done. He re-established Fort Lisa, roved the wilderness as far upriver as the Mandan villages and did a thriving trade in pelts in the years thereafter.

Lisa traveled 26,000 miles on the rough and unpredictable Missouri during his lifetime, ascending and descending it no fewer than 12 times. His last trip, in 1820, brought him back to St. Louis in a state of failing health. But even illness—its nature never determined —could not curb his blazing temper. He was involved in a fight with one Antoine Beaudoin on August 1 of that year. St. Louis court records noted that he "struck with a certain iron bar and his fists the said Beaudoin a great many violent blows and strokes on and about his head, face, breast, back and shoulders and diverse other parts of his body, by means of which the said Beaudoin was greatly hurt."

Death caught up with Manuel Lisa—then 47 years old—in his own comfortable bed just 11 days later and ended his dream of building a fur empire on the headwaters of the Missouri and the slopes of the high Rockies. In opening the upper reaches of the great river to commerce, however, he had already set in motion events calculated to satisfy the most voracious conquistador. Henry Brackenridge had hinted at Lisa's legacy a decade earlier, in the middle of the great keelboat race. The young man had comforted himself, as the boat approached Sioux country, by setting down in his journal: "There is no spot, however distant, where I may be buried but will in time be surrounded by the habitations of Americans and respected as containing the remains of one who first ventured into these solitary regions."

An affectionate tribute to a vanishing breed

The hardy boatmen who fought the Missouri by muscle rather than steam were on duty 16 hours a day and had to subsist, much of the time, on pork, lima beans and rotgut whiskey. Yet the job never lacked for recruits, since it offered moments of camaraderie that more than made up for the hours of toil. This placid, sunlit side of the early rivermen's lives was a source of endless fascination to George Caleb Bingham, a self-taught frontier artist who grew up in Franklin, Missouri, a river town at the head of the Santa Fe Trail.

When Bingham began to work in 1845 on the canvases shown here and on the following pages, the Big Muddy was in a state of radical transition. The keelboat, long the prime means of moving bulk cargo upstream, was near extinction, running only on the shoal-plagued stretch of water between the mouth of the Yellowstone and Fort Benton. The rest of the river — and the future — belonged to the steamboat.

But the day of the muscle-powered vessel was not quite over. Mackinaws and flatboats still ranked as the cheapest form of downstream transport: a Mackinaw able to haul 15 tons of freight could be hired — crew and all — for as little as $2 a day. Despite the complaint of fur-trade memorialist Washington Irving that "the march of mechanical invention . . . is driving everything poetical before it," Bingham's carefree boatmen remained a fixture on the Missouri well into the 1870s.

The young crew and pipe-smoking master of a small flatboat wait for a steamer to buy their load of firewood. These "wood boats" were among the last muscle-powered craft to disappear from the Missouri River.

76

The crucial moment in a card game between two flatboatmen draws a pair of kibitzers to the contest, leaving a single crewman to handle

navigational chores. Gambling and drinking were steady fare on a flatboat voyage — making the craft among the worst insurance risks on the river.

Three opportunistic flatboatmen take their ease on a bank of the Big Muddy and prepare for their evening meal after retrieving the cargo

of a steamboat sunk by a snag *(background)*. Such salvage operations were a lucrative part of the flatboat's role throughout the era of steam.

Loaded to capacity, the stern-wheeler *Rosebud* churns upstream under a full head of steam during a high-water period in the 1880s.

3 | "Steamboat acomin'"

Steam power—scarcely tamed when it came to the Missouri in 1819—was the force that enabled the river to realize its destiny as a life line to the Rockies. By the late 1830s the lower river was raucous with paddle wheelers, some resembling the Mississippi side-wheelers that one skipper hailed as "the most beautiful creation of man."

After the Civil War, a distinctive form of riverboat began to chuff up the Big Muddy to the welcoming shouts of "steamboat acomin'!" It was a no-frills stern-wheeled workhorse especially designed for upper-river voyages. Small and far from sturdy, these boats lasted about eight years on the average, and betrayed their hard lives visibly. One traveler wrote of their "cracked roofs and warped decks, especially adapted to the broiling of passengers in fair weather and drenching them in foul."

Yet during low-water periods, when channels were only waist-deep in spots, the little vessels could carry 200 tons, and they could double that if conditions permitted another foot of draft. Often patched up, sometimes with parts salvaged from wrecks, the doughty stern-wheelers were still busy on the Big Muddy when the glittering side-wheel packets were nearing oblivion.

A pleasing sight on the Missouri was an elegant side-wheeler like *Silver Bow,* shown at Fort Leavenworth in 1869. Although passengers admired her looks, luxury and speed, most steamboatmen chose the homely stern-wheelers, in good part because they were not as vulnerable to snags.

The proud old stern-wheeler *F. Y. Batchelor* had been sunk, raised and converted into a stripped-down freight carrier when this picture was taken at Bismarck in the 1880s. A few years earlier, she set the upstream record from Bismarck to Fort Buford: 307 miles in 55 hours, 25 minutes.

MISSOURI RIVER.

SAINT LOUIS & MIAMI PACKET

TAKING FREIGHT AND PASSENGERS FOR

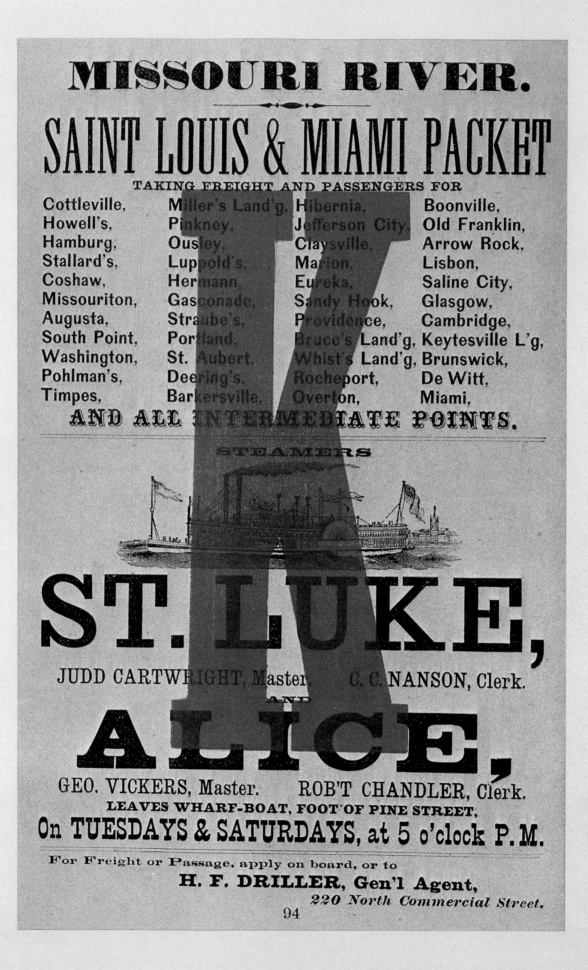

Cottleville,	Miller's Land'g,	Hibernia,	Boonville,
Howell's,	Pinkney,	Jefferson City	Old Franklin,
Hamburg,	Ousley,	Claysville,	Arrow Rock,
Stallard's,	Luppold's,	Marion,	Lisbon,
Coshaw,	Hermann,	Eureka,	Saline City,
Missouriton,	Gasconade,	Sandy Hook,	Glasgow,
Augusta,	Straube's,	Providence,	Cambridge,
South Point,	Portland,	Bruce's Land'g,	Keytesville L'g,
Washington,	St. Aubert,	Whist's Land'g,	Brunswick,
Pohlman's,	Deering's,	Rocheport,	De Witt,
Timpes,	Barkersville,	Overton,	Miami,

AND ALL INTERMEDIATE POINTS.

STEAMERS

ST. LUKE,

JUDD CARTWRIGHT, Master.   C. C. NANSON, Clerk.

AND

ALICE,

GEO. VICKERS, Master.   ROB'T CHANDLER, Clerk.

LEAVES WHARF-BOAT, FOOT OF PINE STREET,

On TUESDAYS & SATURDAYS, at 5 o'clock P.M.

For Freight or Passage, apply on board, or to

H. F. DRILLER, Gen'l Agent,

220 North Commercial Street.

94

"Fill her fireboxes, I want more steam!"

The Big Muddy thrust its tide against a wide promontory above Lexington, Missouri, during the spring flood of 1852 and reacted—on being turned aside—by feeding an angry, ice-littered brown torrent down the channel that boats used to round the bend on their way upstream. The side-wheel steamer *Saluda*—Captain Francis T. Belt, owner and master—was firing hard in consequence as she drew abreast of the town on Wednesday, April 7, and prepared to skirt the point of land ahead. But her double-engine, double-boiler power plant was just not capable of coping with the ugly water into which she thrust her bow. She hurried into it time and time again, hung in the current with her exhaust banging violently and with chunks of ice thudding against her hull, and was each time slowly washed astern. Captain Belt fell back on Lexington in the end, nosed the side-wheeler against a wharf, and tied her up.

The boat's staterooms and lower deck were jammed with Mormon immigrants, most of them from England and Wales, who were bound for Council Bluffs and the head of the long trail to the Salt Lake Valley. Cold, crowding and enforced idleness made them restive. They complained.

Belt took the side-wheeler out into the stream again the following day and was driven back once more. *Saluda*'s machinery was old and worn; she had been snagged and sunk two years before, but Belt—having bought her for a very low price after she was raised and patched—hoped to make big profits from her. Now he

was outraged at the demeaning role he was being forced to play before his grumbling passengers and before an increasingly interested gallery on the shore. On April 9, Good Friday, he resolved to force progress by beating *Saluda* as one might beat a balky horse that refused to pull its weight.

He walked into the engine room shortly after 7 o'clock in the morning and demanded to know how much more pressure her boilers would stand. "Not a pound more than she's carrying now," said the second engineer, Josiah Clancey, according to a subsequent newspaper account of the incident. Belt ordered water injection shut off and the safety valve locked down. "Fill her fireboxes up. I want more steam. I'm going to round that point or blow her to hell trying." He climbed up to the hurricane deck, pulled the clapper of the boat's bell and then—after a Lexington butcher obligingly cast off her lines and the mate and three deck hands poled her bow away from the shore—called for slow speed ahead.

Saluda's paddles splashed through two revolutions and the boilers exploded. The hull disintegrated forward of the engine room and half the upper works went skyward—accompanied by tumbling human bodies and the two iron chimneys—in a great, concussive blossoming of steam, bales, splinters, boiling water and wreckage from the cabins. Captain Belt's lacerated corpse took a high, parabolic course inland with the bell on which he had placed one elbow in the second before death; both landed high on a bluff above the river and rolled downhill together, the bell clanging wildly. A 600-pound iron safe, the boat's watchdog (which had been chained to its door) and second clerk Jonathan F. Blackburn were flung high in the air; they came to rest near one another 200 yards from the river. A local butcher, ashore, was dismembered by a flying boiler flue. A brick house nearby collapsed under the impact

Early steamboats on the Missouri followed no set schedules, but by the 1850s burgeoning passenger traffic spawned a multitude of lower-river packet companies like the K Line—a two-boat, 270-mile operation that advertised fixed departure times.

The skies boil with smoke as St. Louis burns on the night of May 17, 1849. Fire broke out on the steamer *White Cloud*, spread from vessel to vessel along the crowded levee, then ignited adjacent buildings. Twenty-three steamboats and 15 city blocks were razed in the conflagration.

of another chunk of boiler iron. The two pilots were blown into the river with pieces of the wheelhouse and never seen again.

A curious silence followed the deafening roar of the explosion. But a sound of screaming soon began under piles of wreckage on the after portion of the hull — which sank rapidly near the bank. Townspeople, rushing to the river, found — as the *St. Joseph Gazette* reported — "the mangled remains of other human beings scattered over the wharf, and human blood, just warm from the heart, trickling down the banks and mingling with the water of the Missouri River. Groans, shrieks and sobs, mingled with the plaintive wailings of helpless babes, carried grief and desolation to the hearts of those who were exerting themselves to relieve the sufferers. One wounded child called, 'Mother! Father!' But they had gone to the land of the spirits and it was left alone in the world a helpless orphan."

More than 100 bodies were recovered, and about the same number were believed to have washed down the river. Only about 50 of the people who had been aboard survived.

Saluda was long remembered. Her bell was carried to the nearby town of Savannah and placed in the belfry of the Christian Church. Lexington families adopted her orphaned children and raised them — far from England and Wales, far from the Great Salt Lake and Mormonism — as their own. Most of the children lived the rest of their lives in the town.

The disaster at Lexington was the worst in the history of steam navigation on the Missouri River. *Saluda* was representative, nevertheless, of every paddle steamer that operated on the Big Muddy. Like all such vessels, she offered a matchless boon of mechanized ease, yet engaged in a constant flirtation with sudden violence: Missouri steamers blew up by the dozen and sank by the hundreds. Still, excesses of this kind were only to be expected of an instrument that was capable of bringing about a revolution in a world that had known only muscle, animal, wind and water power since the beginning of time.

Two influences — Western rivers and Western builders — produced a boat different from any other ever before known: a ramshackle, flat-bottomed, multitiered structure that was designed to slide over the water rather than to move through it, and that had the most powerful, as well as the crudest, simplest and most dangerous engines then known to man. It was a wasteful device. Its Ohio Valley builders did what little they could to correct this trait, but they embraced wastefulness as a kind of overall philosophy even while doing so. They were quick to recognize the forests along riverbanks as vast, handy sources of cheap energy. And since they valued speed, power and performance over efficiency (or safety), their boats burned cordwood as extravagantly as subsequent American machines would burn gasoline or electricity.

The builders also favored lightweight construction so that the boat, plying shallow rivers, would draw as little water as possible. To save weight, the decks, floor timbers, bulkheads and upper works were made of pine or poplar rather than sturdier—but heavier—oak. A Council Bluffs newspaperman, with tongue only halfway in cheek, said that a Western steamer was put together out of "wood, tin, shingles, canvas and twine, and looks like the bride of Babylon." But the ungainliness of the craft was worth it: such a vessel might have a draft of as little as 14 inches.

The steamer's light construction and gargantuan appetite for fuel forced captains and pilots to become the servants as well as the masters of vessels on the Big Muddy. The Missouri pilot was confronted with a constant dilemma as soon as he steamed into the upper valley: trees were scarce along great stretches of river, but a prodigal use of wood was mandatory in surmounting the bars and rapids with which his vessel was forced to cope. Pilots had to gauge progress with a hard fact in mind: they dared not run out of fuel before reaching some stream-fed side valley where trees did grow or before coming upon a bar where "racks" of driftwood had collected. All tried to find some such source of wood before tying up for the night. Their long-suffering roustabouts then were given the task of cutting it by the light of flickering pine knots and bringing aboard a supply calculated to ensure hours of steady steaming on the following day.

The steamboat's frail construction, meantime, forced pilots into an endless preoccupation with matters riskier than the fuel supply — and into moments of decision during which the fate of the vessel and all aboard could depend on their coolness at the wheel and their judgment

‿⊂ MARK ALL GOODS ⊃‿
"BENTON P LINE,"
Care N. P. R. R., St. Paul, Minn.
Steamer BLACK HILLS,
ROBT. F. WRIGHT,   JAS. B. KEENAN,
Master.   Clerk.

*Crittenden's Island,
July 23d 84.
Steamer "Black Hills" took ten (10)
Cords Wood at four dollars ($4.00) per
Cd.
40 or Bickford*

in ringing commands to the engine room. Light construction allowed steamers to surmount sand bars and conquer low water, but it left them at the mercy of rock reefs, snags, high winds and ice in their voyages to the mountains. With its limitations, thus, the steamboat itself was as responsible as the awful river for creating pilots who emerged as the best in America. And, indeed, while pilots were popular heroes on all the Western waters, none held themselves in such high regard as those who served on the Missouri; they considered themselves princes of their profession, commanded salaries as high as $1,500 a month, and made no secret of their condescending view of counterparts on the Ohio and the Mississippi.

They were not without their quota of eccentrics. There was Joe Oldham, for instance, who wore kid gloves in the wheelhouse, kept a diamond-encrusted watch slung around his neck, and was famous for his highhanded dealings with his employers. Summoned at the last minute to take over one steamer's helm, he delayed the vessel's departure for a full 24 hours by first spending the morning demanding (and eventually getting agreement to) a fee of $1,000 for a single week's

trip and then the afternoon and evening at a previously scheduled picnic ashore with friends so dear that he could not bear to disappoint them. "Silent Ben" Jewell — one of the most garrulous men ever born — saw Indians behind every tree, solemnly reported them after every watch, and claimed to have escaped the James gang by swimming across the river with a half million in silver coins in his pockets. But both Jewell and Oldham could take a steamboat through dangerous water, and that was all that was asked of them — or, indeed, of Jacques Desiré, a French-speaking, Louisiana-born black who was a respected Missouri pilot even prior to the Civil War.

A pilot had to memorize the Big Muddy's endless bars, bends, rapids and chutes — and also know the cliffs, dead trees, clearings, cabins, hills and outcroppings at which a steamer was aimed when negotiating them. He had to be capable of deciding, very quickly, whether any landmarks had been washed away or had changed in appearance since he had last looked for them through the windows of his wheelhouse. The principal channel of the Missouri shifted unpredictably on an unstable riverbed, and its periods of receding water

93

Farfetched gadgets that sank without a trace

In their efforts to build a better steamboat for the shallow rivers of the West, inventors occasionally strayed into the realm of pure wackiness. One of the best known of these errant creators was Abraham Lincoln, who took time from his law practice in 1849 to patent an "Improved Method of Lifting Vessels over Shoals."

Inspired by the old river trick of shoving boxes and barrels under a stranded boat to float it free, Lincoln designed a set of bellows-like "expansible buoyant chambers" to be carried alongside a steamer just above the water line. When the boat entered shoal water, the chambers — made of waterproofed material and perforated at the top — would be expanded by the downward movement of stout poles, filling them with air and presumably giving the vessel a timely boost.

Despite the future President's enthusiasm for his brainchild, no steamer ever used it — possibly because the weight of the contraption was likely to create the sort of problem it was meant to avert. However, it was less farfetched than some shallow-water panaceas. In 1836, for example, a nautical heretic, Gideon Hotchkiss, had the idea of attaching a spiked wheel — described as a "Pedestrian, Traction, Repulsion, Perambulating or Anchor Wheel" — to the bottom of boats so that they could roll along the riverbed in low water. Fifteen years later, a certain William Storm called for the replacement of paddle wheels with a pair of long, cleated belts of "India-rubber, canvas, gutta-percha, sole-leather, or other fit flexible material." A boat so equipped, boasted Storm, would whiz through shallow water faster than a locomotive.

Not all inventors felt that the steamboat was the last word in river travel. In 1828, a dreamer with the promising name of Hull Chase patented a wind-powered side-wheeler. He claimed that a giant propeller mounted atop the boat and linked to the paddle wheels by gears would permit excellent progress into the teeth of the wind. Unfortunately, fact did not coincide with theory, though the wind might have produced some motion when blowing from other angles.

When it came to getting back to basics, no one excelled Samuel Heintzelman. He focused on a specific problem: the fact that rivers often impeded cavalrymen chasing Indians. His solution, patented in 1857, was the essence of simplicity: inflatable saddlebags. With them, he said, horse and rider could effortlessly float across the water. And he even threw in an instant refinement: that cavalrymen put on "waterproof pantaloons with feet" so that they would not have to suffer the discomfort of getting wet.

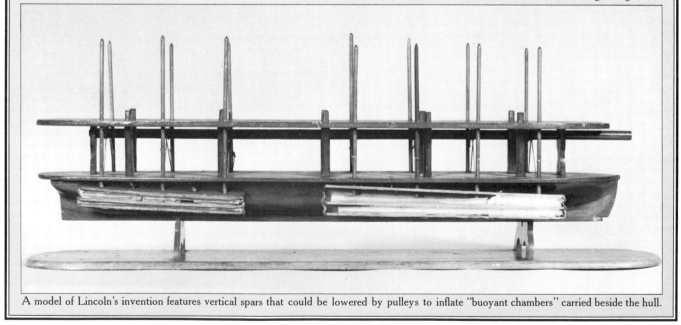

A model of Lincoln's invention features vertical spars that could be lowered by pulleys to inflate "buoyant chambers" carried beside the hull.

were far more extreme than those that pilots encountered on other rivers.

If the water level was high and the moon full, a boat might run at night; the Missouri, with its load of silt, reflected moonlight better than the Mississippi. Usually, however, the prudent pilot tied up at nightfall—unless a landing lay only a mile or so ahead. Steamers often attempted to negotiate such a short stretch of water in the dark after sending the mate ahead to mark the channel. He performed this rite by affixing lighted candles (in cylindrical paper shields) to pieces of scrap lumber and anchoring these crude floats—each tied to a length of rope weighted by a stone—along the stretch of water ahead of the boat. She then churned triumphantly over them to shore—"eating up the lights," as the procedure was called—while fascinated passengers peered into the gloom from the bow.

A pilot tied up as storms approached, too—if he had time—because the flat bottoms and high superstructures of steamboats left them almost incapable of maneuvering when they were caught in open water by one of those boiling valley thunderstorms that, in the words of an Army officer who regularly traveled the Missouri, "caused the river to yield up clouds of spray like the vortex of Niagara."

A pilot had, eternally, to "read water"—to guess at a glance the speed of a current in a bend, and to decide from surface swirls and ripples whether the river concealed rocks, sand bars or snags. Nature intruded as he did so. Wind sometimes helped him, tending to ruffle deep water dramatically. But rain dappled the whole surface and laid a blur of tiny splashes over the river's mysteries. Surface glare masked them, too, when the sun lay lower than 45 degrees above the horizon; and so also, during windy days at low water, did drifting sand from the river's dunelike bars. It took courage and skill to accept such minimal indications as remained and keep a boat moving.

Roustabouts punched a long pole to the bottom, rather than heaving a lead-weighted line, when a pilot began tapping his bell for soundings on the shallow Missouri—and they chanted the depth, while stabbing away, at every contact with the bottom. But good pilots depended on the "feel" of the steamboat as well. A vessel behaved differently as the water grew shallower, or as the speed of the current began to increase. This sense of the vessel's own reaction to the river was crucial; the pilot had only split seconds for decisions that kept the craft whole.

Still, the steamer—like the cowboy's mean and hard-mouthed mount—was exactly what it had to be: cheap enough to float cargo and make money; powerful enough to master a current that, in places, ran 10 miles per hour or even faster; and simple enough to be operated and repaired by uneducated engine-room crews.

The steamboat did not assume its role as the dominant mode of transportation on the Missouri without incessant criticism as well as incessant difficulty. Explosions and snaggings prompted torrents of remonstrance from press and pulpit; and the less-than-luxurious accommodations and the rudeness of propulsive equipment provoked endless complaint from writers, engineers and travelers from abroad. But the operators of the paddle wheelers—as well as the vast majority of passengers who risked their necks on them—responded to steam power with an astonishing optimism.

None maintained a cheerier view than a young inventor-engineer named Nicholas Roosevelt (Teddy's great granduncle), who took the first of all Western steamers from Pittsburgh to New Orleans in 1811—simply to show that it could be done—and by his example opened the whole trans-Mississippi wilderness to paddle navigation. Roosevelt's vessel, built at Pittsburgh by Robert Livingston and Robert Fulton and named, with forthright optimism, *New Orleans,* was wonderfully unsuited to its role: underpowered, deep-hulled like an ocean-going ship, and slow to answer the helm. When the voyage was announced, local rivermen decided Roosevelt was some sort of homicidal maniac. He not only proposed to negotiate the Falls of the Ohio—a two-mile stretch where the Ohio River below Louisville dropped 22 feet over limestone ledges—but to take along his pregnant wife Lydia while thus killing himself. Roosevelt simply smiled and persuaded a large crew to share the boat's fate: a captain, an engineer, a pilot, six deck hands (who were instructed to say, "Aye, aye, sir," when he addressed them), a waiter, a cook, two female servants—and his brother-in-law, who later wrote an account of the adventure.

An enormous Newfoundland dog named Tiger was led aboard on sailing day in late September, and barked in "jolly fashion" at crowds that ran to the riverbank as

The anatomy of a Missouri River stern-wheeler

Smaller, slower and far less glamorous than the floating palaces that plied the Mississippi, the Missouri River stern-wheeler nonetheless was a triumph of shallow-water design. Its draft was so slight that one humorist described the vessel as being "so built that when the river is low and the sand bars come out for air, the first mate can tap a keg of beer and run four miles on the suds."

From its spoonlike bow, shaped for sliding over shoals, to its huge paddle wheel that dipped only a few inches into the water, the Missouri boat was built for muddy going. A typical upper-Missouri "mountain boat" like the celebrated *Far West,* illustrated below and shown in cutaway views on the following pages, could carry 200 tons of freight and up to 30 cabin pas-

sengers through waist-high water. Unloaded, she could proceed safely with as little as 20 inches of river under her flat bottom.

Such remarkable performance was achieved by an ingenious construction that stacked 80 per cent of the bulk above the water line, giving the boat its distinctive wedding-cake silhouette. Directly above the broad, low hull — virtually awash when fully loaded — was the open-sided main deck that housed fireboxes, engines, firewood, cargo and low-paying deck passengers. Covering the main deck was the boiler deck,

where more affluent travelers were assigned small private compartments in an enclosed cabin, topped in turn by an open hurricane deck for promenading.

Some boats rose even higher out of the water than the *Far West* with yet another abbreviated deck, where the boat's officers were quartered. But always at the peak was the boxy wheelhouse, windowed on all four sides to give the pilot a 360-degree view of the hazard-filled river.

As a last defense against sand bars that could not be steered around, slid over or smashed through by the intrepid pilot, every Missouri stern-wheeler boasted a pair of "grasshoppers" — sturdy wooden spars that could be lowered into the mud and used like giant crutches to "walk the boat" to deeper water.

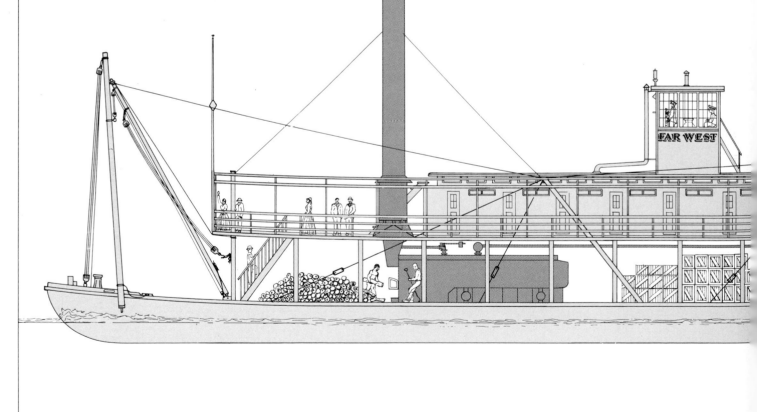

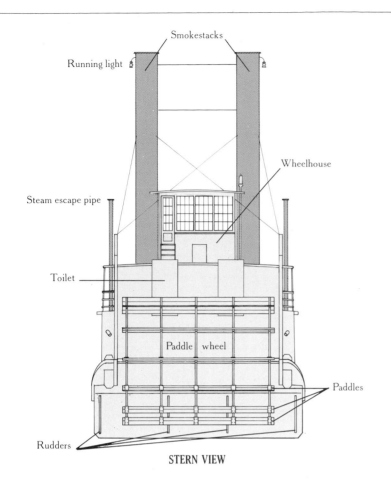

Smokestacks

Running light

Wheelhouse

Steam escape pipe

Toilet

Paddle wheel

Paddles

Rudders

STERN VIEW

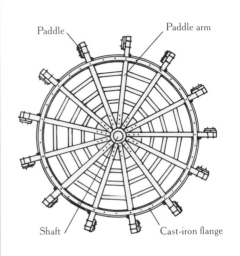

260 DIPS A MINUTE

Far West's paddle wheel, seen below and in the stern view at left, was a simply constructed wooden cylinder 18 feet in diameter and 24 feet wide and belted with cast iron. Two engines rotated the wheel about 20 times — or 260 paddle dips — per minute, providing the thrust to overcome currents that could exceed 10 miles per hour.

Paddle

Paddle arm

Shaft

Cast-iron flange

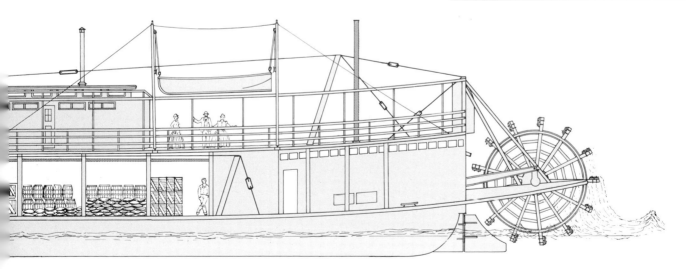

0   5   10   15   20 feet

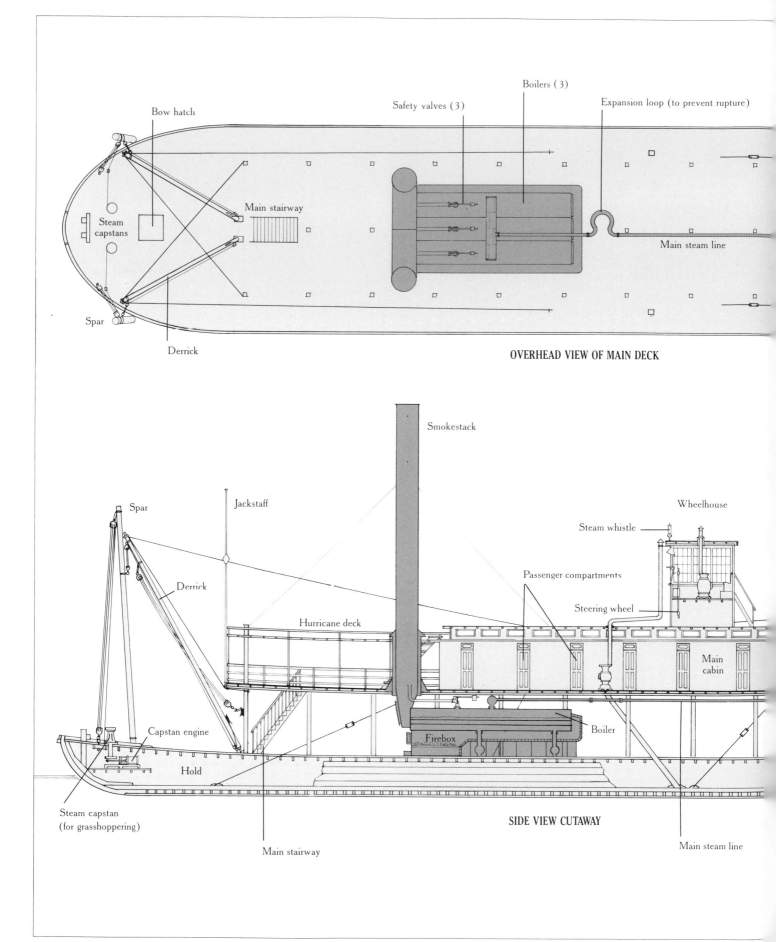

Bow hatch

Safety valves (3)

Boilers (3)

Expansion loop (to prevent rupture)

Steam capstans

Main stairway

Main steam line

Spar

Derrick

OVERHEAD VIEW OF MAIN DECK

Smokestack

Spar

Jackstaff

Wheelhouse

Steam whistle

Derrick

Passenger compartments

Hurricane deck

Steering wheel

Main cabin

Capstan engine

Boiler

Firebox

Hold

Steam capstan
(for grasshoppering)

SIDE VIEW CUTAWAY

Main stairway

Main steam line

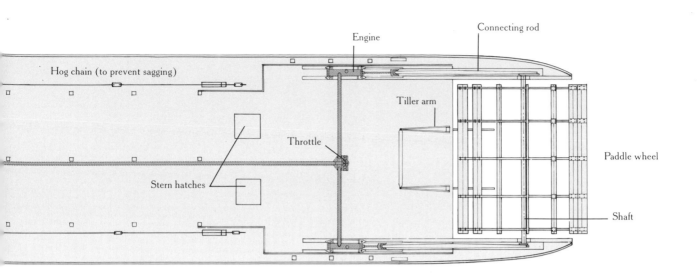

Hog chain (to prevent sagging)

Engine

Connecting rod

Tiller arm

Throttle

Stern hatches

Paddle wheel

Shaft

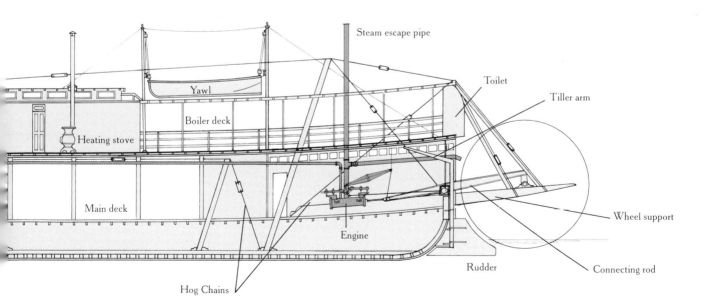

Steam escape pipe

Toilet

Tiller arm

Yawl

Boiler deck

Heating stove

Main deck

Wheel support

Engine

Connecting rod

Hog Chains

Rudder

An 1844 flier announces that part ownership of the steamer *Ione* is up for sale. The winning bidder received a harsh lesson in the chanciness of steamboating on the Missouri: his investment sank in two years.

ADMINISTRATOR'S SALE.

I WILL SELL TO THE HIGHEST BIDDER, FOR CASH, THE

One-eighth part of the Steamboat

IONE,

On THURSDAY, the 28th inst., at 10 A.M.,
OF THAT DAY,
In front of the Store of Messrs. McCalister & Co.,
ON WATER STREET,
Being the interest in said boat belonging to the Estate of
Matthew Hogan, deceased.

SAINT LOUIS, March 6, 1844.

M. BLAIR, Administrator.

the boat went hissing and clanking downstream. Roosevelt and his craft moved from one triumph to another. His wife retired to her cabin after the boat was moored at Louisville and proceeded to give birth to a son. Boat, crew, dog and infant then rushed unscathed through the falls with five inches of draft to spare. They weathered an earthquake that shattered towns in the Mississippi Valley, produced severe flooding and — according to the journey's chronicler — caused general seasickness aboard the boat. They inspired "shouts of exaltation" at Natchez, and were received as symbols of the glorious future when they anchored, after three months of intermittent steaming, at New Orleans on January 12, 1812.

Steamboats began proliferating, almost instantaneously, upon the Western rivers. The early versions were

fully as unsuitable for these shallow waters as *New Orleans* had been, and they had to combat nature without recourse to Roosevelt's luck — or the luxury of always heading downstream. These handicaps did not prevent them from being launched on unlikely adventures. Only seven years after Roosevelt's feat, Secretary of War John C. Calhoun decided to send a fleet of steamboats 2,000 miles up the Missouri to the mouth of the Yellowstone, where a fort would be erected to deter British incursions into American territory. An Ohio River steamboat operator, James Johnson, received a lucrative contract to supply five vessels — plus crews — for the mission. Congress ordered the construction of a sixth, *Western Engineer,* with upper works built to resemble a scaly serpent that would emit steam through its nostrils and thus frighten off any Indians who might be inclined to hostility.

The fleet headed up the Missouri on June 21, 1819 — an ill-chosen starting date, since the river's spring rise had passed. Johnson's boats, designed for deeper waters, failed to make it past the Kansas River, 400 miles upstream. *Western Engineer* ran aground twice in two miles after entering the Missouri and managed to get only as far as the present site of Omaha — 1,135 miles from her destination. Congress took a bitter view of this performance, and when a second expedition to the Yellowstone River was authorized five years later the legislators specified transportation that did not rely on the steam engine.

Legend credits an ex-keelboater named Henry M. Shreve (for whom Shreveport, Louisiana, is named) with creating the powerful, light-draft, multidecked successors to these early paddle boats and with doing so in one fell swoop when he built an improved steamer named *Washington* at Wheeling, West Virginia, in 1816. Shreve put the boat's boiler (though not her engine) up on deck, thus anticipating the idea — soon universally adopted — of taking the whole power plant out of the increasingly shallow hold and installing it on top of the hull. But *Washington* was little different, in other respects, from her sisters of the period.

Western steamers, in fact, were developed over a period of many decades, and vessels used in upper-Missouri travel were still being refined well into the 1870s. The upper-river boat, in its final form, was broad and flat-bottomed for light draft and possessed a spoon-shaped bow for climbing sand bars. It also had accumulated the wedding-cake superstructure — main deck, boiler deck, hurricane deck, officers' quarters and pilothouse — that made its appearance unique; this high superstructure eliminated the need for a deep hold by the upward distribution of passenger and cargo spaces.

Almost all such changes sprang from a kind of workman's practicality rather than from exercises in theory. Most boat and engine builders were refugees from simpler trades: they had been carpenters, flatboat builders, makers of water wheels, blacksmiths, tinsmiths and begetters of backwoods stills. They worked by "cut and try," and "rule of thumb" — under the steady prodding of captains and owners who regularly visited shipyards to express their ideas on the proper design of Missouri

River craft. A philosophy of recklessness — wafted east from the frontier — was a continuous ingredient in the process of evolution. Missouri rivermen showed little inclination to reduce the risks of their trade if it meant paying higher prices for the boats. In 1839, when shipyards experimented with iron hulls — which were far less vulnerable to snags than wooden ones, but twice as expensive — they found no takers among the men who plied the most snag-infested river of all.

It was the rare riverman who did not delight in gimcrackery to add an air of grandeur to his calling. Most vessels bore friezes of wooden scrollwork around cabins and pilothouse; and captains ordered sunbursts, leaping deer or other suggestive heraldry painted in primary colors on their paddle boxes. Whistles did not come into general use until the 1850's — boats signaled with bells alone before this, or sometimes "vented steam" as a salute when meeting another vessel. But, once adopted, whistles lent steamboating its ultimate touch of drama and romance, particularly after manufacturers produced three-toned and five-toned models that played chords and could raise echoes along miles of winding river valley. Sweetness of tone was prized in both signaling devices: Captain John C. Elliott melted 500 silver dollars into the metal from which the bell for his steamer *Emma C. Elliott* was cast, hoping to get a superior sound.

Peripatetic author Robert Forbes refused to be cozened by such theatrics: "The habitual traveler by water," he warned readers in a magazine article, "should carry a bag of vulcanized rubber with means for inflation by mouth, and with 'beckets' or handles to use it as a float." Editors of the *North American Review* seemed resigned, however, to the travelers' preference for swiftness over safety: "It is vain to supply life preservers as a means of inducement to passengers if another steamboat, lying alongside, has proved faster in a trial of speed."

Speed and power to achieve it: these were the fundamental goals of the steamboatman. No single aspect of the paddle vessel's development inspired such an amalgam of rashness and ingenuity, was attended by such a blend of ignorance and intuition, or yielded such flawed but dazzling results as did the struggle to create engines and boilers worthy of the Western rivers. Pittsburgh's mechanics and ironworkers had to puzzle out new methods of working metal as well as new ways of

A flotilla of stern- and side-wheelers lines a boatyard on the Monongahela at Brownsville, Pennsylvania. Though 1,200 miles from the Missouri, Brownsville was the hub of Western riverboat construction in the 1870s, chiefly because the heavy industry for engine-building was in nearby Pittsburgh.

using it, and they had to cope with a mysterious and dangerous new force while doing so.

The direction of their efforts was set by Oliver Evans, a Delaware farmer's son who combined mechanical skill with an imaginative mind and who vastly influenced industrial innovation in the infant United States. Evans engaged in pre-Revolutionary War experiments with steam when he was only 17, invented (but did not develop) a self-propelled carriage, and built scores of engines for factories and steamboats before he died in 1819.

Early American vessels were powered by copies of the Boulton and Watts engine that Robert Fulton imported from England in 1807. These devices used very low pressures, and they condensed steam as it left the cylinder to create a vacuum and thereby induce atmospheric force to help move the piston. They were complicated, unresponsive, excessively big and heavy, and—because they stood upright and their pistons moved straight up and down—they pounded like pile drivers on the framework of hulls. Evans—or rather his ideas—caused these old engines to become outmoded within a very few years and granted the Western steamboat that hazardous practicality that permitted it to perform as an instrument of American destiny in the half century ahead.

Evans had already proved that a light, cheap, simple factory engine with a small piston could exhaust directly into the air and still produce far more power than cumbersome condensing engines if it was fed steam at high pressure. Indeed, it could double or triple this power output if one dared keep the pressure rising through "hard firing" of the boiler. Such engines weighed only five tons, as compared to 100 tons for less powerful low-pressure models, and Evans set out to apply them to boats. But he also incautiously described his ideas in a book entitled (apparently because he was overthrowing previous guidelines to the usage of steam): *The Abortion of the Young Steam Engineer's Guide: Containing an Investigation of the Principles, Construction and Powers of Steam Engines.*

Other mechanics—chief among them Daniel French of Brownsville, Pennsylvania, and Thomas Copeland of Pittsburgh—ignored his patent and began developing high-pressure engines themselves. "They use your strong steam," Evans' son, George, wrote to him in 1814, "and say you dare not molest them." This turned out to be the fact, and the Evans engine —wrenched, no matter how dubiously, into the public domain—was utilized in almost all Western steamers from the 1820s on. It provided the kind of propulsion necessary to cope with fast water, and it made light-draft hulls possible: builders distributed its weight and eliminated pounding by installing the single cylinder on its side and by then connecting the piston rod to the paddle-wheel crank with an iron-bound pine log known as the "pitman."

Steam was generated for paddle-boat engines by batteries of two, four or more long, cylindrical wrought-iron boilers. They were mounted fore and aft and in parallel, and were perforated lengthwise by two or three pipelike flues through which hot gases from the fires were led to increase heating efficiency. Their fireboxes opened toward the bow end of the boat—to utilize the breeze created by forward motion—and were surmounted by a pair of iron chimneys (never called stacks or funnels) that rose up through the vessel's superstructure and towered as much as 100 feet above her upper deck. These steamboat boilers were prodigious sources of energy, but for many decades they visited harrowing risks and hardships upon passengers and crew.

All Western vessels used river water to make steam, and since a cubic foot of brown liquid from the Missouri could contain handfuls of silt and sand, steamboats usually ended a day's run on the Big Muddy by extinguishing the fires, draining and opening the boilers, and sending a hapless fireman inside to shovel them free of steaming mud. The muck caused trouble even after boilermakers devised ways of blowing it out under pressure while a boat was underway, for it still worked its way back into the engines to grind away at valves and pistons. But engine-room crews had concerns more disturbing than this.

Water and pressure gauges did not come into general use until the middle 1850s, and engine crews had to rely mostly on instinct in detecting when boilers were running dry or building steam to dangerous levels. No early engineers really understood—and neither did many of the best technical minds of the day—how fast steam pressures rose as firing was increased. There were experts, in fact, who believed explosions were caused by a mysterious "boiler gas" and not by steam at all. Multiple boilers became doubly dangerous when a boat developed a list; they were connected by pipes calculated to equalize the level of liquid in all of them, but water invariably drained away from the one that was tilted highest by wind or improper loading. Flues turned red hot and collapsed in minutes when thus deprived of internal cooling, cooking everyone within range in a roaring burst of superheated steam.

Not all of the risks originated in the machinery. "The management of engines and boilers is entrusted," wrote visiting English engineer David Stevenson in 1838, "to men whose carelessness of human life is equalled only by their want of civilization." A few years later, one pleader for Congressional reform complained of "filthy engine rooms" being "placed under the charge of mere boys in intellect, in whom enormous wages produce profligacy and recklessness." The more famous mountain pilots could attract steady and knowledgeable engineers, but many captains forgave drunkenness and ignorance in a man who could get his vessel away from landings like lightning, thereby impressing bystanders, and who had some skill as a blacksmith. The Missouri boat that suffered a mechanical breakdown in the wilderness might molder there forever if her engineer could not "pound iron" and make temporary repairs.

An engineer's bargain with the owners was a simple one. They paid him about $200 a month, provided him with an anvil and a forge, applauded him for dealing with dangerous levels of steam pressure, and were always ready to commend him for bravery if he blew himself up, or to deplore him publicly for any accident he might survive.

The competence of engine-room crews rose, in time, and the most horrendous failings of mechanical equipment were gradually eliminated—particularly after Congress voted for federal inspection of steamboats in 1838. But boiler pressures rose, too. Engines used steam at 150 or 160 pounds to the square inch by mid-century—a far cry from the 40 pounds originally prescribed by Oliver Evans. And the boldest engineers overweighted safety valves to push pressures higher when boats approached a stretch of fast water. There was nothing like a "wad of steam"—as rivermen put it—to get a vessel out of trouble in rapids. And there was no way to store this energy for such extraordinary demands save by the ticklish business of bottling up

steam and hoping to release it through the engines in time to avoid disaster.

The lower Missouri was dominated for many years by that classic Western steamboat, the double-engined side-wheeler—prized for the maneuverability it would grant a pilot if one paddle wheel was reversed while the other maintained forward motion. Mountain boats were almost exclusively stern-wheelers. This arrangement saved weight, protected the paddle from snags and permitted a broader-beam hull—hence lighter draft and more cargo capacity. Moreover, stern-wheelers were useful in shallows because their paddles would raise the level of water under the hull if run in reverse while the boat was being grasshoppered over a bar.

Side-wheelers required two engineers at all times —and demanded a high degree of teamwork from them in tricky water. But men at the engine throttles of all boats needed concentration and physical strength when negotiating—as one engine-room veteran put it—"a piece of crooked river with the boat dodging about among reefs and bars and the bells coming faster than you could answer them." There were times when the most conscientious of engineers became so involved that they could not have rectified—or very probably even sensed—an overproduction of steam that was going to kill them in 30 seconds.

A certain fatalism seems to have become ingrained in steamboat crews by the exigencies of their trade. Boatyards found it increasingly difficult, as hulls grew shallower, to achieve rigidity by internal bracing. Most boats were so limber that engines were thrown in and out of line on turns, and steam lines were constantly subject to hissing leaks. The boats had other peculiarities that crews had to anticipate. The paddle of a stern-wheeler would slow down from 24 to as few as 14 revolutions a minute when she got into shallow water, because the paddle could not easily pull water through the narrow gap between the hull and the bottom. Side-wheelers, passing a sand bar to port or starboard, veered toward the shallows, because the paddle on the deep-water side had more pulling power.

It was hard to guess which way to jump—if a prospective victim had opportunity to guess at all—when things went wrong on a Missouri steamer. One fireman drowned when he leaped into the river after a boiler's

A side-wheeler slips cautiously through a cluster of snags — sunken trees that often weighed tons — in this panorama by Karl Bodmer. Many snags

were below the surface, and though pilots were always alert for warning swirls, these obstructions caused almost two thirds of all steamer wrecks.

An 1838 patent diagram reveals the workings of a "snag boat," a double-hull vessel devised by shipbuilder Henry Shreve. It ran directly at sunken trees, scooped them up and hauled them aboard with a windlass.

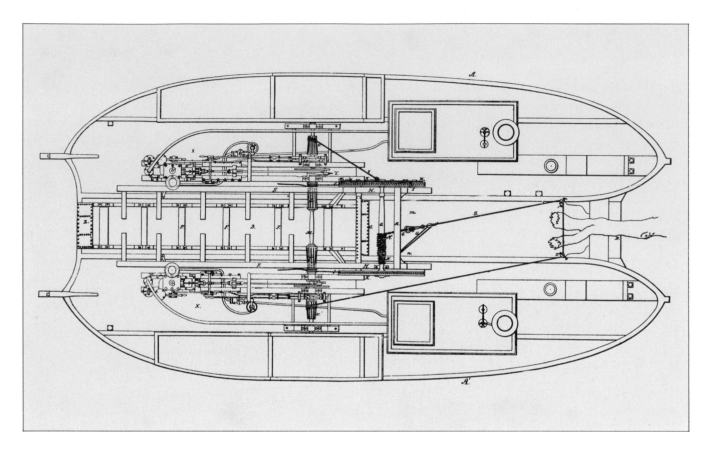

dome gave way on the stern-wheeler *Belle of Jefferson* in 1874. The steam blew harmlessly upward and spared his mates who stayed aboard. Fifty-five German immigrants were scalded to death, however, when boiler flues of the side-wheeler *Edna* collapsed from overheating at Green Island in 1842.

Fate seemed infinitely fickle on the Missouri. The steamboat *Big Hatchie* killed 35 people and wounded many more when she blew up near Hermann, Missouri, in 1845. But most of the side-wheeler *Timour's* passengers escaped a boiler explosion that killed captain, pilot and clerk while she was taking on wood near Jefferson City in August 1854; they were picking wildflowers on a bluff above the river when she went up, and escaped injury even when the boat's safe landed among them like a gigantic cannon ball. Passengers and crew of the mountain boat *Chippewa* got ashore to a man when she caught fire near Montana's Poplar River in 1861, and they watched in complete safety — having cast her adrift — when her cargo of gunpowder blew her into a cloud of splinters and caused one of the biggest

bangs in Western history. The crew members of the mountain boat *Kate Sweeney* also made it to shore without incident when she went down near the Vermilion River in August 1855, but were slaughtered by Indians when they set off downstream on foot.

High winds sometimes wrecked steamboats with no more warning than a boiler explosion. In one such case, the mountain boat *Osceola* was making her way up the Yellowstone River in the summer of 1877 when some cowboys aboard spotted a white stallion in a herd of wild horses on shore. The captain obligingly halted the steamer and waited for two hours while the cowboys roped the stallion, hauled it back to the boat, and tied it to a stanchion. The boat was demolished moments later by a tornado — from which hills up ahead might have shielded her had she not loitered so rashly at the bank. All of the humans survived, but the white stallion, as was noted with satisfaction by the crew, went down with the hull.

Drifting ice was also a menace, although every captain did his best to get back downstream by late au-

The steel-hulled *Horatio G. Wright,* an 1880 embodiment of Henry Shreve's design, lifts Missouri snags. Operated by the Army Corps of Engineers, such boats were known as "Uncle Sam's Toothpullers."

tumn and owners usually delayed upstream voyages until the worst of the river's winter burden had washed away. Still, ice could do terrible damage even in downriver ports. An entire fleet of steamboats was ground to kindling wood at St. Louis during "The Great Ice Gorge of 1856." Rising water broke the solid, heavy ice near the city in late February, piled huge sections of it into vast, noisy hills and ridges and moved these grinding masses slowly downstream with every movable object they encountered. Dozens of boats were torn from their moorings at the St. Louis levee, then solid with steamers for 20 blocks.

"The ice at first moved slowly," reported *The Missouri Republican,* "and without perceptible shock. But the steamers *Australia, Adriatic, Brunette, Paul Jones, Falls City, Altoona, A.B. Chambers* and *Challenge* all were torn away from the shore and floated down with the immense fields of ice. The first obstacles with which they came in contact were a large fleet of barges and canal boats, about fifty in all, which were either sunk, broken or carried away. *Bon Accord* and *High-*

land Mary were carried off . . . both total losses . . . and after them *Lamartine, Westerner* and *Jeanie Deans. Gossamer, Luella, Alice* and *Badger State* were forced ashore only slightly damaged . . . but *Shenandoah* was wrecked, *G.W. Sparhawk* sunk and *Clara* and *Ben Bolt* were badly damaged.

"The character of the ice changed after running about one hour and came down in frothy, crumbled condition. Just before the river gorged, huge piles of ice twenty and thirty feet in height were forced up by the current at the Lower Dyke where so many boats had come to a halt. These boats seemed to be literally buried in ice. At six o'clock P.M. the river had risen at least ten feet. The current was now much more swift and the night very dark, a heavy and steady rain having set in. The terrible sweep of waters with its burden of ice, the mashing to pieces of boats and the hurrying on shore of the excited crowd was one of the most awful and imposing scenes we have ever witnessed."

Grant Marsh, later to become one of the most famous upper-river pilots, was the winter watchman on

109

An extract from a report by Captain Hiram Chittenden of the Army Corps of Engineers spells out the circumstances surrounding some of the 295 steamboat disasters on the Missouri between 1819 and 1897.

List of steamboat wrecks on the Missouri River, from the beginning of steamboat navigation to the present time

Name of boat.	Description of boat.	Trade engaged in, and owners and officers.	Date of wreck.	Locality of wreck.	Cause of wreck.	Remarks.
Dacotah (No. 2)....	Stern - wheel; about 250 by 40 feet; 956 tons.	St. Louis and Kansas City..	Sept. 17, 1884	Near Providence, Mo..	Snag........	Was raised, towed to New Orleans, and dismantled. Her machinery is now on the steamer Imperial, in the New Orleans-Red River trade.
Dallas	Stern - wheel; small boat.	Missouri River trade........	Sometime in the seventies.	Morgans Island..........	......do	
Damsel	Stern-wheel ..	Circus boat. Charles Davis, pilot.	1876	Head of Onawa Bend....	....do	Had on board a circus company. Capt. Joseph La Barge came along on the John M. Chambers and took off the passengers.
Dan Converse.......	....do	Missouri River trade........	Nov. 15, 1858	10 miles above St. Joseph, Mo.	....do	An old boat, valued at $3,000. Boat and cargo a total loss. No lives lost.
Daniel G. Taylor...	Side-wheel; about 240 by 38 feet; 543 tons.	Mountain trade	July 5, 1856	3 miles below Rocheport; head of Paynes Island.	....do	Was afterwards raised and worn out on the Lower Mississippi. She was a peculiar looking boat, having side wheels, but clear back at the stern. Named for a mayor of St. Louis, Mo.
Dart...............	Side-wheel; single engine.	Missouri River trade. Partially owned and commanded by Capt. John Cleveland.	1838	1 mile below Glasgow, Mo.	Rocks	
Dells	Stern-wheel	Missouri River trade........	Oct. 26, 1878	Above Arago, Nebr...	Snag and explosion.	Struck snag and exploded her boilers and sank. Boat and cargo a total loss. No insurance. 2 lives lost.
Dew Drop..........	Stern - wheel; 148 tons.	.....do	June, 1860	Mouth of Osage River.	Fire	
Delaware	Side-wheel....	.....do	1857	Smiths Bar, Missouri.	Snag.....	
Denver (No. 1).....	Side-wheel; 225 by 33 feet; 300 tons.	St. Joseph and Omaha. Owned by the Hannibal and St. Joseph R. R. Co, John Waddell, master.	May 16, 1867	St. Joseph, Mo........	Fire	Named for the first governor of Colorado. The wreck was afterwards rebuilt into the Denver No. 2. The Denver No. 1 burnt while lying at the wharf at St. Joseph, Mo.
Denver (No. 2).....	Center-wheel .	St. Joseph and Omaha, and ferrying.	Mar. 13, 1880	Opposite Fort Lincoln, N. Dak.	Ice	Built out of the wreck of the Denver No. 1.
Diana..............	Side-wheel....	Missouri River trade. Owned by the American Fur Co. Capt. John Shallcross, master.	Oct., 1836	Diana Bend. 2½ miles above Rocheport, Mo.	Snag........	Built for the Cincinnati and Louisville Packet Company by Capt. Joe Swagers, one of the founders of above line. The steamer Diana was wrecked twice; the first time March, 1836, when she was bound for Council Bluffs, by striking a snag near Lexington. Her cargo was put ashore, but high water carried most of it off. The boat was temporarily repaired, brought to St. Louis and fixed up. She was next wrecked by striking a snag 2½ miles above Rocheport, in what is now known as Diana Bend. Part of the cargo was saved. There was some expectation that the boat would be raised, but she was abandoned.
Don Cameron, J....	Stern-wheel ..	Government transport......	May 17, 1877	Omaha and Winnebago Agency.	......do	This boat was built by the United States Government for the Yellowstone River. She was transporting baggage and private property for the Fifth Infantry, from Fort Leavenworth to Fort Keogh, on the Yellowstone River, and sank on her first trip. No Missouri River pilot was on the boat. The boat was being steered by an officer. Boat and cargo a total loss. Several lawsuits grew out of this disaster. No lives lost.
Dugan, R. W......	Stern - wheel; 160 by 32 feet.	Missouri River trade. Capt. Joe Kinney, sr., owner. Capt. Joe Kenney, jr., master.	Oct. 21, 1878	2 miles below Dewitt, Mo.	......do	Boat and cargo total loss. No lives lost.
Duncan Carter.....	Side-wheel; 221 by 33 feet.	Missouri River trade........	Aug. 28, 1858	Augusta Bend..........	......do	Sank on down trip from Weston to St. Louis, in 12 feet of water. Boat and cargo a total loss. She was 2 years old and was valued at $44,000.
Durfee, E. H.......	Stern - wheel; 175 by 36 feet.	St. Louis and Kansas City..	May 23, 1881	Mouth of Gasconade River.	Overloaded .	This boat was named for one of the members of the firm of Durfee & Peck, fur traders. She was on a down trip and was fully loaded, but, on arrival at Portland, 8 miles above the Gasconade, she took on a large amount of wheat. She commenced sinking soon after swinging into the stream and went down at the mouth of the Gasconade River in deep water. Boat and cargo a total loss. Boat was valued at $18,000. No lives lost.
Durock	Side-wheel....	Missouri River trade; John McCloy, master.	1852	St. Charles Bend.......	Snag.....	
Eagle.............	Stern - wheel; 125 by 25 feet.	Ferryboat	Feb. 27, 1897	Lexington, Mo.........	Burnt	A gasoline stove exploded and set boat on fire. Boat was a total loss. Wreck removed by U. S. snag boat C. R. Suter, June 16, 1897.
Eaton, N. J.......	Side-wheel....	Glasgow packet.............	Apr. 9, 1856	Augusta Bend..........	Snag........	Wrecked on her first trip up the Missouri River. Boat a total loss. She was valued at $38,000. The deck load was saved, balance of cargo was lost.
Eclipse	Stern - wheel; 178 by 31 feet.	Fort Benton trade. I. G. Baker, owner.	Sept. 3, 1887	15 miles below Sioux City, Iowa.	....do	Boat and cargo a total loss. No lives lost.
Edgar	....	Missouri River trade.......	Mar. 26, 1884	Near Omaha, Nebr....	Ice........	Boat valued at $3,500; insured at $2,000.
Edna	Side-wheel....	Glasgow packet.............	July 3, 1842	Green Island at the mouth of the Missouri River.	Boiler explosion.	Named for one of Captain McCord's daughters. The flues collapsed in both boilers and killed about 55 German emigrants.
Ella Kimbrough...	Stern-wheel; 243 tons.	Missouri River trade. Capt. T. N. Kimbrough.	Sept. 20, 1884	St. Charles Chute.....	Snag........	This boat was formerly the General Sherman, a United States steamer. She was bought from the Government by P. P. Manion, who sold her to Captain Kimbrough, who named her for his wife. When wrecked she had on board 3,000 sacks of wheat. Boat and cargo a total loss; cargo was insured for $8,000. No lives lost.
Elk................	Side-wheel; small steamer, single engine.	Missouri River trade........	1838	Massie's wood yard, 5 miles below Hermann, Mo.	....do	Passengers taken off by Capt. Joseph La Barge on the steamer Kansas.
El Paso............	Side-wheel; about 180 by 28 feet; about 267 tons.	Missouri River trade. Capt. Bill Terrell, owner; Capt. W. R. Massie, master.	Apr. 10, 1855	Foot of Franklins Island, just below Booneville at Whites Landing.	Snag........	Boat and cargo a total loss. No lives lost.

A.B. Chambers that day, and he stayed aboard as ice swept her away. Both he and his ship were lucky; *A. B. Chambers* was borne gradually back toward shore during the night and came to rest, still afloat, three miles from her original mooring place.

Marsh had yet another glimpse of the forces inherent in river ice, and survived an even closer brush with death, during the winter of 1859. Both he and a young riverman named Samuel Clemens were serving aboard a boat called (by curious coincidence) *A.B. Chambers No. 2* when she ran aground near Commerce, Missouri. Marsh was the mate and Clemens, soon to take the pen name of Mark Twain, was second pilot. The vessel burned up her wood supply while vainly attempting to extricate herself, and Marsh set off in her yawl with a crew of husky oarsmen — and with Clemens acting as steersman — to order a barge load of fresh fuel from a woodyard on shore.

The river's main channel was clogged with moving floes, but Clemens directed the yawl around them to the shore opposite the woodyard, crept cautiously past an island, and eventually — below an ice jam where drifting cakes were fast collecting — found clear water leading across the stream to her destination. But the ice jam rumbled and broke as the boat entered the space below it, and Marsh found himself yelling, "Turn back quick, Sam! Back!" Clemens looked over his shoulder and said almost conversationally, "No. Go ahead as fast as you can." He was right. Acres of grinding ice closed up behind the yawl and her wildly laboring oarsmen, but patches of water opened ahead and she narrowly scraped through to safety.

But ice, no matter how dangerous, was not nearly so much a source of peril as were snags, rocks and shoals. Missouri steamboats spitted themselves by the score, year after year, on these obstructions and seemed to do so, at times, out of some perversity of their own. In 1867 the side-wheeler *New Sam Gaty* — for reasons that were never determined — suddenly veered out of control near Arrow Rock, Missouri, smashed into an obstruction, listed wildly, caught fire and burned up, all in the space of one hectic hour.

Reminders of the steamboat's fallibility were visible everywhere. Cora Island was created in 1869 when the side-wheeler *Cora Number 3* struck a snag and sank near Bellefontaine Bluffs, Missouri, altering the hydraulics of the river and attracting rising layers of mud and sand that eventually supported grasses, bushes and trees. The river simply moved away from other disabled boats. When the stern-wheeler *James H. Trover* suffered a broken boiler pump and was caught immobile against the bank in eastern Montana Territory in 1867, the stream abruptly altered its course, leaving her high and dry forever.

But if the steamboat was subject to constant tribulation on the Missouri, it was often able to survive the worst the river had to offer. For decades boats multiplied faster than they went down. In 1859 alone more than 100 vessels plied the river regularly, splashing over the bones of their predecessors in bend after bend. The steamboat's record of accomplishment, all things considered, was astonishing; and in the final analysis the catalogue of its mishaps is significant only as a measure of the odds surmounted and the prices paid by the men who created for it such a strategic role in Western history.

The steamer was indeed served, in many cases, "by men of coarse habit, recklessness, and uneducated mind," as an 1838 government report declared. But critics forgot, while complaining, that men like these were exactly the sort who braved the Blackfeet to trap beaver, and who thronged mining camps, roped and punched cattle and crossed the mountains to California and Oregon. It is quite possible that fewer steamboats would have exploded had they been in the hands of engineers with more training or wisdom, and it is certain that fewer would have gone up in flames had they been manned by teetotalers, since crewmen, in the hope of stealing whiskey, were known to light their way into steamer holds with candles.

Yet it seems doubtful that the paddle vessel could have so routinely exceeded its own potentialities in the West — or have exerted the influence it did — had it been in the hands of more prudent men. Boat builders did not really expect their steamers — even those designed for the upper Missouri — to cope with the swift, rock-strewn Yellowstone; and they certainly did not believe their deep-hulled, heavy lower-river boats could survive the Missouri's 198-mile stretch of shallow rapids and rock reefs between Cow Island and Fort Benton. But captains damned the risk and took them there anyhow — and, if a boat survived, took it back another time.

111

Casualties of a cantankerous river

If a flimsy Western steamer ever ventured out to sea, mused a 19th Century wit, "the ocean would take one playful slap at it and people would be picking up kindling on the beach for the next eleven years." Even on the Missouri River, steamboats were victimized by a whole catalogue of calamities: they were consumed by fire, crushed by ice, impaled by snags, torn apart by high winds, blown to smithereens by devastating boiler explosions, and occasionally brought to an ignominious end in collisions with sturdy railroad bridges.

Many wrecks, however, were not the catastrophes one might imagine. Passengers and crewmen learned to flee to the high, open hurricane deck when the alarm bell sounded, confident that even if the pilot could not quickly ground his stricken craft on the nearest bank or sand bar, the boat would probably not sink deep enough to wet their feet. The shallowness of the Missouri was also a salvager's boon; at least 20 of the steamers wrecked on the river were easily refloated.

Surely the hardiest of these resurrected vessels was the mountain boat *Benton*. She first came to grief when she hit a snag in 1889. Raised and repaired, she had an uneventful second life until 1895, when she again struck a snag and sank. Restored to service again, the *Benton* lasted another two years before a bridge collision reduced her to the hopeless hulk shown here.

Her chimneys askew and her back broken, *Benton* draws a curious crowd near Sioux City after her third wreck in 1897. While approaching a drawbridge, she ran into submerged pilings, careened out of control, slammed into the bridge and drifted to her final rest not far downriver.

Crushed against the St. Louis levee by ice floating down-river, steamers gradually crumble into ruin in a drawn-out disaster that continued through much of the winter of 1865-1866. Twenty-one steamboats were destroyed in all — six of them during a surge of ice that lasted only five minutes.

Beset by a savage storm at the Bismarck levee in 1879, the brand-new *Montana*—one of the largest stern-wheelers—had most of her superstructure torn off. Some pieces were discovered 500 yards away. She was repaired and sailed five more years before her second and fatal mishap *(over)*.

117

The luckless *Montana* rests on the bottom of the shallow river at St. Charles, Missouri, in 1884, after a capricious current forced her against the supports of the railroad bridge in the background. Although some of her cargo was saved, the boat—valued at $40,000—was declared a total loss.

Hung up on a sand bar, the steamer *Yellowstone* has her cargo lightened in order to refloat her in this 1833 scene by artist Karl Bodmer.

4 | No buoys, no beacons, no maps

Before a pilot could take a steamboat into the Missouri he was expected, in the words of a veteran riverman, to "know the river as a schoolboy knows a path to the schoolhouse, upside down, endways, inside, outside and crossways." But even with an encyclopedic knowledge of snags, sand bars and landmarks, earned during a period of grueling apprenticeship that might last as long as five years, a steamboat pilot could rarely let down his guard and relax on a river regarded as one of the world's most difficult to travel safely.

"Navigating the Missouri at low water," wrote one observer, "is like putting a steamer on dry land and sending a boy ahead with a sprinkling pot." Yet the hardy band of pilots attacked this task with great gusto. Without buoys, beacons or reliable maps to guide them along the ever-shifting channel, they steered deftly around freshly formed sand bars when they could—or ran smack across them full steam ahead if necessary. The inevitable groundings were shrugged off; any pilot worth his salt soon developed ingenious ways to free his boat.

By the 1850s the cockier pilots had even begun to run the lower river after dark, calculating their position by moonlight, by the echoes of their steam whistles and by familiar sounds ashore. It was a risky technique. One pilot, in the habit of steering to the sound of a dog yelping near a river-front cabin, ran hard aground one dark night when the dog decided to do its barking elsewhere.

The unsinkable wizards of the wheelhouse

Captain Joseph Marie La Barge — a handsome, muscular, vigorous man of French-Canadian lineage — was the most heralded mountain pilot of his day, and one of the two most famous steamboatmen ever to operate on the Missouri River. Few equaled him at working a steamer through unfamiliar channels; he possessed an intuitive sense of water and an uncommon feel for the vessel beneath his feet, and he embodied an amalgam of steadiness, daring and endurance that made him unique among his peers. And he had qualities beyond these. He had been a fur trader and understood Indians and their ways. La Barge was so confident of his ability to deal safely with them that, in 1847, he took his wife, Pelagie, to the upper river with him in the side-wheeler *Martha* (and, in so doing, showed her a corner of the West no white woman had seen before). But he found himself in trouble with Indians after he tied *Martha* up at Crow Creek in Dakota Territory.

Tribesmen of the Missouri valley were more intricately involved with white rivermen than legend suggests, particularly after steamboats began delivering government "annuities" — shipments of cloth, food and beads specified by treaty and intended to woo Indians away from their warring life style. Crow Creek's Yanktonai Sioux were not pleased when the government agent aboard *Martha* sent only part of their promised goods ashore and told them that the rest could be available at the American Fur Company post in Fort Pierre, 92 miles upstream. The Sioux were all too familiar with this form of frontier graft: fur companies bribed Indian agents to "store" annuities at their warehouses and

then sold the goods to the same tribesmen to whom they had been consigned in the first place. Disgruntled Sioux now drifted toward the bank and stared blackly at the steamer — the most obvious symbol of white corruption at hand.

A high wind was blowing, its gusts whipping smoke from *Martha*'s chimneys and flattening the tall grasses ashore. La Barge decided, black looks or not, that it was safer to stay where he was than to pull out into the stream and risk the chance of being blown into shoal water. But he had 10 cords of wood piled on the bank — fuel he had originally intended to pick up on his return trip — and, having seen Indians react before to the kind of miserable little farce that had just been enacted, he decided to take the wood on board before one of the Sioux hit on the idea of setting it on fire.

In addition to its cargo of annuities, *Martha* was transporting a contingent of loud-talking mountain men toward the Rockies. La Barge sent for their commander, Etienne Provost — a renowned trapper, hunter, explorer and guide — and asked for help. Provost grinned and jerked his head at the Indians: "We are going to have some fun before we get that wood on board." Then he bawled, "Woodpile! Woodpile!" and waved his men ashore with *Martha*'s deck hands. The Sioux did not move until the gangplank was jammed with men; at that point they ran up with rawhide whips, which had been wrapped around their waists, and began flailing at the hapless whites — who threw their burdens in all directions and tumbled over one another in getting back on deck.

Provost bent double with laughter at his place beside La Barge on the boiler deck. "I told you," he yelled. "I told you!" He then went below, strolled down the plank and said, "Now, men, come back out here and get this wood." The wood gang returned to the bank and loaded up again. "Now go on board," said Provost. He turned

to the Indians. "Why don't you stop them? Are you afraid of *me*?" Not an Indian spoke. Not an Indian moved. The wood was rescued. The Sioux moved sullenly away.

La Barge watched them depart, left his windy station on deck, walked into the steamer's big passenger cabin, sat down to read and, in an hour, was caught off guard by an Indian attack for the first and only time in his long career on the river. The Sioux had been insulted beyond endurance; they fired a volley into the boat, killed one deck hand, rushed the gangplank unopposed, and — having learned something of steamboats in years of observing them on the river — seized buckets, opened the vessel's fire doors, and flooded the banks of embers under her boilers.

La Barge — returned to reality by gunfire, the tinkle of broken glass and the howls of the invaders — scrambled out the cabin's after door, ran to his wife's stateroom and dragooned a man into helping him pile mattresses against its door. When he burst back into the passenger cabin, the Sioux had begun crowding through its forward entryway with a fur company boss named Colin Campbell. "They want the boat," said Campbell. "They say they'll let the crew go if they get it. If not, they're going to kill everybody."

La Barge was struck by the fact that the Indians, having pushed into the unfamiliar cabin, made no move to advance farther. How long would their doubts and suspicions keep them huddled where they were? The undercarriage of *Martha's* brass cannon had been damaged and the weapon was — alas — in the engine room awaiting repair. But La Barge nevertheless decided to try to bring it into play. He held up a reassuring hand, walked slowly out of the cabin, leaped down to the engine spaces, yelled for engineer Nathan Grismore — a "brave and noble fellow" he later said — and began stuffing powder into the gun. Grismore shoved in a double handful of boiler rivets. The two men rigged a pulley, swayed the weapon up to the next deck, and maneuvered it into the cabin's after end. La Barge lighted a cigar, puffed on it, lowered it toward the cannon, looked up at Campbell and said, "Tell them that if they don't get off the boat I'll blow them all to hell!"

The gesture was enough. The horrified Indians fought one another to escape and, though La Barge and Grismore pushed the gun out on deck behind them, the intruders were in full flight and the incident was over by the time the two steamboatmen swung it into position to command the shore.

Or almost over. "I looked for my crew," La Barge remembered after the voyage, "I looked for the brave mountaineers. Where had they hidden, leaving the boat defenseless? They were hanging thick as sardines all over the paddles. I was so disgusted that I was disposed to set the wheels in motion and give them all a ducking, but the Indians had put out the fires and we had no steam."

La Barge indeed possessed the power to chastise his passengers as he wished; like many of his peers, he filled two roles, serving both as *Martha's* captain — the highest legal authority on board and the overseer of all administrative matters — and also as her pilot, or helmsman. Hundreds of captain-pilots contended with the Missouri during the long day of paddle navigation on Western waters. Theirs was a contest that demanded moral stature, courage and a kind of stage presence as well as knowledge of water and wilderness. Two men emerged as archetypes of the breed: La Barge, who was the most acclaimed of rivermen during the era of the Rocky Mountain fur trade, and Grant Marsh, the greatest of the steamboatmen drawn up the Missouri by the Montana gold boom and the Indian campaigns that followed the Civil War.

La Barge began his career in 1832 when few but keelboatmen had ever ascended the river and when the steamboat itself was in its infancy. Marsh, on the other hand, did not feel his way upstream to Fort Benton until 1866 — when railheads had been established on the lower river and dozens of steamers were taking part in the summer race to the mountains. But the two men were alike in many aspects of character and attitude;

For the Indians, an invisible cargo of death

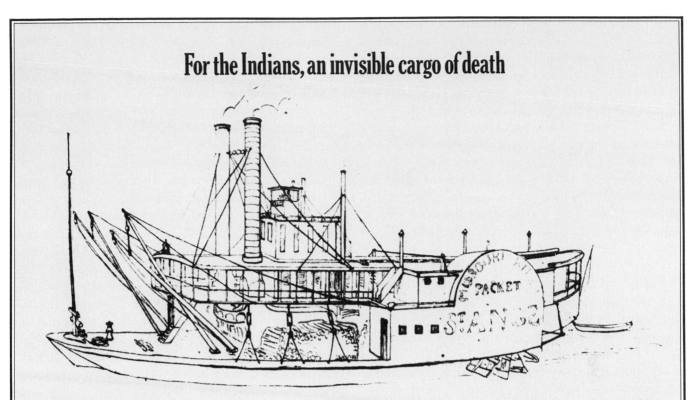

St. Ange was both blessed and cursed: in 1850 she set a speed record on the Yellowstone, but in 1851 the vessel was swept by a cholera epidemic.

In the history of the West, there was no more dangerous carrier of disease than the early steamboat with its confined spaces and fetid atmosphere. The specter of a ship-wide epidemic haunted every captain. The redoubtable Joseph La Barge underwent just such an ordeal in 1851 when his steamer, *St. Ange,* was swept by an outbreak of cholera that infected 100 passengers and crew, killing 11 before it was checked.

Nor were the dangers confined to the people on the boat. Upriver Indians had little or no resistance to many of the white man's illnesses, and contact with steamboats often had devastating results. The 1837 trip of *St. Peters* from St. Louis to Fort Union earned it an especially infamous niche in the annals of Western medicine by touching off an epidemic of smallpox that afflicted nearly every

tribe from the Platte to the Rockies.

The outbreak began among the Mandans at Fort Clark when a chief stole the blanket of an infected roustabout. *St. Peters'* officers tried to retrieve it by offering a new one, and to warn the Indians away from the boat. But the Mandans, convinced that the whites were denying them the right to trade, refused to leave.

Three days after the boat's arrival the Mandans began falling sick. Hundreds died each day, their bodies swelling and turning black. Since burial of so many was impossible, the living disposed of the corpses by throwing them over cliffs — then committed suicide by the scores, preferring a quick, clean death to the grim fate unfolding before their eyes. After a few weeks, only 30 survived of a tribe that had numbered 1,700. By that time the plague was wreaking its

horrors on the nearby Arikaras, Pawnees and Minnatarees.

St. Peters, meanwhile, callously pressed on upriver — there were, after all, profits to be made — and at Fort Union delivered the virus along with the cargo. The first of the Indian victims were 30 Assiniboin women who were fatally injected by a well-meaning but medically ignorant post employee with a vaccine made of the live virus. More Assiniboins came to the post to trade, and naturally caught the disease. As the stricken staggered home to die and *St. Peters* steamed home to St. Louis, smallpox spread to the Crows and Blackfeet.

By the time the smallpox plague had run its course the next year, at least 15,000 Northern Plains Indians had died of it — more than would fall in combat with the Army in the remaining 62 years of the century.

and both, above all, were helmsmen of consummate coolness, judgment and skill. La Barge never lost or even badly damaged a boat — an almost impossible record in the first years of steam — although few men made as many voyages into dangerous water as did he. Both he and Marsh were at their best in taking a steamer up unfamiliar channels, and both were admired by fellow rivermen as well as by passengers. Horace Bixby, a grand old man of the New Orleans packet trade, was in no way disturbed by a Montanan who called him "the Grant Marsh of the lower Mississippi." "By the Lord, sir," he said later, "it was a high compliment, for any man who can run a boat for 20 years on that rainwater creek above Bismarck is surely the king of pilots."

Both captains were entrepreneurs and businessmen and often had a financial interest in vessels they commanded; each was capable of handling every aspect of a boat's employment — from assessing freight rates and booking passengers to finding channels in time of low water. Neither, however, was a man who would have looked at home amid the dust of the countinghouse; upper-river captains not only had to run the gauntlet of the Missouri tribes but to preside (there being no other law for a thousand miles) over wild and undisciplined men among the passengers and crews of their steamboats. This inevitably involved a certain acceptance of violence. La Barge gave the most obstreperous of his roustabouts every chance to fight one another after his boat left St. Louis, thus easing disciplinary problems by establishing a kind of pecking order that lasted until a voyage was done. Both he and Marsh were hard men — though each met the world with a quiet and courteous air — and neither stood for any nonsense from the roughnecks who rode their steamers.

A self-proclaimed "bad man" named Gilmore did a good deal, though this was not his intention, toward instilling caution in those who dealt with Marsh after he became a captain on the upper river. Gilmore came aboard the steamer _Luella_ at Fort Benton, attracted a following of noisy louts, and made life miserable for other passengers Marsh carried downstream on his first mountain voyage. He ceased his bullying after Marsh threatened to throw him off and leave him for the Indians, but publicly swore revenge. On a day when winds forced _Luella_ to tie up at the bank, he announced that he was about to do so. He took his entourage

ashore, waited until Marsh followed with a woodcutting party, and cried: "Watch me make this low down dog of a captain jump the mark!" The captain went red with rage, yanked out a pistol, walked up to the bully and his grinning cronies and said, "Gilmore, the time has come. You've been looking for trouble and you're going to get it." He nodded at his would-be tormentor's revolver, waved to a space near the bank, and said, "Come over here and fight. I'll give you a fair chance."

Gilmore turned pale and began shaking his head. Marsh stepped closer, hit him across the face and yelled, "Now will you fight?" and, as the trembling man backed off, said, "I'll kill you right here if you don't!" Startled passengers moved between the pair. Marsh allowed himself to be led away and, once he had recovered his composure, began regretting the violence of his reaction. He decided, in the end, that he owed all concerned some gesture of conciliation. When the boat reached Sioux City, he followed some of his passengers, Gilmore among them, to a waterfront saloon and invited all present to advance to the bar and allow him to buy them a drink. This effort at making amends collapsed almost instantly: Gilmore sullenly refused his hospitality. The Marsh legend, however, attained new dimensions in the same moment. The exasperated host seized a heavy beer mug, and yelled, "Come up here and drink, Gilmore, or by the Eternal I'll break this glass over your skull!" He kept the impromptu weapon firmly in hand until his unwilling guest advanced amid catcalls and choked down a glass of whiskey.

News of such confrontations traveled fast along the Missouri, and so did word of unusual navigational episodes that proved a pilot's skill. Marsh became as acclaimed, in time, as La Barge himself. And La Barge was a celebrity indeed in the early West: bankers, traders, scientists and the odd Indian chief were flattered to be invited to his wheelhouse; dignitaries went out of their way to meet him on trips to St. Louis; and many of the Union generals of the Civil War became his admirers during tours of duty in Indian country. So did Mormon leader Brigham Young, Senator Thomas Hart Benton, and — on one pre-presidential trip to Council Bluffs — Honest Abe himself.

Joseph La Barge was not only a pioneer among pilots and one who made himself a model for those who followed, but was also a man whose family background and early experiences as a fur trader and Indian fighter made him a link between the French-Canadian wanderers who first explored the Missouri wilderness and the Yankee captains, miners and settlers who took it from the Indians in the end. He never lost a cold realist's eye for the wilderness through which the river led him, and never abandoned a hot, Gallic insistence on personal independence—a quality he inherited from his father, a notable riverman on his own.

The father sprang from a family of Norman peasant blood that had lived in Quebec since 1633, but he celebrated his 21st birthday, in 1808, by setting forth in a birch bark canoe to seek his fortune on the Missouri. He settled in St. Louis, served in upriver trapping expeditions, and took no back talk from any man. When a St. Louis judge fined him four dollars for caning a trapper, the old man handed over double the amount, since he proposed—as he politely informed the magistrate—to whip the fellow all over again for taking him to court, and saw no point in sitting through a second trial.

All three of his sons became steamboat pilots. All three seem to have possessed his extrasensory feel for moving water as well as his sense of command, but Joseph, the oldest, was shaped by an apprenticeship unusual even in that rough day and, having lived through it, seemed to carry some unique and permanent gift of survival with him through the rest of life.

Young Joseph began his career on the Missouri at the age of 16 as a fur trader for Pierre Chouteau Jr.'s American Fur Company, which exerted something close to dictatorship in the upper valley, and he quickly achieved a reputation for hardihood and wit. Stragglers from a Sioux war party spotted him on an open plain as he headed for a trading compound with a companion and five mules loaded with buffalo meat. He leveled his rifle and faced the Indians down while his partner whipped the loaded beasts to safety, sounded the alarm and finally returned with help. The redoubtable Etienne Provost happened to be present at the trading compound. He seized La Barge's hands and cried—as the wilderness grapevine was not slow in reporting—"I am glad you did not show the white feather to those rascals. You are a man for this country!"

La Barge won the admiration of his superiors in the company during these adventurous early years ashore and he served the firm well as a pilot and charter cap-

CHANGES OF THE CHANNEL
OF THE
MISSOURI RIVER
THROUGH MONONA COUNTY, IOWA.
Present Channel Distance, 44 Miles.
(COMPILED BY MITCHELL VINCENT, ONAWA, IOWA.)

	1804	LEWIS AND CLARK
	1852	U. S. LAND SURVEY.
	1879	MO. RIV. COM. SURVEY.
	1894	COUNTY SURVEY

tain later on. But he was audacious enough to compete with it, too. In 1840, when he was 25 years old, he quarreled with an American Fur Company official, turned down a berth in its steamboat *Trapper,* and went ashore to trade with Indians on his own. This was risky, for the company stopped at almost nothing to maintain its ascendancy and ensure its profits.

He went broke, as things turned out, and the company invited him—through the offices of an Indian runner—to a conciliatory meeting at Fort Pierre. La Barge was surprised to note that the Indian had come to his wilderness post unarmed and at once assumed that the man had been instructed to murder him after they set off together for the fort. He slipped away alone, backtracked the runner, found a rifle the fellow had hidden under some foliage, and hid it all over again. He betrayed not the slightest indignation at this duplicity,

A desolate depot, 60 miles from the Missouri River's last landing at Fort Benton, is heaped with supplies that will be carried by wagon train to inland trading posts. The groceries, furniture, medicine and whiskey stacked on the riverbank were brought upriver from Bismarck, North Dakota.

though he took a certain poker-faced satisfaction — after rejoining the guide — at watching the man's equally poker-faced efforts to spot the missing weapon.

La Barge regarded the company's monolithic unscrupulousness almost as philosophically as he regarded the excesses of the Sioux — or of the weather — and made a point of anticipating its dirty tricks rather than losing sleep over them. The company's men were equally realistic: they betrayed neither surprise nor disappointment at his arrival, treated him with punctilio, and bought out his trade goods at 10 cents on the dollar. But the incident did not quite end there: a band of Yanktonais Sioux — who went wild at learning he had sold out and had put them again at the mercy of the company's exorbitant prices — tried to waylay and kill him on his way home. La Barge ran 40 miles across the plains, guiding himself by the light of the aurora borealis as the temperature dropped to 30° below, before losing his pursuers near the mouth of the Cheyenne River.

La Barge had begun learning rivermanship while still engaged in the fur trade, and on one upriver trip aboard the American Fur Company's *Yellowstone,* he received a grim foretaste of the role that would make him famous. Cholera swept the boat and killed half her crew — including her pilot, her engineer and all her firemen. The captain tied up opposite Kansas' Kaw River, turned the boat over to young La Barge, climbed into the yawl with the other survivors and headed back to St. Louis to find a new crew. After the captain left, local Missouri settlers — in mortal fear of the plague — threatened to march on the vessel and set her ablaze. But La Barge fired the boilers, engaged the engine, steered her across the river and managed to tie her up in safety against the Kansas shore.

La Barge became a steamboat clerk after his youthful years as a fur trader and soon moved up to the wheelhouse as an apprentice steersman and then a pilot on the lower river. He bought the steamer *General Brooks* for $12,000 in 1846 when he was 31 years old, and built up a fortune over the years by buying, selling, building, chartering and operating other vessels. His capacity for pragmatism — and for the sardonic view — played no small part in his career as a steamboatman in the wilds. He had no quarrel at all, for example, with so elemental an aspect of the fur trade as the sale of whiskey to Indians; he was delighted, in fact — when

chartered by the American Fur Company — to outwit inspectors whom the government stationed at lower-river checkpoints to halt the liquor traffic into the Rockies. He put his whiskey barrels ashore with other freight after stopping at Bellevue, Iowa, on one upstream trip, invited the clergyman in charge of inspection to search the boat — and ordered the booze back on board after that gentleman had congratulated him on his sympathetic attitude and had retired to quarters ashore.

The famed naturalist John James Audubon helped La Barge play an even more ludicrous trick on an inspecting Army officer when they traveled upstream together on the steamer *Omega* in the spring of 1843. Steamboatmen — La Barge included — considered Audubon a pompous and overbearing ass; and Audubon, in his turn, regarded rivermen as a trying lot of simpletons and dolts. Audubon liked to drink, however, and was horrified when a young Army man put a rifle shot across *Omega*'s bows at Bellevue and waved her in to the bank to be searched. The naturalist introduced himself to the young officer, asked for the "privilege" of inspecting the post at which the man was stationed and was led, instantly, ashore and treated as a guest of honor by the camp's dazzled commandant. La Barge, who was the boat's pilot, and Joseph Sire, its captain, used the time to get their whiskey barrels below decks and loaded on a narrow-gauge tramway that ran in a circle around the shallow hold. The inspector was not only lighted down into this black tunnel by candles on his return, but was urged to crawl, at times bumping his head, around the whole circuit while roustabouts pushed the whiskey-laden cars ahead of him in the gloom.

La Barge had a much better understanding of Indians than the Army officers and Indian agents who were given the task of dealing with them; he was known and trusted, indeed, by many chiefs along the river. Yet the Sioux, who boarded and stormed his *Martha* in 1847, remained a continual source of danger. No Missouri steamer was ever subject to such persistent attack as was his chartered vessel, *Robert Campbell,* in the summer of 1863. This was a year of low water and intense tribal hostility. La Barge took the heavy-laden *Campbell* upstream with a smaller steamer, *Shreveport* — planning to cope with the first problem by transferring part of his cargo from *Campbell* to *Shreveport* when they reached the shallow upper river. He presumed, that the second problem would solve itself; he had shipments of annuity goods for the Mandans, Sioux, Crows and Blackfeet, and Indians usually swallowed their anger, at least temporarily, when it was time to line up for their peace bribes from the government.

He reckoned, however, without passenger Samuel M. Latta, an Indian agent in charge of disbursing goods for all tribes but the Blackfeet. Angry spokesmen from the Two Kettles band of Sioux came to see La Barge after he tied up at Fort Pierre, pointed out that they had received only two thirds of their goods, and — for all their friendship with the captain — demanded the rest on pain of armed retaliation. He told them the truth: that his cargo belonged to the government and that he had no control over its division among people on shore.

Peace reigned as the steamer lay at the bank, but La Barge — and everybody else aboard her — soon discovered that the Sioux meant business. When *Robert Campbell* headed upstream, the Two Kettles band mounted their horses and set out in dogged pursuit. The steamer seldom stopped for wood without enduring scattered fusillades from the angry Indians. La Barge piled cargo around the pilothouse and engine spaces and kept his attackers at a distance by arming his roustabouts and returning the fire. But the Sioux refused to give up. They chased the boat upriver for 600 miles, got ahead of her, and finally found a perfect place to wait in ambush for her arrival. The channel curved in against the bank at this spot, and no boat could pass — thanks to a long sand bar out in the stream — without moving within 30 yards of the shore.

But the fates — and a hunter named Louis Dauphin — sided this time with La Barge. Dauphin was almost as well known for his daring and woodsmanship in the golden era of the steamboats as Etienne Provost had been in the day of the mountain men. He had signed on to provide meat for *Shreveport* and *Campbell* and had been ranging the country between the big bends of the Missouri even as the Sioux had been scouring the shore. He had managed to deliver game to both boats by emerging from cover as one or the other of them caught up with him on their circuitous progress upstream. Now he moved even more surreptitiously in warning *Campbell* of the trap ahead. La Barge, still miles below the ambush, saw a hat floating oddly on the river upstream. He put his glasses on it, and presently saw it lift, slight-

ly, to reveal the hunter's head. La Barge rang his engine-room bell for stop and Dauphin pulled himself, dripping, onto the deck: "I had to take to the water. There were too many for me. You're going to have trouble. . . . There are 1,500 of them waiting."

Shreveport lay cautiously dead in the water a hundred yards below the point of ambush as *Campbell* approached; La Barge pulled slowly around her, saw his pursuers gathered en masse on the bank and stopped, too. A parley began across 60 yards of water. The Indians spoke in conciliatory tones: they wanted nothing but their rightful goods. Indian agent Latta indignantly refused. But he then asked La Barge to send his yawl to shore "for some chiefs and head men so we can talk and give them sugar and quiet them." La Barge was dumfounded by Latta's assumption that Indians willing to ride 600 miles after his steamer were not to be considered a deadly serious and dangerous lot — and refused, as indignantly, in return. "Well," said Latta, "I'm not afraid of them," and asked for the right to seek volunteers among the crew. La Barge hesitated but, staring hard at the agent, finally agreed.

Here the tale diverges as such reminiscences often do. Passenger Henry A. Boller (*page 74*) insisted afterward that members of *Campbell*'s crew ran to the opposite side of the boat as Latta turned toward them, lowered themselves over the side and hung there, refusing to go near the yawl. They acquiesced, said Boller, when the mate got an ax and "threatened to cut their fingers off."

La Barge (who denied Boller's story until his dying day) did not let the seven men aboard the yawl set off for shore until he had ordered both steamboats' cannons (two on *Campbell*, one on *Shreveport*) loaded and aimed, and had armed the crews of both vessels with rifles. Latta, watching, decided to stay behind after all — a wise, if unpraiseworthy, decision.

Several warriors waited at the water's edge as the yawl approached. When the boat ran up on the shore, they leaped in and killed three roustabouts with lances and rifles; an Indian archer, back on the shore, wounded another. The two remaining oarsmen threw themselves to the bottom of the yawl, but the steersman — a quick-witted fellow named Andy Stinger — jumped overboard, crouched behind the gunwales and tried to haul the boat away from the bank. At that point, the men back

Men who mastered the mighty Missouri

"In order to be a pilot a man had to learn more than any man ought to be allowed to know," wrote Mark Twain about the virtuoso performances demanded of riverboat pilots and captains, adding: "He must learn it all over again in a different way every 24 hours."

The captains learned the fundamentals of their craft as lowly deck hands or cabin boys. All earned renown for their ability to cope with Indians, unreliable machinery and roisterous crews as they guided their boats, according to an entry in the log of one ship, "just a little beyond no place."

Joseph LaBarge, as a youth, disqualified himself for the priesthood, confessing a great fondness for the ladies. As Captain La Barge, he was asked how he was affected by the Missouri's constant hazards. His reply: "I am actively engaged and forget the river's dangers."

Grant Marsh, a cabin boy at 12, spent a total of 32 years on the Missouri defying the river's reputation as a graveyard for steamboats. Only one vessel under his command — *Little Eagle No. 2* — was ever lost: it flipped over during a twister and sank into the Big Muddy in 1894.

Daniel Maratta, whose flamboyance and "petroleum tongue" made him a pet of the press, began as cabin boy in the 1850s and capped his career in command of *Fontanelle,* one of the fastest boats on the river, before leaving its wheel to oversee a company fleet from a desk.

Charles Blunt Sr. rose from deck hand to captain in just three years. But his fortunes turned sour as an owner. Transporting Civil War troops, he lost one boat to a boiler explosion and another in an ambush by Rebels. Congress turned a deaf ear to his loss claims.

Charles Blunt Jr., unlike most rivermen, stayed with the same company for 45 years. Imperturbable, he once rode out a tornado during which, wrote the *Bismarck Tribune*, "he stood in the pilot house as the boat's superstructure was cleaned off right behind his head."

Carrol J. Atkins, who left Vermont for the Missouri, suffered an epic humiliation in command of *Live Oak* in 1865. Seeing an alluring lady on a bluff waving her hat, he gallantly put in to shore — whereupon her hidden confederates robbed passengers and crew.

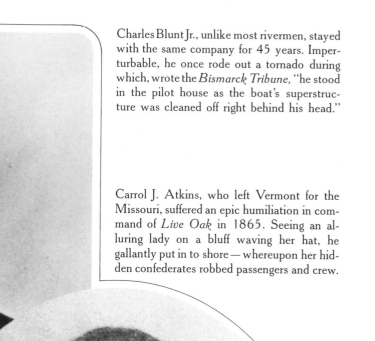

John M. Belk boarded his first steamboat when he was 13, as owner-operator of a refreshment stand. He got his first experience at the wheel five years later when he signed on *Evening Star* as errand boy and a kindly pilot allowed him to use his spare time steering the boat.

William ("Captain Billy") Sims was 27 when this photo was taken in 1869 and just establishing himself as one of the steadiest and most respected masters of the river. He began his career at the age of 15 as a cub pilot under his uncle, Captain Charles Blunt Sr.

on the steamboats, thinking that Stinger and his crew had been killed, opened up with their three cannons and small arms. The storm of shot swept the attackers away from the yawl, felling nearly 40 Sioux and 20 horses in all.

Steersman Stinger managed to get the yawl into open water by paddling furiously with one hand, climbed back into it, and directed its two unwounded oarsmen toward the sand bar. Both leaped out on arrival there, and Stinger was left — cursing brilliantly — to bring the boat, its dead men and wounded survivor, back to the steamer by himself. But that was the end of the Indians' long chase. The runaway crewmen were retrieved, the Sioux further discouraged with cannon fire, and *Campbell* churned on to the mouth of the Yellowstone with passengers, crew, corpses and freight.

This battle reflected a new belligerency on the part of Indians. Missouri tribes had not regarded white men as real threats to their hunting grounds during the years of the fur trade, and Indians who fired at passing vessels had usually done so out of individual pique, or as a matter of casual sport. But Montana gold — which prospectors began discovering at Gold Creek and Bannack in 1862 — was already altering these attitudes and this state of affairs when the Two Kettles band was moved to its anguished if angry feud with *Campbell*.

Gold drew hundreds and then thousands of miners to camps like Virginia City and Last Chance Gulch and threatened the last, vast Indian domains as a few scattered trappers had never done. It turned bands of Sioux and Northern Cheyennes into impassioned enemies who harassed steamers and Army posts alike, and did so as a matter of principle and on every possible occasion. Gold, too, finished the era of lonely mountain voyages that Joseph La Barge so typified, and launched a new era of massive upper-river traffic and of steamer-assisted military campaigns.

This is not to say that La Barge failed to respond with ardor and alacrity to the new chances for wealth that gold so suddenly provided shippers and traders. His organization of La Barge, Harkness & Company — to which he and his brother John and three St. Louis investors each contributed $10,000 in 1862 — was an ambitious but perfectly logical reaction to new times in Montana. The firm proposed to deal in annuities and take goods of its own upstream — as well as cargo for

customers — and to sell them at big profits in mining camps. But La Barge and his associates soon became mired in financial disasters. La Barge's partner, James Harkness, took a wagon-train load of the firm's goods to the Deer Lodge Valley in one instance, and then — startled by life among whiskery miners — turned it over to a sharp trader named Nick Wall and hurried back to his fireside in St. Louis. Wall — a Confederate sympathizer whom La Barge had extricated from federal authorities in Missouri, and whom he had grubstaked and given free passage upriver — then sold the consignment, kept the money and embroiled his benefactor in a long, costly and losing damage suit in the Montana courts. The company ultimately collapsed — having cost La Barge $100,000.

He set forth alone to retrieve his fortunes and made a gallant fight of it. He scraped up $40,000 to buy a three-quarters interest in the steamboat *Effie Deans* in 1864, took a cargo of mining supplies upstream, turned the boat over to his brother John when it was stalled by low water, rounded up wagons, drivers and oxen and took his goods on to Fort Benton and Virginia City by land. This venture in trading left him the possessor of $100,000 in gold dust — and made him a target of opportunity for the gangs of road agents that spied on well-heeled men in the gold fields and robbed them if they attempted to travel beyond. La Barge reserved a seat on an eastbound stagecoach (which highwaymen duly stopped and searched), but sneaked safely out of town a day early on another stage bound for Salt Lake City. He dropped in on his old friend, Brigham Young, bought a team and wagon, drove it into the valley of the Platte, hid for days on a river island to avoid an Indian war party, got back to the Missouri with his treasure — having traveled 8,400 miles since spring — and boarded the season's last downstream vessel for home.

La Barge brought back $50,000 in gold dust from another personal trading venture the following year. But *Effie Deans* then burned to the water line at the levee in St. Louis, and La Barge, whose stubborn sense of honor precluded his taking any other course, used much of his newly gained profit and his remaining energies in settling debts that haunted him in his declining years. He remained a figure of patriarchal authority on the river until he was 70, and a celebrity on the streets of St. Louis until he died in 1899 at the age of 84.

Grant Marsh would prove a worthy heir to La Barge's mantle as the Missouri's premier pilot and captain; but the motley citizenry of Fort Benton was hardly aware of him or his steamboat *Luella* when he tied up there on June 17, 1866, to discharge a cargo of groceries and mining machinery and to loose a cabinful of argonauts upon the wilderness. Rich gold strikes, coinciding with Lee's distant surrender at Appomattox, had triggered such waves of invasion and exploitation as the northern Rockies had never known, and the Montana gold boom was roaring in earnest at last. Thirty-one steamers had reached, or were approaching, the head of navigation—though not more than a half dozen had done so in any previous year —and they now lay bow to stern along a half mile of riverfront. Huge freight wagons stood in Fort Benton's rutted lanes; and its shabby bars and dance halls were jammed with plainsmen, unfrocked Confederate soldiers, Mexicans, Missouri, plowboys and miners.

But Marsh, though only 34 years old and making his first voyage as a captain, was not a man who went unheeded in any company. He was a clear-eyed and open young man with an easy manner and a deceptively soft voice; but he was, as well, a big, lean, hard-muscled fellow who wore an unmistakable air of decision and command. His *Luella* made history before the summer was over.

Marsh had never laid eyes on the upper reaches of the river before feeling his way to Fort Benton in *Luella*. But that was lesson enough. In the same season, he took his steamer back through its shoals and rapids twice again after discharging his original cargo — once to rescue the passengers and machinery of a steamer wrecked in white water 70 miles downstream, and once to aid in closing up the old fur-trading post of Fort Union at the mouth of the Yellowstone. And, having done so, he made a decision that reflected that ultimate quality of great pilots: an intuitive ability to see some constricted but logical route through water others considered wholly dangerous; and beyond that, the confidence to assume that, in the end, almost any stretch of river would be negotiable, given time and resolution.

Captains made a practice of turning their boats around after unloading at Fort Benton and of heading downstream in a hurry to avoid entrapment by the shallowing water of midsummer. But Marsh, having kept *Luella* at work on the upper river into August, decided to delay until September—although she was the last vessel at the riverbank—and thus to accommodate crowds of miners who wished to stay at the diggings as long as possible before taking their earnings home. His mind made up, he headed into the Highwood Mountains and hunted deer for a week with a party of his officers and passengers-to-be. *Luella* headed for home, as a result of her late departure, with the most valuable cargo ever borne downstream: $1,250,000 in gold dust. And she collected an impressive weight of the precious metal for herself in the process.

Miners paying for tickets in dust made a practice of debasing it with sand, but Marsh had heard of this ruse during the summer; he countered it by making every passenger pan his offering clean before weighing out the price of a voyage to St. Louis. *Luella* delivered them there with remarkable ease and dispatch, though she was bushwhacked near the mouth of the Milk River by Indians, who found her stuck on a sand bar and began firing down at her from the summit of a high bluff. Marsh simply called his 230 passengers to the deck with their shooting irons and drove the tribesmen off the skyline with the first, noisy fusillade. He got boat, passengers, gold and crew to St. Louis without further incident. He had worked *Luella* as few boats had ever been worked on the upper river, had handily disposed of an Indian war party, and made a profit of $24,000 in the bargain—all of which earned him a respect rarely accorded new captains on the Missouri.

Marsh was more firmly grounded in the fundamentals of paddle navigation than a good many of his new admirers realized. He had been working on the Western rivers for 22 years, having run away from his parents' home near Pittsburgh to become a cabin boy on the Allegheny River steamer, *Dover*. He had served as a stripling roustabout and as a husky young mate on the Ohio, the Mississippi, the Tennessee and the lower Missouri; and had lived through the great St. Louis "ice gorge" of 1856. There were few "trades"—commercial runs—on any of the Western waters in which he had not handled cargo or commanded deck crews.

Marsh served as mate of the New Orleans packet *John J. Roe* that supported General Ulysses S. Grant's forces at the Battle of Shiloh on the Tennessee River in 1862. *John J. Roe* was celebrated for lack of speed

The accidental conquest of the Cascades

By every yardstick of size or traffic, the Missouri was the greatest of Western waterways, but the Columbia — churning 1,210 miles through the Pacific Northwest — ran a strong second with its burden of fur trappers, prospectors, settlers and freight. Unfortunately, traffic on it was blocked at several points by stretches of white water that confined a steamboat to the section of river on which it was built. Passengers and cargo had to be unloaded to bypass these rapids via portage railway and then resume the journey on relay boats.

One of the deadliest of the foaming obstructions was the Cascades, a six-mile gauntlet of rocks midway between a town called The Dalles and Portland, Oregon. From the first appearance of steamers on the Columbia River in 1836, pilots regarded the Cascades as a sure deathtrap; but in 1858 the stern-wheeler *Venture* proved them wrong. Her pilot, setting off upstream from above the rapids, failed to call for enough steam and the boat was swept back over the rapids stern first. Incredibly, *Venture* fetched up in calm water with all hands safe — but for one hapless soul who had panicked, leaped overboard and drowned.

This lucky accident coincided with the growth of Portland as a major shipping center. Emboldened by the news that the Cascades could be crossed, shipowners operating above it encouraged their captains to shoot the rapids — bow first — and join the Portland-to-Pacific trade.

Prudent pilots tackled the Cascades when the water was high; but in 1888 one of the most renowned captains on

White-water champion James Troup

the river, James W. Troup, dared to make the run at low water in the 462-ton *Hassalo*. On the great day — May 26 — thousands of thrill seekers gathered to watch the bold Troup do or die. Photographers snapped and supporters cheered lustily as *Hassalo (left)* barreled through the obstacle course in a breathtaking seven minutes and wound up with only minor scrapes. Troup moved on to seek new challenges in British Columbia, and eight years later a canal-and-lock system was built to end forever the hazard of the Cascades.

An act of Congress in 1852 made pilots' licenses mandatory. Its aim, stated in small print, was to "provide for the better security of the lives of passengers on board vessels propelled in whole or in part by steam."

("so slow," wrote Mark Twain in *Life on the Mississippi,* "that when she finally sank in Madrid Bend it was five years before the owners heard of it."). She was, however, one of the largest boats on the river and was used to move two complete regiments of Union infantry from the captured bastion of Fort Donelson to Pittsburgh Landing, 300 miles upstream. The armies fought close to the river there — 55,000 Union soldiers trying to dislodge 42,000 Confederates from the key position at Shiloh Church. Marsh watched in admiration as a furious officer of General Grant's staff stopped an incipient retreat at pistol point — and he saw a man standing within a few feet of him on deck decapitated by a Confederate cannon ball. Every man aboard *John J. Roe* knew the price paid for Shiloh Church; she took 600 wounded soldiers with her when she headed back to St. Louis. The Union forces had suffered 13,000 casualties overall, and the Confederacy nearly as many.

Marsh was guided in later life by impressions formed during these thunderous and bloody days: by an admiration for good soldiers and a sense of duty to them, and by a personal belief in the efficacy of daring and resolution during moments of stress or danger. These traits were mandatory on the Missouri during the years of gold boom in Montana and Idaho, for the Sioux reacted with savage bitterness to the encroachment of white travelers and soldiers. Red Cloud, the great Oglala Sioux war chief, besieged Forts Kearny, Reno and C. F. Smith so successfully in 1866 and 1867 that the government was forced to close the Bozeman Road — the overland emigrant route from the North Platte River to Virginia City, Montana.

With east-west travel thus confined to the Missouri, other warriors harassed the miserable little log-built posts the Army established on the upper river. Sitting Bull of the Hunkpapa band waged a kind of psychological warfare on the garrison at Fort Buford in the winter of 1867; he not only bottled its shivering soldiers inside its walls for months, but kept his warriors banging continuously on a circular saw, captured from the post's sawmill, to dramatize his presence outside the fort's log stockade.

This hostility was extended to steamers when and if they could be attacked from the shore. Marsh, having weathered one ambush in *Luella,* was compelled to cope with another and more serious attack when he took the steamboat *Ida Stockdale* to Fort Benton the following year.

The Sioux liked heights, since the vulnerable wooden roofs of armored wheelhouses were exposed to snipers firing from above. *Ida Stockdale* ran into trouble at a point where an island divided the river and pushed the steamer channel close to the north bank under a precipice known as Plenty Coal Bluff. A big war party — which had been riding along the south shore when they saw the vessel's smoke — divided to waylay her. Dozens of horsemen swam their mounts across the river and scrambled up the bluff; others crossed to the island; and the rest — just in case — stayed where they were. No steamer had ever chanced the fast, narrow chute between the island and the southern bank; but Marsh, watching the hurried deployment of the Indians, decided to risk it — and accept gunfire aimed at river level rather than expose the boat to fusillades from on high. He headed into the quickening water of the chute, scraped across a sand bar with bullets clanging on his boiler plate, put his wheel hard down to avoid a jutting snag, ground along the bottom for awful seconds — and glided into open water beyond the island with the sound of Indian musketry dying into frustrated silence astern.

There was a curious inconsistency about these brushes with Indians and, indeed, about the whole pattern of their reaction to whites. Almost all bands took recesses in enmity at times, and the captain who came downstream with bullet holes in his upper works might find himself starting back with cargo for the very warriors who had put them there. Marsh attached less importance to his adventure at Plenty Coal Bluff than to the fact that he had made a profit of $24,000 during the voyage on which it occurred. And he agreed, the following year — when the government asked him to deliver annuities it had pledged in making peace with Red Cloud — to one of the most outlandish proposals ever put to a riverman: to risk almost certain freeze-up by taking the steamer *Nile* upstream in October with cargo for an Indian agency at the mouth of the Grand River in Dakota Territory.

One can only speculate about those aspects of character that prompted Marsh to attempt this difficult project. He was intensely proud of his skill at the wheel. He also had reason to expect that his attempt to get up-

IN ACCORDANCE WITH THE ACT OF CONGRESS,

APPROVED AUGUST 30, 1852.

Second Renewall

No. 96

PILOT'S CERTIFICATE.

The undersigned, Inspectors for the District of *St Louis* Certify that *Thos. W. Brierly* having been by them this day duly examined, touching his qualifications as a _____ Pilot of a Steamer on *the Mo. River from & to St Louis & Milk River* they do certify that they are satisfied he possesses the requisite skill as a Pilot, and is trustworthy and faithful, and do license him to act as such, within the said bounds for one year from this date.

Given under our hands, this *15* day of *May* *1856*

James H McCord
for self and
H. Singleton

I, *James H McCord* Inspector for the District of *St Louis* certify that the above named *Thos. W. Brierly* this day, before me, solemnly swore that he would faithfully and honestly, according to his best skill and judgment, without concealment or reservation, perform all the duties required of him as Pilot, by the Act of Congress, approved August 30, 1852, entitled "An act to amend an act entitled An act to provide for the better security of the lives of passengers on board of vessels propelled in whole or in part by steam; and for other purposes."

Given under my hand, this *15* day of *May* *1856*

James H McCord

James Lucas & Son, prs. Baltimore.

river would be construed as an act of patriotism by the Quartermaster Department of the Army on which the burden of delivery had been placed; and he was shrewd enough to realize that there was profit for the steamboatman who retained the good graces of governmental agencies. But it is hard not to believe that he was attracted as well by the risky drama of the proposal. The odds against his returning before spring were astronomical and no steamer had previously weathered a winter on the upper river. Marsh seems, however, to have remembered his earlier escapes from ice; to have felt that a vessel could live if frozen into protected water; and to have looked forward, with a certain curiosity, to exile in the wilderness. *Nile,* at any rate, became the first steamer to endure freeze-up and return unscathed. Marsh fell far short of the Grand River: low water forced him to secrete part of his cargo on an island just above Yankton and to unload the rest at the mouth of the Cheyenne River. But he got less than 100 miles back downstream before closing ice forced him to choose a mooring against the east bank and there await the coming of warmer weather.

Nile came to rest near an encampment of Lower Brulé Indians, a particularly unruly lot of Sioux. This band was so intent on staying warm, however, and so dependent on supplies from the agency at Fort Thompson, that it saw no profit in wading through snow to raid a well-armed and empty steamboat. Marsh, as a result, was able to devote himself to heroic walking expeditions along the frozen river. He made frequent hikes to Fort Thompson, which lay 20 miles from the boat, and took longer excursions almost weekly: 47 miles to the island on which he had stored his cargo and 47 miles back the next day.

Men from the Indian agency were abashed, and a little nettled, to discover — on accompanying him back to the boat on one occasion — that they simply could not match strides with him. They sought to even the psychological score with frontier humor and asked him to dinner at the fort, where they slyly served him a "special dish" of stewed dog. Marsh assumed it was venison and ate with such relish — though those around him confined themselves to bacon — that his host could not bring himself to confess until 38 years later.

The captain's victims now sought a hiker who could outwalk him over the 47 miles to Cul-de-sac Island.

rant Marsh would prove a worthy heir to La Barge's mantle as the Missouri's premier pilot and captain; but the motley citizenry of Fort Benton was hardly aware of him or his steamboat *Luella* when he tied up there on June 17, 1866, to discharge a cargo of groceries and mining machinery and to loose a cabinful of argonauts upon the wilderness. Rich gold strikes, coinciding with Lee's distant surrender at Appomattox, had triggered such waves of invasion and exploitation as the northern Rockies had never known, and the Montana gold boom was roaring in earnest at last. Thirty-one steamers had reached, or were approaching, the head of navigation—though not more than a half dozen had done so in any previous year—and they now lay bow to stern along a half mile of riverfront. Huge freight wagons stood in Fort Benton's rutted lanes; and its shabby bars and dance halls were jammed with plainsmen, unfrocked Confederate soldiers, Mexicans, Missouri, plowboys and miners.

But Marsh, though only 34 years old and making his first voyage as a captain, was not a man who went unheeded in any company. He was a clear-eyed and open young man with an easy manner and a deceptively soft voice; but he was, as well, a big, lean, hard-muscled fellow who wore an unmistakable air of decision and command. His *Luella* made history before the summer was over.

Marsh had never laid eyes on the upper reaches of the river before feeling his way to Fort Benton in *Luella*. But that was lesson enough. In the same season, he took his steamer back through its shoals and rapids twice again after discharging his original cargo—once to rescue the passengers and machinery of a steamer wrecked in white water 70 miles downstream, and once to aid in closing up the old fur-trading post of Fort Union at the mouth of the Yellowstone. And, having done so, he made a decision that reflected that ultimate quality of great pilots: an intuitive ability to see some constricted but logical route through water others considered wholly dangerous; and beyond that, the confidence to assume that, in the end, almost any stretch of river would be negotiable, given time and resolution.

Captains made a practice of turning their boats around after unloading at Fort Benton and of heading downstream in a hurry to avoid entrapment by the shallowing water of midsummer. But Marsh, having kept *Luella* at work on the upper river into August, decided to delay until September—although she was the last vessel at the riverbank—and thus to accommodate crowds of miners who wished to stay at the diggings as long as possible before taking their earnings home. His mind made up, he headed into the Highwood Mountains and hunted deer for a week with a party of his officers and passengers-to-be. *Luella* headed for home, as a result of her late departure, with the most valuable cargo ever borne downstream: $1,250,000 in gold dust. And she collected an impressive weight of the precious metal for herself in the process.

Miners paying for tickets in dust made a practice of debasing it with sand, but Marsh had heard of this ruse during the summer; he countered it by making every passenger pan his offering clean before weighing out the price of a voyage to St. Louis. *Luella* delivered them there with remarkable ease and dispatch, though she was bushwhacked near the mouth of the Milk River by Indians, who found her stuck on a sand bar and began firing down at her from the summit of a high bluff. Marsh simply called his 230 passengers to the deck with their shooting irons and drove the tribesmen off the skyline with the first, noisy fusillade. He got boat, passengers, gold and crew to St. Louis without further incident. He had worked *Luella* as few boats had ever been worked on the upper river, had handily disposed of an Indian war party, and made a profit of $24,000 in the bargain—all of which earned him a respect rarely accorded new captains on the Missouri.

Marsh was more firmly grounded in the fundamentals of paddle navigation than a good many of his new admirers realized. He had been working on the Western rivers for 22 years, having run away from his parents' home near Pittsburgh to become a cabin boy on the Allegheny River steamer, *Dover*. He had served as a stripling roustabout and as a husky young mate on the Ohio, the Mississippi, the Tennessee and the lower Missouri; and had lived through the great St. Louis "ice gorge" of 1856. There were few "trades"—commercial runs—on any of the Western waters in which he had not handled cargo or commanded deck crews.

Marsh served as mate of the New Orleans packet *John J. Roe* that supported General Ulysses S. Grant's forces at the Battle of Shiloh on the Tennessee River in 1862. *John J. Roe* was celebrated for lack of speed

The accidental conquest of the Cascades

By every yardstick of size or traffic, the Missouri was the greatest of Western waterways, but the Columbia—churning 1,210 miles through the Pacific Northwest—ran a strong second with its burden of fur trappers, prospectors, settlers and freight. Unfortunately, traffic on it was blocked at several points by stretches of white water that confined a steamboat to the section of river on which it was built. Passengers and cargo had to be unloaded to bypass these rapids via portage railway and then resume the journey on relay boats.

One of the deadliest of the foaming obstructions was the Cascades, a six-mile gauntlet of rocks midway between a town called The Dalles and Portland, Oregon. From the first appearance of steamers on the Columbia River in 1836, pilots regarded the Cascades as a sure deathtrap; but in 1858 the stern-wheeler *Venture* proved them wrong. Her pilot, setting off upstream from above the rapids, failed to call for enough steam and the boat was swept back over the rapids stern first. Incredibly, *Venture* fetched up in calm water with all hands safe—but for one hapless soul who had panicked, leaped overboard and drowned.

This lucky accident coincided with the growth of Portland as a major shipping center. Emboldened by the news that the Cascades could be crossed, shipowners operating above it encouraged their captains to shoot the rapids—bow first—and join the Portland-to-Pacific trade.

Prudent pilots tackled the Cascades when the water was high; but in 1888 one of the most renowned captains on

White-water champion James Troup

the river, James W. Troup, dared to make the run at low water in the 462-ton *Hassalo.* On the great day—May 26—thousands of thrill seekers gathered to watch the bold Troup do or die. Photographers snapped and supporters cheered lustily as *Hassalo (left)* barreled through the obstacle course in a breathtaking seven minutes and wound up with only minor scrapes. Troup moved on to seek new challenges in British Columbia, and eight years later a canal-and-lock system was built to end forever the hazard of the Cascades.

An act of Congress in 1852 made pilots' licenses mandatory. Its aim, stated in small print, was to "provide for the better security of the lives of passengers on board vessels propelled in whole or in part by steam."

("so slow," wrote Mark Twain in *Life on the Mississippi,* "that when she finally sank in Madrid Bend it was five years before the owners heard of it."). She was, however, one of the largest boats on the river and was used to move two complete regiments of Union infantry from the captured bastion of Fort Donelson to Pittsburgh Landing, 300 miles upstream. The armies fought close to the river there — 55,000 Union soldiers trying to dislodge 42,000 Confederates from the key position at Shiloh Church. Marsh watched in admiration as a furious officer of General Grant's staff stopped an incipient retreat at pistol point — and he saw a man standing within a few feet of him on deck decapitated by a Confederate cannon ball. Every man aboard *John J. Roe* knew the price paid for Shiloh Church; she took 600 wounded soldiers with her when she headed back to St. Louis. The Union forces had suffered 13,000 casualties overall, and the Confederacy nearly as many.

Marsh was guided in later life by impressions formed during these thunderous and bloody days: by an admiration for good soldiers and a sense of duty to them, and by a personal belief in the efficacy of daring and resolution during moments of stress or danger. These traits were mandatory on the Missouri during the years of gold boom in Montana and Idaho, for the Sioux reacted with savage bitterness to the encroachment of white travelers and soldiers. Red Cloud, the great Oglala Sioux war chief, besieged Forts Kearny, Reno and C. F. Smith so successfully in 1866 and 1867 that the government was forced to close the Bozeman Road — the overland emigrant route from the North Platte River to Virginia City, Montana.

With east-west travel thus confined to the Missouri, other warriors harassed the miserable little log-built posts the Army established on the upper river. Sitting Bull of the Hunkpapa band waged a kind of psychological warfare on the garrison at Fort Buford in the winter of 1867; he not only bottled its shivering soldiers inside its walls for months, but kept his warriors banging continuously on a circular saw, captured from the post's sawmill, to dramatize his presence outside the fort's log stockade.

This hostility was extended to steamers when and if they could be attacked from the shore. Marsh, having weathered one ambush in *Luella,* was compelled to cope with another and more serious attack when he took the steamboat *Ida Stockdale* to Fort Benton the following year.

The Sioux liked heights, since the vulnerable wooden roofs of armored wheelhouses were exposed to snipers firing from above. *Ida Stockdale* ran into trouble at a point where an island divided the river and pushed the steamer channel close to the north bank under a precipice known as Plenty Coal Bluff. A big war party — which had been riding along the south shore when they saw the vessel's smoke — divided to waylay her. Dozens of horsemen swam their mounts across the river and scrambled up the bluff; others crossed to the island; and the rest — just in case — stayed where they were. No steamer had ever chanced the fast, narrow chute between the island and the southern bank; but Marsh, watching the hurried deployment of the Indians, decided to risk it — and accept gunfire aimed at river level rather than expose the boat to fusillades from on high. He headed into the quickening water of the chute, scraped across a sand bar with bullets clanging on his boiler plate, put his wheel hard down to avoid a jutting snag, ground along the bottom for awful seconds — and glided into open water beyond the island with the sound of Indian musketry dying into frustrated silence astern.

There was a curious inconsistency about these brushes with Indians and, indeed, about the whole pattern of their reaction to whites. Almost all bands took recesses in enmity at times, and the captain who came downstream with bullet holes in his upper works might find himself starting back with cargo for the very warriors who had put them there. Marsh attached less importance to his adventure at Plenty Coal Bluff than to the fact that he had made a profit of $24,000 during the voyage on which it occurred. And he agreed, the following year — when the government asked him to deliver annuities it had pledged in making peace with Red Cloud — to one of the most outlandish proposals ever put to a riverman: to risk almost certain freeze-up by taking the steamer *Nile* upstream in October with cargo for an Indian agency at the mouth of the Grand River in Dakota Territory.

One can only speculate about those aspects of character that prompted Marsh to attempt this difficult project. He was intensely proud of his skill at the wheel. He also had reason to expect that his attempt to get up-

IN ACCORDANCE WITH THE ACT OF CONGRESS,

APPROVED AUGUST 30, 1852.

Second Renewal

No. 96

PILOT'S CERTIFICATE.

The undersigned, Inspectors for the District of *St Louis* Certify that *Thos. W. Brierly* having been by them this day duly examined, touching his qualifications as a _____ Pilot of a Steamer on *the Mo River from & to St Louis & Milk River* they do certify that they are satisfied he possesses the requisite skill as a Pilot, and is trustworthy and faithful, and do license him to act as such, within the said bounds for one year from this date.

Given under our hands, this *15th* day of *May* 1856

James H McCord
for self and
W. Singleton

I, *James H McCord* _____ Inspector for the District of *St Louis* _____ certify that the above named *Thos. W. Brierly* _____ this day, before me, solemnly swore that he would faithfully and honestly, according to his best skill and judgment, without concealment or reservation, perform all the duties required of him as Pilot, by the Act of Congress, approved August 30, 1852, entitled "An act to amend an act entitled 'An act to provide for the better security of the lives of passengers on board of vessels propelled in whole or in part by steam,' and for other purposes."

Given under my hand, this *15th* day of *May* 1856

James H McCord

James Lucas & Son, prs. Baltimore.

river would be construed as an act of patriotism by the Quartermaster Department of the Army on which the burden of delivery had been placed; and he was shrewd enough to realize that there was profit for the steamboatman who retained the good graces of governmental agencies. But it is hard not to believe that he was attracted as well by the risky drama of the proposal. The odds against his returning before spring were astronomical and no steamer had previously weathered a winter on the upper river. Marsh seems, however, to have remembered his earlier escapes from ice; to have felt that a vessel could live if frozen into protected water; and to have looked forward, with a certain curiosity, to exile in the wilderness. *Nile,* at any rate, became the first steamer to endure freeze-up and return unscathed. Marsh fell far short of the Grand River: low water forced him to secrete part of his cargo on an island just above Yankton and to unload the rest at the mouth of the Cheyenne River. But he got less than 100 miles back downstream before closing ice forced him to choose a mooring against the east bank and there await the coming of warmer weather.

Nile came to rest near an encampment of Lower Brulé Indians, a particularly unruly lot of Sioux. This band was so intent on staying warm, however, and so dependent on supplies from the agency at Fort Thompson, that it saw no profit in wading through snow to raid a well-armed and empty steamboat. Marsh, as a result, was able to devote himself to heroic walking expeditions along the frozen river. He made frequent hikes to Fort Thompson, which lay 20 miles from the boat, and took longer excursions almost weekly: 47 miles to the island on which he had stored his cargo and 47 miles back the next day.

Men from the Indian agency were abashed, and a little nettled, to discover—on accompanying him back to the boat on one occasion—that they simply could not match strides with him. They sought to even the psychological score with frontier humor and asked him to dinner at the fort, where they slyly served him a "special dish" of stewed dog. Marsh assumed it was venison and ate with such relish—though those around him confined themselves to bacon—that his host could not bring himself to confess until 38 years later.

The captain's victims now sought a hiker who could outwalk him over the 47 miles to Cul-de-sac Island.

Steamboat Captain Minnie Hill

First lady of the Columbia

When 20-year-old Minnie Mossman married Columbia River Captain Charles Hill in 1883 she meant to be more than a mere mate to him. Joining Charles in the pilothouse, she learned the river currents and skills of boat-handling so well that in 1886 she was able to astound two skeptical inspectors with her expertise — and become the first licensed female steamboat captain west of the Mississippi. For the next three years the Hills operated a ramshackle trader boat on the lower Columbia. Then, in 1889, they purchased the 112-foot stern-wheeler *Governor Newell* to haul freight downriver — with Captain Minnie in command and Charles in the engine room answering her bells. In time, the couple acquired four more boats and a baby son. The boy lived aboard *Newell* until 1900, when Minnie moved ashore with him so that he could go to school. But whenever a Hill boat was short a captain, the enterprising Minnie filled in — still unchallenged as the Columbia River's only woman at the wheel.

An agency Indian named Bad Moccasin was nominated for the contest but fell behind, panting, after only an hour. One Dutch Jake — a laborer at the fort — went the distance but finished two miles behind. Some Lower Brulé Indians then suggested a genuine prodigy — a skinny little Sioux called Fast Walker — and his services were duly enlisted.

Fast Walker, it developed, did not walk at all; he ran. He vanished from Marsh's sight after only a few miles, trotted blithely to the island, ran 20 miles more, rolled up in a blanket for a few hours, and then ran another 70 miles to visit some relatives who were camped farther along the river. Marsh accepted defeat with good humor and was on hand to applaud, during a layover the next summer, when Fast Walker took on a thoroughbred horse and beat it, too, while covering 24 miles between the fort and American Creek.

Marsh won the friendship and admiration of an increasing number of Army men in the West — and not only of the quartermasters who were indebted to him for this winter voyage in *Nile*. There was a certain dash about him that appealed to line officers — as did his skill, hardihood and good sense. And he had a way of associating himself with their problems that, in their minds, separated him from other civilians. Marsh ran big risks for mundane, but enormously appreciated, ends during October of 1869: he chanced another entrapment by ice with the steamboat *North Alabama* to deliver winter supplies of vegetables to all the forts along the river. This mission inspired an almost feverish gratitude in men who were prepared to face Indians without complaint but were absolutely appalled at the prospect of living until spring on a diet consisting of only hardtack and salt meat.

Marsh had been earning the princely sum of $1,200 a month as a captain and pilot, but in 1871 he became party to a steamboat combine as an investor in his own right. His contacts with the Army lent new dimensions to his career; they not only provided increasingly remunerative charters and cargo contracts for the line's fleet vessels, but made him a really fabled figure in U.S. military history.

Marsh was one of eight captains, financiers and shippers who created the Coulson Packet Line, a principal instrument by which the Army moved troops and supplies into Indian territory; and his services, in particular,

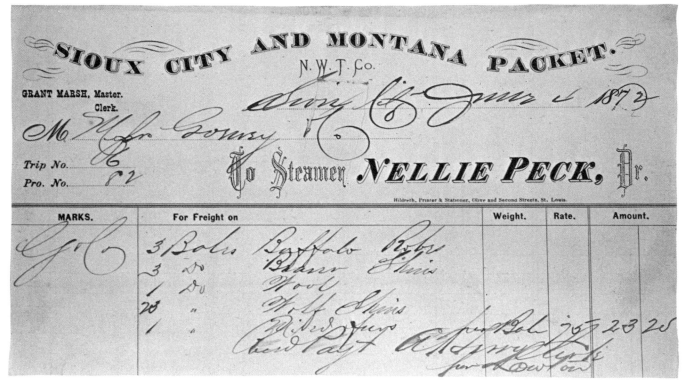

were coveted by officers charged with carrying out ticklish amphibious missions. These expeditions grew more crucial and more dangerous with the passage of time. Red Cloud and his free-roaming Sioux had been granted possession of all country "north of the North Platte River and east of the summits of the Big Horn Mountains" after their bloody closure of the Bozeman Road. But the pressure of white immigration was making this treaty agreement less tenable by the month. Chiefs Gall, Black Moon and Crazy Horse began preaching anew the gospel of the warpath, the government moved the 7th Cavalry under George Custer into Fort Abraham Lincoln as a counterthreat, and the Army began preparing itself for inevitable and final conflict in southern Montana and northern Wyoming.

It was obvious that the Yellowstone River would be a key to military operations against the Sioux. Its tributaries watered the heart of the Indians' remaining hunting grounds. But the Yellowstone presented the Army with a dilemma: generations of trappers and explorers had walked its banks, and surveyors for the Northern Pacific Railroad had penetrated its valley in plotting a route to the coast, yet no man knew whether the stream was navigable for more than a few miles above its

mouth. Lieutenant General Phillip H. (Little Phil) Sheridan, the Civil War hero who now commanded the Army's Division of the Missouri, chose Marsh to explore it by steamboat: 460 miles to the mouth of the Powder River in 1873, and up vastly greater distances of its higher reaches in 1875.

These two expeditions marked the chutes and channels through which troops were ferried and supplied before, during and after the tragic Battle of the Little Bighorn in 1876. Both of them penetrated country marked "hostile" on Army maps and did not go upstream without deckloads of escorting infantrymen. But neither voyage, for all these military trappings, heard so much as an unfriendly rifle shot. They were essentially exercises — though, indeed, ultimate exercises — in river navigation and both turned, almost completely, on the skill, judgment and experience of Grant Marsh.

Key West, the Coulson steamer assigned to the first expedition, seemed to have come to the end of her voyage almost as soon as she turned into the Yellowstone on the morning of May 6, 1873. The water was very low and Marsh found himself facing a labyrinth of shallows and sand bars that spread from shore to shore. He set forth in *Key West*'s yawl to seek some semblance

146

On the St. Louis waterfront in the 1880s, captains and pilots meet in front of a favorite hangout between voyages. Emporiums like this were vital social centers, where boatmen traded gossip and news of available commands.

of a channel—not, in this case, water deep enough to float his vessel but simply water that would permit her some essential buoyancy as she was sparred over obstructions. He got her through, only to find similar shallows and to repeat the exasperating process a few miles farther on. These bars finally gave way not only to definite channels but to sharp rock reefs as well. And there were other hindrances to progress: generations of Indian ponies had grazed on the green bark of cottonwood trees along the stream and had so thinned, stunted and killed them that fuel was hard to find.

Marsh was soon convinced, for all this, that the Yellowstone was indeed navigable and that a good pilot could be expected to compensate for its dangers and difficulties in the future. The river's banks were stable, and the scattered pieces of driftwood that had been stranded along them at high water promised summer levels that would make its channels feasible for shallow-draft steamers. They were channels, moreover, that would not shift. The stream bed was mostly composed of gravel, and its bars—though they could tear out a vessel's bottom—were immovable obstructions that, once charted and memorized, could be avoided by a man who knew his business.

Marsh was as charmed as his crew and his two companies of soldiers at the vistas that opened before the steamer as she churned cautiously upstream. The riverside willows were turning green; vast herds of buffalo moved on the rising prairies; and elk and antelope wandered in herds, like cattle, across bottom land near the water. The boat boasted the presence of an eminent guide and hunter: Luther S. (Yellowstone) Kelly, a New Yorker who in his youth had headed to the frontier for adventure, awed the Sioux with his daring, and had coursed the West for years with "Old Sweetness," his trusty rifle. The boat's company dined on venison that Kelly shot during jaunts ashore. They named points along the stream for one another, their wives and friends: Forsyth Butte, Mary Island, De Russy Rapids. And *Key West* did her work more nimbly than anyone had believed possible: she went to the mouth of the Powder and back to the Missouri in just nine days.

This lighthearted sense of holiday was prolonged: George Custer and his 7th Cavalry were ordered into the Yellowstone valley to escort a party of railroad surveyors, and Marsh was asked to take his vessel back up-stream as a supply boat for the horse soldiers and their flamboyant commander. Custer's support of the Northern Pacific involved sharp little clashes with Indians during the summer and was—with his subsequent reconnaissance of the Black Hills—instrumental in rousing the Sioux against the Army in 1876. The boat was not involved in these skirmishes, however, and Custer behaved, despite them, as though he were engaged in some grandiose sporting expedition. The cavalry, at one point, kept the vessel waiting in the river for two weeks; but its commander sent his regimental band ahead and the musicians, who came aboard as soon as they dismounted, played a crashing concert for captain, crew and the silent hills by the light of a summer moon. Three packs of hounds—one owned by Lord Clifford, an Englishman whom Custer brought along as a guest—came into the valley with the troops. The dogs, having been equipped with little moccasins to protect their paws from the thorns of prickly pear, were sent baying off after jack rabbits when their masters relaxed between bouts of military duty.

Two summers later, Phil Sheridan ordered Marsh into the farthest reaches of the river on another exploratory expedition. He explained in a letter: "It may be necessary, at some time in the immediate future, to occupy by a military force the country in and about the mouths of the Tongue River and the Big Horn." Since there was a possibility of trouble from the Sioux, the steamboat *Josephine* carried 100 soldiers of the 6th Infantry, four mounted scouts and a one-inch Gatling gun with 10,000 rounds of ammunition. But this voyage, too, though it penetrated hundreds of miles of unknown water and skirted hills plumed with the smoke of distant Indian signal fires, evolved into a peaceful, even dreamy summer idyl. It presented Marsh with chains of navigational problems, but it also presented him with splendid water and splendid weather as he encountered them; he thus had every possible means of dramatizing his own remarkable talent at the wheel. *Josephine* came into the Yellowstone at the peak of its spring flood and not only passed serenely over the sand bars that had delayed *Key West* in 1873, but steamed all the way to the Powder River without once having to set her spars or to warp upstream with her steam capstans.

Marsh had doubts as to what he would encounter as *Josephine* passed beyond this point and into water no

PORTAGE BOOK.

NAME.	OCCUPATION.	No. Days.	Wages per Month.	AMOUNT.		Amount Retained.	Amount Paid.
R. F. Woolfolk	Master	30	125	175			
Chas M Blunt	Clerk & Pilot	30	125	175			
Jno Bress	Pilot	30	100	100			
Ole Strom	Engineer	30	100	100			
Harry Larson	Watchman	36½	35	42	60		
Jos Thompson	Mate	30	50	50			
M. S. Moore	Carpenter	30	50	50			
Geo Isam	Cook	5½	50	9	13		
		20½	50	8	5		
Ole Nelson	"	5	20	3	35		
Thos Grover	Cabin	33	18	19	80		
Joy Fosdick	"	36½	18	21	90		
Fannie Davis	Chambermaid	34½	18	20	70		
Dan Johns	Fireman	19½	30	19	50		
Phillip Furber	"	26	30	26			
Hugh McLaughlin	Engineer	25½	60	51			
Peter Martin	Rooster	17	30	17			
Jos Quinn	"	4½	30	4	50		
E. Lindeman	"	17	30	17			
W. E. Wilson	"	3	30	3			
K. Hendrickson	"	26½	30	26	50		
C. Mason	"	17	30	17			
Con Mahoney	"	3½	30	3	50		
L. Johnson	"	26½	30	26	50		
R. Nick	"	26½	30	26	50		
Geo Williams	"	26½	30	26	50		
Christ Padlok	"	26½	30	26	50		
Wm Gliepen	"	3	30	3			
Nick Hill	"	10½	30	10	50		
P. Schwarlz	"	3½	30	3	50		
Andrew Johnson	"	26½	30	26	50		
Gilbert Gullickson	"	13½	30	13	50		
Sam Burgier	"	1½	30	1	50		
Henry Butler	"	4	30	4			
Jno Powers	"	2½	30	2	50		
Jos Binford	"	10	30	10			
Jno Savage	"	4	30	4			
Geo Clark	"	13	30	13			
Jno Hersby	"	8½	30	8	50		
A. A. Gillett	"	1½	30	1	50		
Wm Briggs	"	1½	30	1	50		
Geo Shipley	"	9½	30	9	50		
Robt Powers	"	9	30	9			
albert Surland	"	3½	30	3	50		
Irvin Briggs	"	3½	30	3	50		
Willis Doan	"	3½	30	3	50		
R. Vossul	"	6	30	6			
Wm Pallett	"	6	30	6			
Wm Hiscock	"	6	30	6			
Wm Briggs	"	6	30	6			
C M Blunt in port	"	5½	60	11			
				1163	33		

Luther Kelly, at 24, had already spent five years trapping along the Yellowstone. Since few knew the area as well as he, Grant Marsh hired him for the first steamboat exploration of the river in 1873.

pilot had ever seen. But the river led on and on through usable if reef-bordered channels, and its valley grew more beautiful with every passing day. The steamboat sighted one Sioux encampment on shore but had only the briefest look at its inhabitants: they fled so precipitously that they left their tipi fires burning. The sparse and stunted trees of the lower valley gave way to great stands of enormous cottonwoods, some as much as six feet through the trunk. Wooded islands appeared in midstream. "They are so handsome," wrote General James W. Forsyth, the Army commander on board, "that they almost make the voyager believe he is seeing the well kept grounds of an English country house." Draws and bottom lands along the stream were choked with wild plums, cherries, gooseberries, currants and strawberries; and the prairies were alive, at times, with herds of migrating buffalo. Soldiers and crew feasted on wild fruit and on fresh meat from the rifle of hunter Charley Reynolds. A sense of timelessness—of savoring Eden—settled over all aboard as *Josephine* churned, day after day, up dazzling, sunlit reaches of water toward the retreating horizons of an untracked and smiling world.

Marsh, for all this, kept a painstaking record of the marks at which he aimed his steamboat and of the methodology by which he moved her up the river: "Run left hand shore up past big bluff. Plenty of dead timber at this bend. Then cross from the deadwood to the left hand bluff over a short, right hand bend, then circle out between two islands (first named Crittenden Island for General T. L. Crittenden, 17th Inf.; second named Elk Island) and come back to a right hand prairie bend." He did not pass the mouth of the Bighorn River without pushing up it, too, for a few miles and scribbling similar instructions to himself. Marsh kept this detailed log for very personal reasons: to ensure his own primacy as a pilot on the Yellowstone. He had no idea that the Army would judge it the one most valuable by-product of the whole expedition, would demand it from him and would parcel out copies to the captains of other steamers it eventually chartered.

The river grew gradually faster, gradually narrower, and finally, 27 miles above the Bighorn, squeezed its clear, green flood into an 85-foot-wide channel between towering and intractable cliffs. *Josephine* plunged into this enormous millrace, slowed and hung motionless

with her paddles thrashing madly. She did not fall back, but she could not move forward, and Marsh was forced, while his engines labored at high pressure and his deck hands toiled frantically with derricks and capstans, to set spars and inch ahead, reset them and inch a little farther and to repeat the process amid the racing water for hour after hour as rock walls sent back echoes of his vessel's banging exhaust. But *Josephine* and all aboard her were rewarded when she emerged at last. Easier water lay ahead, and on the horizon was a sight even Marsh had not hoped to see: Pompey's Pillar—the lone, towering, sandstone butte that Lewis and Clark had discovered and celebrated 69 years earlier.

Marsh tied up at its base in the early afternoon, gave soldiers and crew the rest of the day ashore, and—on noting the legend, "Wm. Clark, July 25, 1806," carved on the pillar's face—climbed it himself, erected a makeshift pole and raised one of the boat's two U.S. flags to the gentle Montana breeze. *Josephine* labored on for two more days and 46 more miles, sparring or warping almost continuously through faster and faster water. Forsyth and Marsh finally called it quits at the head of a savage stretch of rock and foam the crew christened Hell Roaring Rapids. The pilot went ashore with an ax and a knife, chopped a blaze on the trunk of a huge cottonwood, and carved, "Josephine, June 7, 1875." The boat had come 483 miles upstream to a point within 60 miles of modern Yellowstone National Park—a feat no other steamer was ever to duplicate.

Marsh turned her around at two in the afternoon, and —exhilarated by success, by the clear summer flood the river still provided and, apparently, by some kind of hypnotic communion with his own skills—sent her swiftly reeling back through the upper rapids, the cliff-bordered narrows and the turbulent reaches below them at a pace that seemed, to some of her soldiers, like flying. This marvelous use of rudders and engines went on: *Josephine* averaged more than 100 miles between each sunup and sundown on her downstream journey and slid back into the Missouri River, without having so much as touched a shoal or bar, in just four days. But Grant Marsh had no way of knowing that he had simply conducted a rehearsal for tragedy, that time was closing in on him—and on his friend George Custer—or that sorrow, danger and real fame still awaited him on the river he now knew better than any man alive.

The fateful intrusion of the "fire canoe"

To the captains who plied the upper Missouri, the Indians along the shore were a perfidious lot who might be grateful consignees one day and bloodthirsty bushwhackers the next. But to the Indians the awesome steamboats embodied all the fears and frustrations linked to the white man's presence.

The first "fire canoes" brought the Indians not only useful goods and gaudy trinkets, but also the illegal whiskey —and the deadly diseases that wreaked havoc among tribesmen, who had no natural immunity to them. Later on the vessels carried in settlers, then soldiers who crushed resistance. Finally, it was the steamboats that took the vanquished to reservations, where they were sustained by riverborne government supplies—regularly pilfered by un-scrupulous traders and corrupt agents.

Artist William Cary, who sketched these deceptively placid scenes on a trip to the upper Missouri in 1861, caught the moods of defiance, hope and resignation among the Indians, who by then had come to regard the steamboat —according to a perceptive commentator—as a symbol of "friend and foe, truth and falsehood, honor and shame."

Watched by a gesturing brave, a stern-wheeler steams through a herd of migrating buffalo that might take hours to cross the river.

A crowd of curious Mandans — one of a dozen tribes served by trading posts on the upper Missouri — lines the riverbank at Fort Berthold to watch a steamboat arrival. The Indians were so awe-struck by the smoke-belching behemoths that they sometimes accompanied them along the shore for miles.

July Fourth celebrants enjoy sunshine and ice cream while strolling aboard the garlanded *Newella* at Leavenworth, Kansas, in the 1860s.

5 | Good times, bad times

The tempo of life along the Missouri was irresistibly linked to the moods of what newspaperman-humorist George Fitch once described as "a river that plays hide-and-seek with you today, and tomorrow follows you around like a pet dog with a dynamite cracker tied to its tail."

Residents looked to the river for essential sustenance, including a limitless quantity of cloudy but wholesome drinking water and an abundant supply of tasty catfish, dubbed by one fancier as "this best of all fishes." And every spring, the arrival of the season's first steamboat bearing produce and supplies touched off a celebration rivaled on the calendar only by the Fourth of July.

The capricious river brought prosperity to some towns and disaster to others. A well-located steamboat center like Yankton, Dakota Territory, in the 1870s, provided the zesty spectacle of roustabouts, bullwhackers, prospectors, land speculators and homesteaders rubbing elbows in the town's four hotels, 73 stores, 30 saloons and one ice-cream parlor. Yankton also boasted a college, an insane asylum and a double-edged reputation. Residents saw no inconsistency in acknowledging that it was "one of the worst of the river towns" for its wide-open ways, while also praising "the tone, refinement and culture pervading its society."

Many locations were not so fortunate. A record 41-foot flood in 1881 wiped out Green Island, Nebraska; and Brunswick, Missouri, found itself a mile inland after the river abruptly changed course in 1875. As for Carroll, Montana, which once hoped to rival bustling Fort Benton, an itinerant grocer wrote its epitaph in 1874. Stuck on a stranded steamboat, he lamented that the only potential customers for miles around were in Carroll "and they haven't got a hundred dollars all told."

Completing a Missouri crossing, local residents and their horses wait for the ferryman to secure his rope-drawn craft at Wilder's Landing, Montana Territory. Such ferries did a brisk business, charging tolls that ranged from a dime for a pedestrian to 75 cents for a loaded wagon and team.

The inevitable saloon, with the owner's wife standing demurely beside the doorway, beckons from the riverbank at Rocky Point, Montana. The saloon, which doubled as a restaurant, was one of a dozen rude buildings clustered at the site of a popular ferry crossing below Fort Benton.

163

A bustling hotel in Bismarck, Dakota Territory, shows off its guests, staff and station wagon while roofers work on unconcernedly. Named for the famed Iron Chancellor in the hope of attracting German investors, Bismarck was known for years by its homely original name: The Crossing.

Recently unloaded steamboat cargoes rest on the levee at Fort Benton, Montana Territory, the boomtown that sprang up at the site of an old fur-trading post. From here during the Montana gold rush, teamsters carried supplies 150 miles to the mining area of Last Chance Gulch.

Commodores, woodhawks and the struggle to survive

Chief Strike-the-Ree is not as well remembered as bloodier-minded leaders of the Sioux Nation, but he was better attuned to the realities of his times. The chief—more familiarly known as "Old Strike"—was hauled off to Washington, D.C. for one of those improbable political consultations to which Indians were occasionally subject in the 1850s and announced to his people on his return to the Dakota Territory: "The white men are coming like maggots. We must get the best terms we can."

This caused some unrest among his E-hank-ton-won (Yankton) band, for the white men wanted to take over the Indians' gathering ground near the juncture of the James and Missouri rivers. Old Strike prevailed, however, and not only got a steamboat load of calico, blankets and farm implements in exchange for the place, but also 400,000 acres of substitute prairie on which he and his band relocated, upriver, in 1859. He got out just in time. A crude new river town—also named Yankton—evolved, almost overnight, on the old Indian campground. Dakota Territory's first legislators convened there just three years later—making it the symbol as well as the scene of Old Strike's augury, and embodying an era of enormous change on the upper Missouri as they did so.

Members of this legislative gathering had no idea that they might be playing so consequential a role when they rode into Yankton in March 1862. The town boasted only one street and 19 inhabitable buildings, all made of logs or whipsawed cottonwood, plus a dismal collection of sod houses, shacks and cabins scattered at random on the bare plain. The village and its surrounding district housed but 287 whites and nine half bloods. But the presence of legislators—and, indeed, the very existence of Yankton itself—heralded irrepressible new forces and anarchic new times on the Missouri. White men had previously dominated only one aspect of the wilderness—the river itself; the banks had belonged to river tribes. But immigrants were now rushing for prairie land along the shore. They were soon to be followed by townsite speculators, gold prospectors, railroad men, soldiers, dealers in Indian annuities and organizers of steamboat lines—all creatures of a "manifest destiny" no longer to be dammed back by distance or peril—who would forever alter the simple patterns of life, commerce and travel that had prevailed since the day of Manuel Lisa.

These patterns had been based on certain immutable facts: that the upper valley boasted but one source of wealth, furs; that the river provided the valley's only channel of communication with the outer world; and that the whole, vast country from the Mississippi to the Rockies was financed, supplied and controlled by businessmen in St. Louis. But these assumptions were undermined, one by one, in the late 1860s.

St. Louis lost its position as supplier and citadel of the Missouri when railroads reached new ports (at Sioux City, then Yankton, then Bismarck) a thousand miles and more above it on the upper river itself. Steamboats in fleets began churning upstream from the new railheads to deliver short-haul cargoes to a growing population in the wilderness. A network of stagecoach routes evolved between prairie settlements along the river. Heavy freight wagons linked Fort Benton with Montana's inland gold camps. And Indians were suddenly regarded as maverick animals to be herded off, fenced up and hand fed on reservations.

The new ports on the upper Missouri were the most important instrumentalities of change—the pumps, as it

An expert Allegheny riverman by age 20, Sanford Coulson began on the Missouri as an engineer for William Kountz, the man he later bested for control of the river.

been inevitable from the moment Manuel Lisa had set off upstream in 1807.

Both Sioux City, which was incorporated in 1857, and Yankton, founded in 1858, were logical townsites, since each faced vast, tillable vistas of open country, and since the Missouri's deep channel hugged a solid shoreline at both locations and assured mooring space for future steamboats. Bismarck (so named in the odd hope that Germany's Chancellor Otto von Bismarck would buy land there) materialized farther upriver in 1872 when it became obvious that the Northern Pacific Railroad would reach, and eventually cross, the Missouri at that point. But none of the towns developed without a dependence on the luck, guile, credit and political connections of speculators — promoters who engaged in a kind of blindfold roulette in the hopes of getting rich quick.

One James A. Jackson, an Omaha storekeeper, bet a small fortune on Sioux City, Iowa, in 1856 after his father-in-law bought up empty land there and began offering lots for sale. Jackson spent $24,000 to charter a steamboat at St. Louis, and another $70,000 to load her up with a kind of portable village: dry goods, groceries, hardware, machinery for a sawmill, and precut lumber for a store and instant houses. But while Jackson earned immediate rewards, most of Sioux City's founders, like those of Yankton, did not prosper before having to endure awful setbacks: drought, flood, Indian scares, blizzards, clouds of grasshoppers and a draining away of men, money and interest in the West during the time of the Civil War.

An engineer named Alexander McCready improved Sioux City's early communications by plowing a 150-mile furrow between it and Fort Dodge, Iowa, to keep stagecoach drivers from losing their way while carrying passengers between the two settlements. But the new river town was annually isolated by winter snow, which lay so long in one bad year that magpies pecked holes in the backs of cattle and lived on their bleeding flesh; and it was not really in touch with the world again before the first steamboat of spring.

All this changed, however, when the first train reached Sioux City on March 7, 1868, and made the town "the new gateway to the West" — 1,100 miles above St. Louis and only 1,900 miles below Fort Benton. "Saved at Last!" announced the local *Journal*.

were, by which white civilization was pushed up the river and through Indian lands to the Rockies. The towns' bankers and entrepreneurs lent dynamism and direction to the white invasion, and their newspapers and retail stores, their entertainments and politics — upon which the most remote of mines and settlements drew for new attitudes and new styles — contrived an increasing urbanization of the wilderness. No keelboater or early steamboater had imagined so complex and overwhelming an exploitation of the Rocky Mountain West, or had remotely suspected that his own difficult and dangerous feats were simply prelude to it. But these new upper-Missouri ports harbored a last generation of pioneer rivermen who presided over a spoliation of wild herds, a domestication of wild tribes and wild country, and a triumph of the plow and the scythe that had

"Look out for the Cars! All Hail Chicago! All Hail New York! All Hail Creation!"

One Joab Lawrence, back North after making a fast dollar in postwar cotton speculation at Mobile, Alabama, based a fleet of five steamers at the Sioux City levee, posted upriver schedules that were 20 days faster and only two-thirds as expensive as service from St. Louis, and began loading mountains of freight — some of it only eight days out of New York itself. The population, which stood at 1,030 in March, began to swell: the road from Fort Dodge was blocked, at times, by immigrant wagons and herds of milk cows. Lawrence splurged on a marine railway and steamer repair yard, and doubled his fleet in 1869. Sioux City now received furs, and monopolized shipping to seven Army posts and eight Indian agencies that had sprung into existence on the upper river. Optimism reigned: Minzesheimer's Store installed eight gaslights fed by fumes from "gasoline oil."

Tempers grew short, however, in Yankton because Dakota legislators had failed to get federal backing for a railroad, and the town was now stranded 65 miles upstream of Sioux City with a population of 737 and nothing but a pork-packing plant to lend it distinction. The legislators soon concocted a new scheme: they proposed to build a railroad of their own with local money and to connect it — ah, ultimate insult — with Sioux City's own road. They would be able, thus, to snatch the rival town's own river freight on arrival from the East and spirit it by rail to Yankton, where boats would be waiting to haul it farther upriver. The citizenry voted a $200,000 bond issue, bridges were built, rails were laid and, in January 1873, a locomotive named C.G. Wicker — for a railroad executive — pulled the first cars through cheering crowds to a new depot. Yankton boosters disparaged the Northern Pacific's all but simultaneous entry into Bismarck, way up there on the river above *them*. But all three river ports were launched on a contest for commercial dominance of the Missouri.

This rivalry, and a stimulation of trade by 1) new settlers, 2) a gold rush to Montana, and 3) the Army's increasing involvement with Indians, mandated the use of river vessels in fleets. A plethora of steamboat companies materialized on the upper river, then split, merged or subsided — until the lion's share of all commerce fell to four of them: the Coulson Line, the Peck Line, the Kountz Line and the Power Line. With them emerged a new sort of Western speculator: rivermen bent on using political leverage, banking connections and a kind of blackjack dealer's intuition in grabbing and delivering cargoes. Lesser mortals tended to deride these new operators — but only at a safe distance; they inspired caution at close range, and none more so than William J. Kountz and Sanford B. Coulson, who were giants of their era on the river.

The two men had a great deal in common; both came west from the town of Allegheny City, Pennsylvania, both basked in the self-chosen title "Commodore," and both had a lively sense of opportunity. They launched themselves almost simultaneously as fleet operators on the upper river — Coulson at Yankton in 1873, Kountz at both Bismarck and Sioux City during the same year. But there their natures and methods diverged. Kountz, a bearded and patriarchal figure, may well have been the most experienced and, in many ways, the most efficient and practical operator of river boats in the U.S. when he advanced on the upper Missouri at the age of 56. But he was also one of the most bullheaded, opinionated and tactless men ever born; and he handicapped himself on the upper river, as he had on the Mississippi during the Civil War, by an inability to temper the guiding principle of his life: that William J. Kountz was always right and the Army, the government and his competitors almost certain to be wrong.

It seems doubtful that any civilian ever turned a more penetrating eye on Army malpractice than did Kountz after General George B. McClellan asked his assistance in river transportation early in the Civil War — or made a bigger nuisance of himself in the process. Kountz had operated Mississippi steamboats and understood all aspects of river navigation, but it never seemed to occur to him that the rest of the Army was not a kind of minor appurtenance of his river boats (and, thus, of William J. Kountz). He was tireless in his efforts to stamp out bribery, corruption and waste of the taxpayer's money — or what he took to be corruption and waste in cases where the Army sacrificed good bookkeeping and proper selection of vessels for speed in moving troops by water. He ignored orders and bypassed the chain of command to write complaining letters to Congressman James K. Moorhead: "Captain Able is still robbing the government . . . but I will stay

here and expose all such stealing as I can find out."

Reputable officers were almost as appalled as the crooks: "He may know how to spy out a rascal," wrote one, "but he doesn't know how to be a gentleman. I am at a loss to know what to do with him." But Kountz met his match when he decided it was his duty to demolish General Ulysses S. Grant in the interest of public morals. Kountz declared he "could not tolerate a drinking man," and wrote to Congressman Moorhead: "I have preferred charges against Gen. Grant for drunkeness—he, on three different occasions . . . drank with trators [sic] until he became beastly drunk. At another time he was so drunk at the Hotel for three days he was not fit to attend to business."

Grant simply had him arrested, though without actually filing charges against him, and blandly suggested that "he be sent to some other field of usefulness." Kountz continued firing off alarmed messages to Washington while confined to the city limits of Cairo, Illinois, but he was dropped from the Army rolls and was returned, still breathing heavily, to civilian life and the management of his own vessels.

Sanford Coulson, known as "The Napoleon of the Big Muddy," was fully as abrupt, egotistical and de-

172

manding as Kountz; but he had a shrewder view of human nature and was wilier, by far, in using others to achieve his own goals. Coulson was only 34 when he started his steamboat company at Yankton, but he, too, was well grounded in the techniques of river navigation, having been a steamboat engineer, a pilot and a captain on the Missouri. And, young or not, he had a voracity of ambition and a flexibility of mind that Kountz could never quite match. Coulson went out of his way, for all his essential aloofness, to cultivate congressmen, generals and steamboat inspectors. He tolerated both individuality and eccentricity in those who worked well for him: many of his boats—including *Far West, Key West, Rosebud, Western* and *Montana*—were so named because his brother-in-law and associate, William S. Evans, was allowed to exercise a superstitious belief in the efficacy of seven-letter words. Coulson had no trouble at all in raising money to finance his company nor in attracting men of talent to put his subsequent schemes into operation.

None of these associates was more useful to him than Daniel Webster Maratta, a steamboat captain who had deserted Kountz to become Coulson's partner, confidant and front man. Maratta—known as "Slippery

173

Dan"—combined an inner pugnacity with a beaming gregariousness. He loved to talk, had a compulsion for shaking hands, enjoyed—and played for—applause, wore flashy clothes, exuded a kind of muscular benevolence and never failed to describe Coulson's fleet as "The Old Reliable Line."

Maratta courted publicity, even such a gibe as was run in the *Bismarck Tribune* after he remonstrated at being asked to pay in advance for a room at a local hotel. "Everybody on the Missouri slope knows me," the paper quoted him as having told the clerk, "and you ought to know who I am without an autobiographical sketch to assist you, although I suppose"—this last more philosophically—"that if Jesus of Nazareth had nowhere to lay his head why should 'the Little Jesus of Dakota' complain." But Maratta's amiable verbosity cloaked a tough and realistic mind. He would not be pushed: he kept Coulson's steamer crews in line, helped him negotiate contracts, and acted as a Washington lobbyist as well as an omnipresent representative of the company at funerals, church socials, political rallies and important poker games.

Kountz and Coulson were not the only steamboat operators on the upper river; other companies formed

An ungainly pontoon bridge spans the Missouri, linking Nebraska City, Nebraska, with settlements across the river in Iowa. Built in 1888, the

and re-formed to compete for the fortunes that were to be made there. But the two irascible giants were its most dominant personalities and conducted its bitterest rivalry. Kountz, who formed an instant alliance with the Northern Pacific Railroad, had the advantage of position high on the river. But Coulson and Maratta were simply too astute.

Representatives of the Coulson Line did their best, for one thing, to cultivate officers of the Army — not excepting a Second Lieutenant Drubb who was empowered to reassign Dakota cargo if an original contractor failed, as was often the case, to load it aboard a steamer on schedule. Coulson Line captains, like Grant Marsh, won the good will of field officers — and charters for the movement of troops — by their willingness to take risks in support of expeditions against hostile Indian tribes. Kountz, on the other hand, clung stubbornly to his dire view of military men. He lost his temper after failing to win an Army contract from Coulson in 1873, and threatened General Phil Sheridan with exposure in the United States Senate — at which Sheridan invited him to "take the matter to hell if it pleases you."

Coulson and Maratta used other devices: they tailored their freight rates to a variety of influences — par-

structure was designed to part at the point of the V to permit the passage of steamers. A flood wrecked it after only four months of service.

ticularly the level of water in the river—rather than basing them on simple poundage of cargo. They were quick to cut prices for big shippers, though with provisos for protective increases in unforeseen cases of low water, wood shortages or Indian trouble. They dramatized the fact that rail rates from Chicago to Yankton were half the rates from Chicago to Bismarck and sold shippers on the idea that the long way upstream was the cheap way upstream for customers of The Old Reliable Line.

They infuriated Kountz. At one point, using a Pennsylvania newspaper in which he owned stock, Kountz printed up a spurious and highly critical article about his enemy's operations, disguised it by running an advertisement for an Illinois drugstore on its reverse side, and—having thus produced what seemed to be a clipping from the independent *Quincy* (Illinois) *Herald*—mailed off copies to companies upon which Coulson depended. But few of his efforts at reprisal really worked —if only because the Army became so heavy a user of steamboats in the 1870s—and he was forced, in the end, to move most of his Bismarck boats back to the lower river and the Mississippi. The Coulson Line —though always heavily engaged by its competitors, and particularly by the relatively stable and successful Peck Line and Power Line—reigned supreme on the water above Yankton.

The Yankton and Bismarck fleets of Coulson and his rivals were inexorably involved in the problems, ambitions and pursuits of burgeoning white civilization along the shore: those of miners and settlers, of Army men, of merchants, bankers and railroad officials in new towns. But, like the solitary mountain boats that went upstream before the Civil War, they were also dependent on the bravery and cunning of men who lived in lonely groves along the upper river: the woodcutters, known to steamboatmen as "woodhawks."

These woodhawks led a desperate and, often, a suicidal existence, for Indians tried to deny boats fuel as a corollary to more serious harassment and they murdered

NEW ARRIVAL
OF
Two Hundred
STOVES
CHRISTIAN DEUSER.
Brownville, Nebraska.
ANNOUNCES to the public that he has just received, per Steamer Ryland, a very large, and well assorted stock of Parlor and Cook Stoves, of new and improved patterns, as follows:
Buck's Pattern,
Plymouth Rock,
Elevated Oven, New Er,
olden Era. and every variety o
Parlor and Office Stoves.
Also,
Japaned Ware, Brass Kettles, Lantherns, Copper Ware. Shovels and Tongs.
All of which I pledge myself to sell at as fair rates and on as accommodating terms as any other establishment in this region of country.
I have also now on hand every requisite variety of Tin, Copper and Sheet Iron ware, and am prepared to put up guttering and spouting and all other work in my line, at short notice, and in a workmanlike manner, which I warrant to give satisfaction.
I pledge myself not to be **undersold in the upper country.**
Brownville September 2, 1858.   u10-1y

seven woodhawks in the area between Fort Benton and Bismarck during 1868 alone. Indians, in fact, having created shortages, sometimes went into the wood business themselves. They proved, however, to be rather tricky sources of supply. Some dyed the ends of green cottonwood logs with their face paint to simulate more flammable cedar, and others—having erected woodpiles beside shallows—squatted up to their necks in the water to create an impression of depth and waved enticingly at passing steamers to ground one for a quick raid.

But if steamer captains did their best to avoid buying fuel from Indians, they also tried to avoid paying cash to white woodhawks; they much preferred to barter with flour, ax handles, whiskey or other goods—when they could not use their own roustabouts as cheaper wood gatherers yet. Woodcutters, thus, could very well go broke at their risky trade. The diary of Peter Koch, a Danish youth who cut wood near a trading post at the mouth of the Musselshell River in 1869 and 1870, reflects the misery, discouragement and occasional peril that were the lot of many such toilers. There is an inconclusiveness about this record suggesting that men needed a certain resignation as well as hardihood in coping with life on the empty Missouri shore:

"Oct. 4. Commenced chopping. Blistered my hands and broke an ax handle.

"8. Twenty five years old and poor as a rat. Cut down a tree on the cabin.

"20. Cutting while Joe is on guard. Snow tonight.

"24. Killed my first buffalo. He took 7 Spencer and 6 pistol balls before he died. River full of ice.

"Nov. 7. A Gale of wind. Those Arapahoes who camped abt. 10 days at Jim Wells woodyard have moved down the river after shooting into his stockade.

"15. Chopped hard all day. B.M. says 3 cords. Fred came back all wet. He had started in a skiff with Dick Harris, both drunk, and upset at Squaw Creek.

"25. Fred and Olsen started out wolfing. We stopped chopping on account of shooting and shouting

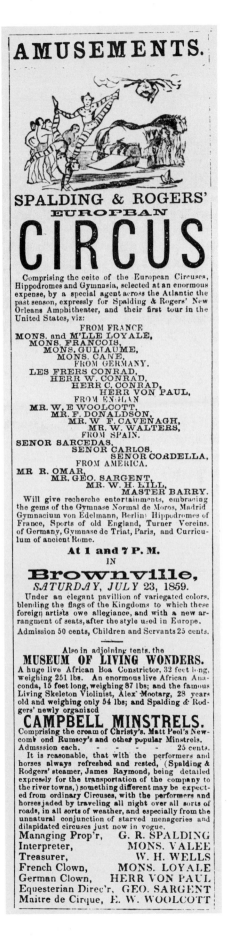
The first circus toured along the Missouri in 1857 and was a staple amusement when this ad appeared in 1859. The copy stressed the advantages to a circus that traveled by steamboat rather than overland.

in the hills. Joe and I found 4 wolves at our baits.

"Dec. 10. Sick. No meat.

"11. Sick yet. Bill, Joe and Mills went to Musselshell, said Indians had attacked and stolen 3 horses and mule but lost one man.

"24. Christmas eve. No wolves.

"Jan. 16. Awful cold. Froze my ears.

"17. Too cold to work. Went up to Musselshell. Froze my nose.

"24. Thawing heavily. Mills drunk.

"Mar. 22. Saw three geese. (Spring has come, gentle Annie.) Martin sick.

"Apr. 24. Sixty Crows went up the river after Sioux to avenge the killing of 29 Crows. They were all looking dreadful, had their hair cut off, their fingers and faces cut, with the blood left on their faces.

"May 9. One hundred and seventy cords on the bank. We put fire to the brush piles. The fire spread and burnt up 50 cords. We were played out before we got it checked. Nothing to eat.

"13. Wind turned and started the fire again. About 20 cords burned.

"22. The 'Nick Wall' passed about two o'clock in the morning without stopping.

"23. 40-50 Indians showed themselves at Musselshell the 20th. The crazy Frenchman started toward them and was badly beaten but when firing started they turned and ran.

"24. Raining. The 'Ida Reese' passed about daybreak without our knowing it.

"28. Sold 'Deerlodge' about 10 cords of wood.

"June 13. The 'Sallie' passed after midnight and took on 15 cords of wood.

"16. The 'Ida Stockdale' passed without stopping. We threw 6 cords back from the bank to keep it from falling into the river.

"July 4. Indians firing at us from nearest cottonwood trees and all through the sage brush. The balls whistled pretty lively but we returned the fire and drove them from their shelter. We went out and found one young warrior killed by a shot through the upper thigh. We got his gun, bow and arrows and two butcher knives and threw his body in the river. Waring scalped him."

No more steamers bought wood from Koch and his companions; he gave up in the fall, headed southwest toward the Big Belt Mountains, became an Indian trader

Fort Benton in 1880 still maintained the illusions of a growing river city. That year, 30 million pounds of freight were
landed and, though railroads already presented a threat to
business, its citizens felt so expansive that they tore down
much of the wood-and-adobe town and rebuilt it with brick.

and surveyor—and, eventually, a director of Bozeman's First National Bank. He was typical, for all his European background, of many nameless wanderers who drifted into woodcutting for steamers and, on occasion—having been trapped by Indians in remote camps—simply vanished from the ken of man.

But there were celebrated woodhawks, too—or, at any rate, celebrated mountaineers and plainsmen who adopted woodcutting as the means of turning a fast dollar. None of these achieved a more astonishing reputation—nor was more adept at disposing of Indians who got in his way—than a burly, red-headed hunter, trapper, woodcutter and brawler named John "Liver-Eating" Johnson.

Johnson was one of the last—and very probably, the canniest and most ferocious—of the old-fashioned mountain men. He came up the Missouri in 1843, started a woodyard above the Musselshell in 1846 and had, thus, been producing cordwood as an adjunct to trapping and more sporting pursuits for a quarter century before later and less wily woodhawks materialized in the new era of steamer fleets.

Johnson believed implicitly in the adage: "Never give an Indian a chance." He was one of those rare white men who was quicker, stronger, more sensitive to the wilderness and more proficient at the lethal arts of the ambush than the tribesmen of the plains themselves, and he slew Indians by the scores during a long and bloody career in the wild country north of the Yellowstone River. Johnson was death on Crows. He began killing, scalping and eating—or making a show of eating—their livers in 1847 after discovering, on his return from a trapping expedition, that a Crow war party had invaded his mountain cabin and had murdered his pregnant Flathead Indian wife.

Leaders of the Crow tribe charged 20 picked warriors with the duty of tracking down the Liver Eater after word of this demeaning practice had begun to spread. These warriors were told to attack Johnson singly—at a place and time of their own choosing—to better prove Crow valor.

This was a tactical error, for Johnson killed, scalped and plucked them, too—or, at any rate, reported having disposed of 18 of them by 1855. His contemporaries argued about his peculiar form of cannibalism; some swore he chewed the raw livers down, "only spitting out the gristle," and others maintained that he simply made gobbling sounds while rubbing the bloody mementos in his whiskers. All were in agreement, however, that he was a sight to give the strongest man pause when he was engaged in consummating the rite, and that he widened the practice to include Sioux after eventually reaching a kind of quasitruce with the Crows. Johnson's reputation and certain decorative touches made him all but proof against attack from Indians at his woodyard—and kept steamboat clerks from demurring at the payment of cash for his wood.

Johnson was aging by the time Indians began ambushing lesser woodhawks in the 1870s; he had, in fact, taken on a partner—a pistol-packing lout known only as X. Biedler—to help him cope with increased business. Tribal raiders gave him very little difficulty, nevertheless. Notes by a traveler who came upriver on the steamboat *Huntsville* during the period make this caution understandable: "Along the brink of the riverbank on both sides of the landing a row of stakes was planted and each stake carried a white, grinning, Indian skull. They were evidently the pride of the inhabitants and a little to one side, as if guarding them, stood a trapper well-known throughout eastern Montana by the sobriquet of Liver-Eating Johnson. He was leaning on a crutch with one leg bandaged, and the day being hot his entire dress consisted of a scant, much shrunken red undershirt reaching just below his hips. His matted hair and bushy beard fluttered in the breeze and his giant frame and limbs, so freely exposed to view, formed an exceedingly impressive picture."

Woodhawks were not the only people to take an uncertain foothold on the dangerous shore above Bismarck after the Civil War, or to endure the hostility of tribes being squeezed between the mining towns of Montana and the railroad towns in Dakota Territory. New Army posts sprang up along the far reaches of the river, and life in these forts was lonely and confining as well as perilous—particularly for service wives. But it was a life with its own amenities, excitements and satisfactions, too, as Sarah Elizabeth Canfield noted in a diary she kept while following her husband Andrew Canfield, a second lieutenant of infantry, into Indian country during the spring and summer of 1867.

Sarah Canfield, an Ohio girl who had been a schoolteacher, came up the river to Fort Berthold aboard the

John ("Liver-Eating") Johnson — a "wood-hawk," or supplier of steamer fuel — enjoyed a remarkable immunity from raids by Indians, who believed the frightening legend that he had devoured the raw liver of a brave who had the temerity to attack him.

steamboat *Deer Lodge* and was dismayed by the landscape through which the vessel bore her. "This is a worse country than I ever dreamed of. Nothing but hills of dry sand, with little streaks of short, Shriveled grass in the hollows and on the river bottoms." She was delighted after her long trip to see "the dear old flag" flying over the crude fort's watchtower and to be reunited "with my dear husband" (to whom she referred, throughout, as "Mr. Canfield"). But she wished there "were more signs of civilization" and seems to have been alternately startled, fascinated and appalled by the 2,000 Arikaras, Mandans and Gros Ventres who had settled — for protection from the Sioux — in a noisesome village of tipis just outside the post's palisade.

She stared in some admiration at the chiefs of the three tribes when she spied them drinking coffee and smoking a peace pipe in the office of the commandant, and was not above noting: "Their robes were only held by hands and had a way of Slipping down and displaying their Splendid brown shoulders. They were magnificent specimens of manhood." But Chief Fooldog of the Yankton Sioux struck her as a ludicrous figure when he paid the fort an official visit. "He wore a row of ornaments attached to the rim of his ears which had been perforated for that purpose. For bracelets he wore tin tomato cans with the ends taken out but the pictured paper all there. To add a touch which was quite becoming to his style of beauty he had painted his face a beautiful blue with clay from the riverbank and made it Striped by scratching before it dried, and he had a bright red streak around each eye giving him an 'Owly' Appearance."

But life became at once harder and more interesting when the Canfields were sent upriver to Camp Cooke, Montana Territory, in July. "This fort," she wrote on arrival, "is built in design like all I have seen, with bastions, Stockade moat etc., but there is timber on the river bottoms and So there is a sawmill here and the rows of houses are framed of wood and filled in with 'adobe' bricks. The roofs are made of poles with brush and a foot or more of earth spread over all. The walls of the rooms are white-washed and the floors of rough boards. When carpeted they make nice, cozy homes. Had a loaf of bread, a can of turkey (no salt), a can of tomatoes and coffee without Sugar or cream for our first meal this morning, but we enjoyed it. Our table was a goods box and our chairs cracker boxes."

Camp Cooke was situated on the south shore of the Missouri near the juncture of the Judith River. When winter closed in and the river froze, Mrs. Canfield became very conscious of the fact that she and three other officers' wives "are the only ladies for 60 miles," that "we do not go outside the stockade but take our exercise walking up and down the long porch in front of our rooms" and that "we see a good deal of each other. ...Still, we have had little dinner dances and card parties to pass the time." "The ladies of the Ft. received" on New Years Day, and "the officers came calling in full uniforms."

But with spring — while Sarah Canfield's husband was "gone with 25 mounted men to the mouth of the Mussle Shell" — the fort was "attacked by Indians in

A gallery of Benton Company executives in the 1880s focuses on owner T. C. Power *(center, left)* and his brother John.

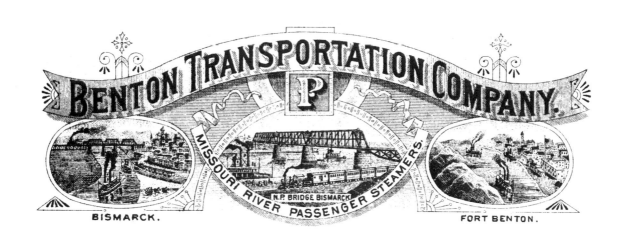

T.C. Power and his far-flung enterprises

Most firms engaged in steamboating on the upper Missouri in the 1870s had scant interest in overland operations. Not for the rivermen were the mud and dust of carting passengers and cargo over prairie and mountain. But there was one thriving exception: the Benton Transportation Company, which boasted a complete system of stagecoaches, muletrains and ox-drawn wagons that, together with its steamboats, connected Eastern commerce with the Dakotas, Montana and "all points in the Northwest territories of Canada."

The company was the brainchild of T. C. Power, a onetime surveyor who moved from Omaha to Fort Benton in 1867, thinking only to open a general store. With hordes of miners passing through the river port to join Montana's gold rush, the store was an instant success. Power sent for his brother John to assist him, and immediately set up branch stores in isolated settlements to the north, including Calgary and some Northwest Mounted Police outposts in Canada. As his mercantile chain grew, the overland freight line he organized to supply the stores attracted such an abundance of outside business that it flourished in its own right.

By 1875, Power was making his mark in steamboating, as well. It was a time of huge government contracts for the shipping of Indian annuities and military supplies — and ferocious competition among the major steamboat lines to win them.

At first, the wily Power did not challenge the established companies. Instead, he contracted privately with the Northern Pacific Railroad to haul its freight upriver 1,100 miles to Fort Benton from the railhead at Bismarck. In this fashion, Power found enough business to build a substantial fleet of steamboats — and did it without enraging Sanford Coulson, whose line was the dominant force on the upper Missouri and specialized in government business. Indeed, so amicable were re-

T. C. Power's headquarters in Helena

lations between the two that in 1877 Power and Coulson even discussed the possibility of a merger.

But their relations deteriorated rapidly from 1880 on, as river transport firms began losing huge amounts of business to the westward-questing railroads. Seeking to snatch what business remained, Coulson launched a vicious rate war against Power — only to discover that Power's diversified outfit was ready and able to fight back. With his overland freight and passenger operation assuring healthy profits for the company regardless of the river fleet's earnings, Power systematically underbid Coulson on government contracts and cornered most of the private freight as well. By 1885, Coulson was out of business and the Benton Transportation Company ruled the upper river.

Power went on to become a successful politician — he was elected to the United States Senate in 1890 — and an even more successful financier, with an investment empire that included banks, flour mills, granaries, cattle and sheep companies, and mining concerns. As for Benton Transportation, it kept steamers on the Missouri River for the rest of the century and was the last refuge for a number of great steamboatmen, among them the fabled Grant Marsh.

One of Power's freight wagons, loaded with goods for remote northern settlements, stands ready to depart from Fort Benton in the 1870s.

Fort Claggett, seen from the deck of a steamer in the 1870s, was one of the first trading posts Power established on the Montana frontier.

Helena, pride of Benton Transportation's five-year-old boat line, docks in 1880 at Milk River Landing, 460 miles below Fort Benton.

great numbers. The alarm was sounded and soon every man was at his post at a loop hole. The officers and ladies watched the coming of the Indians and we Saw they were painted and mounted for war having no women or children with them. We Ladies held a 'council of war' when we saw what might happen and decided that if the Ft. could not be held that we preferred to be shot by our own officers rather than be taken captive. The officers promised to do so before Surrendering—Dr. Porter was to see to Mrs. Auman, and Capt. DeCourcy took me. . . . But both Artillery and Infantry fire scattered the Indians in short order and we are spared to tell about the attack by three thousand."

Camp Cooke and its people were but instruments, however—and their Indian attackers but victims—of white pressure for land and for exploitation of the wilderness. In an essential sense, thus, all the combatants in such Indian battles were reacting to the rise of the new steamboat ports and to the national aspirations on which these ports battened as they grew. The real future of the whole, vast region from the Platte to the Rockies was taking form, for better or for worse, in the minds of railroad builders and steamboat operators and, increasingly, in the habits, philosophical attitudes and day-to-day enterprises of the townsmen in Sioux City, Yankton and Bismarck.

All three straggling river villages had set out with solemn, if rather schizophrenic, vigor—each beadily watching the other—to become the "Queen City" of the Missouri Valley. Three-story frame buildings replaced false-fronted shacks along their central streets—only to be shouldered aside, in many cases, by ugly, wonderfully permanent buildings of sawed chalkstone or red brick. Yankton was able to boast of eight separate schools in 1875 (though none had more than one room). Banks, churches and courthouses rose, and a contingent of "Rooshian" settlers (Germans who had farmed in Russia but had come to the U.S. after being uprooted by Czar Alexander II) built a club: the brick Germania House on Douglas Street.

Yankton built marine ways to match those in Sioux City, and so did Bismarck. Yankton also pointed with pride to a steam-driven flour mill, an ironworks, a harness factory. The town also boasted a "painless dentist" who offered patients "Chloroform, Nitrous Oxide or Narcotic Spray"—and who supplied bed and board to "parties from a distance." But evolution—Yankton being a good example—went only so far. People still drew water from wells or the river. The streets were unpaved, unlighted, and subject to disturbances. "Three dog fights occurred simultaneously on Broadway this forenoon," the *Press and Dakotian* reported on November 30, 1875, "and something like thirty dogs took part." And all three ports were resigned to similar behavior by similarly excited humans. Drunken Indians had a habit of starting bonfires on the steps of buildings on cold nights, and steamer crews of taking over the streets on holidays.

"Eight steam boats tied up to the bank in front of Sioux City," wrote a local citizen in describing the ruder aspects of its observance of Independence Day, 1870, "and the crews and passengers turned themselves loose and paraded about town in gangs. There were some old grudges and rivalries—a gang would march into a saloon and soon a crowd would come boiling out in a fight. It was a miracle that no one was killed, as it seemed as though there was a fight every five minutes, sometimes indoors, sometimes out. There were two open dance houses in full blast and one, lone city marshal to try to keep order when there were pitched battles between crew of different boats."

Steamer officers permitted themselves a similar bellicosity at times—even though they were considered members of local "society." The captain of the steamboat *Viola Belle* submitted quietly when a U.S. marshal arrested him at Yankton for throwing one of his passengers overboard while approaching the landing; he explained in pained tones that he had done so only as a joke. The marshal, lacking a jail, placed a friend on board to make sure the boat stayed there until a trial could be held. But the captain and his officers threw the friend overboard, too, and proceeded to sail blithely upstream while their roustabouts brandished pistols to discourage any reapplication of the law as the vessel moved away from the landing.

Bars, brothels and dance halls flourished along every levee but most noisily in Bismarck, which was considered, and not without a certain grim satisfaction on the part of many local citizens, to be the hardest town in the West. Its seamier attractions linger in the diary of a Canadian with a sardonic, if outraged, eye—one

The adventurous Pennsylvanian who made it big in Sioux City

One of Sioux City's first and foremost citizens was John H. Charles, a onetime Pennsylvanian who had traveled to Panama and Nicaragua, and had panned gold in California before deciding, at the age of 30, to plant his roots along the Missouri. Charles arrived in Sioux City on December 1, 1856, just two years after its founding, and firmly vowed, "I'll be in Sioux City on the morning of January 1, 1900 and as the sun rises I'll say, 'Hail old fellow! I'm still here.' "

Charles was as good as his word. In the years between, he saw the town grow from a population of a few hundred to 44,000 and chronicled his experiences in a volume of wry reminiscences that paints a revealing picture of an early Missouri River town.

On Charles's first night in Sioux City, a fierce blizzard was raging and he sought shelter in the hotel. Its name was the Hagy House, but "it was ordinarily referred to as 'The Terrific,' " Charles recalled, without explaining why. Irony might have had something to do with it, because, Charles continued, "the hotel consisted of two log cabins connected by roughhewn boards, and in the lobby one old man sat by the stove with an umbrella raised over him." Charles quickly recognized the wisdom thereof: the storm was blowing clouds of snow into the room, and "above the stove the heat changed the falling flakes to rain."

Charles inquired about a room, only to find that "there were no rooms and I'd be lucky to get a bed." Considering "the hard-looking set, harder even than I had seen in the California mines," Charles was perhaps luckier

John H. Charles in the 1860s

to wind up outside, spending the night huddled under a buffalo robe. He awakened in the morning to find himself blanketed with several inches of snow, his eyelids glued shut by ice. "On the whole," Charles concluded, "I thought I had been given a rather cold reception in Sioux City."

The infant town had a sheriff but no jail; its "stagecoach" was "only a lumber wagon used to haul the mail." But it certainly had a going real-estate market. "One-fourth of the state of Iowa was for sale at Sioux City's land offices," Charles recorded, "and even the dirty and ragged men of the Hagy House talked chiefly of how much money they had made."

Charles soon began investing profitably in land and buildings. By August 1857 he had attained sufficient stature in the community to be elected justice of the peace, then won an alderman's seat. When it was decided

that Sioux City needed more lawyers, Charles and another stalwart were drafted. That neither had any legal training was of little consequence. "Judge Marshall F. Moore appointed a committee to examine us," Charles wrote. "They asked us only one or two questions, then certified we were admitted to the bar — or, as the boys put it, 'admitted to be eternally at law and solicitous of good chances.' "

Charles noted that on January 1, 1858, he performed "the first wedding in Dakota Territory after white settlers came to Sioux City" — though with some reluctance. He was no longer a justice of the peace, but his protestations were lost on the Crow bride and the French groom, who understood neither his language nor each other's. They did, however, understand frugality, and paid Charles with a bowl of dog soup and a bite of roasted beaver tail.

As Sioux City grew into a refined and commercially diverse community, Charles helped establish a public library and a scientific association; he went into retailing in the 1860s and steamboating in the 1870s, becoming a manager of T. C. Power's Benton Transportation Company (page 182, pictured in the third row, second from the left). To the end of the century, he helped guide Power's empire in his crusty frontiersman's style. He once advised the firm not to bid too low on a government contract because, while they might land the business, they would stand to make no profit. Actually, Charles concluded dourly, "We can make more money staying at home and hauling manure."

187

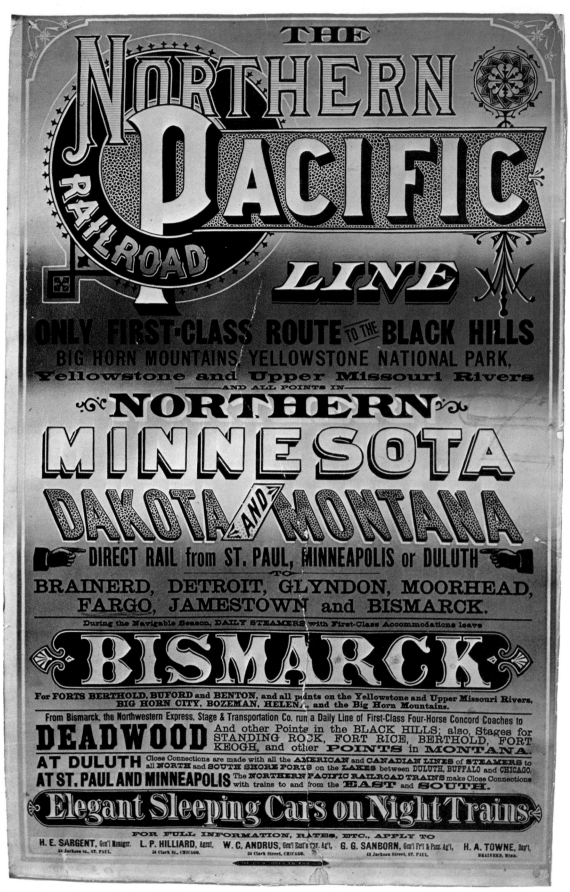

In dazzling color, the Northern Pacific announces 1870s service to the West by steamer and stage from Bismarck.

A first-class ticket in the 1870s from Helena, Montana Territory, to Chicago covered the stage to Fort Benton, boat to Bismarck (misspelled), and rail to Sauk Rapids, St. Paul and Chicago. Fare: $71.

D. McEachran, who passed through in 1881 on his way to Fort Benton.

"Bismarck," he wrote, "was started by the opening of a whiskey shop and though it now contains a population of over 2,000, the example set by the pioneer has been faithfully followed, since at least three-fourths of the buildings are grog shops, gambling houses or places of amusement. Having three days to wait for our steamer we took advantage of a high Government functionary's offer to show us the 'city by gaslight.'

"Our first visit was to a 'keno' house where we stayed but a short time for the disgusting sight of gambling in its worst form, and the foul air and still fouler language drove us away. We next visited a faro bank where similar scenes presented themselves. We could not help remarking on the general expression of abandonment depicted in the faces and nervous expressions of the frequenters of these dens.

"Our next place of visit was to the 'opera house,' a wooden structure, the entrance of which is a barroom. At the counter tickets had to be procured, the charge for entrance to the ground floor being twenty five cents, to the boxes fifty cents. We looked into the pit. Here we saw a sawdust covered floor, rough, unplaned board seats and forty or fifty frontiersmen, all with large, wide brimmed hats and nearly all smoking or chewing tobacco.

"Ascending the narrow stairway we reached the gallery which was partitioned into curtained boxes — which are connected to the stage and in which actresses spend their time between the acts being regaled by beer or champagne according to the extravagance of the occupants. About half a dozen women acted as waiters and their dress

and manners indicated the life of immorality which they lead. The scenery on stage was of the most primitive nature and the acting was execrable. While we were looking on, a large woman with a voice like a cow horn attempted a vulgar ditty, 'Champagne and Oysters.'"

The attitudes that so startled McEachran in Bismarck's dens sometimes spilled over into more august premises. In one such case in 1873, merchants and civic leaders called for a meeting in the courthouse at Yankton to discuss a bond sale proposed by directors of the Dakota Southern Railroad. Liberals and Democrats (known as the Broadway Gang) opposed the idea while Republicans (the Capitol Street Gang) supported it vehemently. General Edwin Stanton McCook, a huge ex-Civil War officer, then serving as the territorial governor's secretary, had supported the sale for weeks — but not without bitter objection from a leading member of the opposition, banker Peter Wintermute. The two men nodded politely when they encountered each other before the meeting in the bar of the St. Charles Hotel, which stood next door to the courthouse. But when Wintermute discovered that he was out of cigars and asked the other man to loan him one, the general turned him down; and then, after an argument, beat him up.

General McCook was a man of robust instincts — the Dakota *Herald* regarded him as an "ignorant, vainglorious, drunken lout, who is an eyesore to our people and a depression upon the good morals of this community." Peter Wintermute weighed only 135 pounds, and the general proceeded, according to later testimony, to push the banker's head into a cuspidor. The vic-

189

A stern-wheeler rests on wooden ways at Bismarck in 1886. Boats were winched up by steam engine allowing workmen to repair hulls, rudders and steering mechanisms. In winter, as many as five steamers could be hoisted and stored side by side, safe from the Missouri's crushing ice.

tim cleaned himself up and went to the meeting anyhow —but with a pistol, which he used to shoot his tormentor as soon as he saw him again. The big man charged once more—though this time with blood dripping down his coat front—seized the little banker, who was still firing, and tried to throw him through a window. But the general was mortally wounded and died on the following morning.

A jury eventually found Wintermute innocent of manslaughter, but he died of tuberculosis caught in the dank cell that he inhabited while awaiting trial. News of the deaths was received by the men's colleagues with grave headwagging; incidents of similar violence by roustabouts caused little stir, but prosperity was producing men of property—with wives who harbored social ambitions—and, thus, an awareness of class that had not existed a decade before.

Yankton's leading lights boasted in the mid-1870s that the population included 90 college graduates, and applauded a high-toned female visitor who opined: "The tone and refinement and culture pervading Yankton's society might at first incline a traveler from the East to suppose he had been moving in a circuit which had brought him to the point from which he had started rather than in the wilds of a territory."

The lust for culture and refinement engendered absurd strictures on occasion. In 1876 the territorial legislature passed a statute, universally ignored, which prohibited Sunday buggy riding save by those on their way to church, to a doctor's office or to a funeral. But solid citizens laid a stratum of respectability over the yeastier impulses of Yankton for all that—as did solid citizens in other steamboat towns—and dominated the affairs of the upper river as they did so.

Ladies were conscious of style; they had their pick of silks, prints and various furs at the local dry goods stores. Hostesses did not lack for fancy groceries—almonds, lemon syrup in cans, oysters in glass jars and brandied cherries. Young men of promise matched wits at weekly meetings of the Literary and Debating Club. But they were also privy to social intercourse with the fair sex at spelling bees, dances on the decks of steamboats that were docked at the levee, and group excursions through the countryside around the town to hunt wild fruit for canning. Lecturers were prized: frontier ladies applauded loudly when suffragette Susan B.

Anthony urged them into the battle for women's rights.

But it took even more glamorous visitors to Yankton —Lieutenant Colonel George Armstrong Custer, his wife, Elizabeth, and officers of the 7th U.S. Cavalry —to prompt the steamboat era's supreme social occasion; the one that was envied by other river towns and that served as a kind of catalyst by which those who were safely embosomed in polite society and those who were simply scrabbling about on its fringes were sorted out for good and all.

The 7th came into Yankton by rail on April 9, 1873, bound for its historic and tragic service on the frontier, and camped under canvas near Rhine Creek on the outskirts of town. Local merchants were pleased. Custer had 800 officers and enlisted men in his command, plus 700 horses, 200 mules and 40 laundresses. Joseph R. Hanson and C. H. McIntyre contracted to supply 300 tons of hay and James M. Stone to deliver 300 cords of wood; a vanguard of officer's wives took rooms in hotels, and Mrs. Custer rented a small house in town and moved into it with her servants, Mary and Ham. But Yanktonians were thrown into a more intimate and difficult relationship with the visiting cavalrymen a week later.

A cold rain began spattering the area. Soon the rain turned to dry snow, the wind rose, the temperature fell alarmingly, and both town and camp were engulfed by a blinding spring blizzard. The storm lasted for 36 hours; tents blew down, the snow piled into deep drifts and troopers began staggering through the white gloom toward town leading horses in dire need of shelter. Others sought cover for themselves. Mrs. Custer opened her door to a half dozen of them and rolled them up in carpets to restore warmth to their bodies. But this time civilians came to the rescue of the cavalry. Barns, livery stables and warehouses were reopened to the regiment's horses and mules; and parties of muffled townsmen succored shivering soldiers and frightened laundresses—one of whom had just given birth to a baby.

Yankton experienced a heady sense of possessiveness in the process of delivering the soldiers from the elements. Custer was not just any colonel (the town referred to him by his grander Civil War title: Brevet Major General); and the very word *cavalry* suggested an élan, a certain steely chic, that infantry simply could not match. The snow had barely begun to thaw before

the best people were jostling each other to plan and prepare a celebration by which the 7th and its gaudy commander could be formally welcomed into their hearts —and by which those citizens who received invitations could bask, modestly, in the reflected glamor and cozy sense of exclusivity the event was certain to provide.

The proceedings were duly reported by the Yankton *Press,* issue of April 30:

"The social event of 1873 occurred in Yankton on Thursday evening last on the occasion of the Reception Ball given by the citizens of Yankton to the officers of the 7th Cavalry.

"The Reception Ball was held at Stone's Hall, which was profusely decorated with Flags, the walls being completely hid from view by starry banners arranged in the most attractive and tasteful manner, while the ceiling was hung with like emblems gracefully festooned. These striking ornaments with the bright full-dress uniforms of the military gentlemen present was sufficient to call to mind Byron's famous 'Battle of Waterloo.' There were present about 120 couples embracing the leading commercial men of Yankton with their ladies; while the officers were fully represented.

"The Seventh Cavalry band led by our former townsman Felix Vinatieri, furnished the music which could not have been better. Vinatieri also added much interest to the entertainment by his wonderful skill as a violinist, in rendering the 'mocking bird.'

" 'Rosy Morn' peeped through the windows before the company thought of separating, and when the 'adieu and safe return' signalled the closing of the Reception Ball the parting was most reluctant."

It was a far more symbolic occasion than the Yankton *Press* could have imagined. The "leading commercial men" of the river ports wanted to obtain white control of the wilderness upriver; they wanted the anarchic Sioux contained in reservations at last — and living off government bounty that would be shipped from warehouses along their levees. George Custer and his cavalrymen paid for the Reception Ball on the Little Bighorn; they were human sacrifices who forced the Army into final containment of the wild tribes, and ensured that future upon which speculators had so rashly gambled after gaining the riverbank from Strike-the-Ree.

193

A few embellishments to lure commerce

By the late 1860s, when steamboat ports were booming on the upper Missouri, the older towns on the lower river had begun to settle into a comfortable municipal middle age. Their chambers of commerce often sought to show off their hard-won respectability by means of a visual device dear to the hearts of western promoters: the panoramic map, a bird's-eye view created by a skilled —and highly imaginative—artist.

While impressively accurate in many details, the panoramas ofttimes indulged in flights of self-serving fancy: steamboats lined levees that had long fallen into disuse; trains sped along nonexistent railbeds and bridges; and smoke belched industriously from vacant factories. The deliberate deceptions, designed to attract new residents and industry, were studiously ignored by the townspeople who prominently displayed the maps on the walls of their homes and offices.

Especially prized were the handsome maps painstakingly crafted by Albert Ruger, a German-born artist who produced no fewer than 198 such panoramas during the course of a long and prolific career. Ruger would sometimes spend weeks walking the streets of a town, sketching every building and landmark. The result, as seen in each of the three maps of old river towns that are reproduced here and on the following pages, was a remarkably detailed vista in which all streets, churches, schools and other noteworthy structures were labeled, and where the pleasing aura of commercial vitality was always present, whether it existed or not.

1 COURT HOUSE
2 COUNTY OFFICES
3 MARKET HOUSE
4 SCHOOL HOUSE
5 ST CHARLES COLLEGE
6 FEMALE SEMINARY

PUBLIC SCHOOL

The oldest white settlement on the Missouri River, St. Charles was 100 years old when this

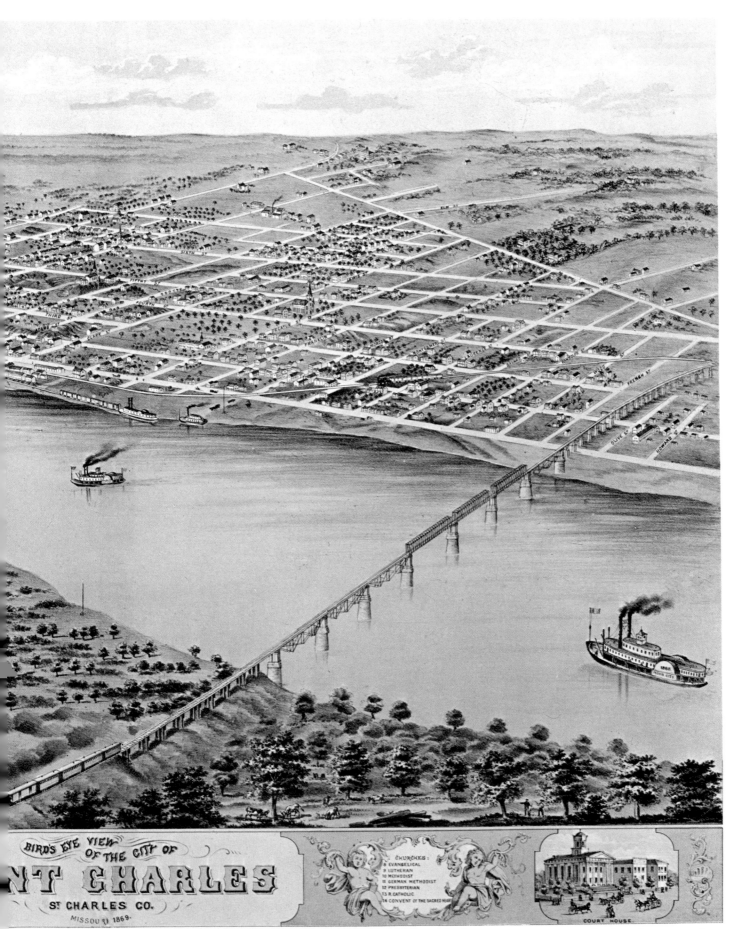

panorama appeared in 1869. But the railroad bridge, one of the longest of its type in the country, was not completed until two years later.

Within the illustration:

COLLEGE ST.

LAFAYETTE ST.

MISSOURI RIVER

DRAWN BY A. RUGER.

1. COURT HOUSE.
2. COUNTY JAIL.
3. PUBLIC SCHOOL.
4. MASONIC COLLEGE.
5. BAPTIST SEMINARY.
6. PRESBYTERIAN SEMINARY.
7. ARGANA HALL, TURNER HALL.
8. MARKET HOUSE.
9. L. & ST. Jos. R.W. DEPOT.

COURT HOUSE.

BIRD'S EY

LEXI

LAFAYET

Once prosperous Lexington—where the *Saluda* exploded in 1852, killing more than 100 Mormons—had fallen on hard times by

1869, despite the illusion given of a busy river port. The walled area at left is the campus of the world's first Masonic college.

REFERENCES
1 Court House
2 Public School
3 Midland Pacific
  R. R. Depot
4 Steamboat Landing
5 Cemetary

NEBRAS

OTOE COUNTY

BIRD'S EYE V

COURT HOUSE

At one time a booming jump-off point for overland freight wagons bound for the West, Nebraska City had begun by 1868 to pin

its future hopes on the railroad. But the tracks seen curving into town at the top of the map did not actually arrive until 1871.

6 | In service to the Army

General Alfred Sully, who employed 15 steamboats to transport troops and supplies while campaigning against the Sioux on the upper Missouri in the early 1860s, later wrote that the "conquest of the Missouri Valley would have been a very different matter had the government been deprived of this important aid in its operations."

The steamboat's role in the service of the Indian-fighting Army was as varied as it was indispensable. Throughout this long and bloody struggle it was the main carrier of supplies to well-established military posts along the upper river as well as to isolated depots, where it left food, ammunition and other provisions for troops on the march.

The steamboat was also invaluable strategically; it was not only the fastest way to move soldiers upstream or down, to points where they were needed in a hurry, but it also maintained communications between units separated by a stretch of river too wide, deep and fast to be forded by mounted messengers. In addition, the steamer was frequently pressed into service as reconnaissance vessel, floating hospital and — armed with howitzers as well as riflemen — powerful gunboat.

Besides being a principal factor in the Army's ultimate victory over the Indians, the steamboat served heroically at the time of the Army's most devastating defeat at the hands of the hostiles. In a harrowing race downstream after the debacle at the Little Bighorn, *Far West,* Custer's supporting supply boat, carried to safety wounded survivors of the battle that cost the lives of Custer and his entire column of troops.

A steamer unloads military supplies at Cow Island in 1880 at a broad bend of the Missouri. The soldiers (*foreground*), belong to the encamped detachment guarding equipment stockpiled at the wilderness depot.

200

Rest about on the far west

Steaming "from a field of havoc to a station of mourners"

Men blunder into history so myopically that they are seldom aware, until they find themselves involved in some enormous drama, of being cast and costumed by the fates. The 7th U.S. Cavalry was immersed in its own mundane exasperations as it rode out of Dakota Territory's Fort Abraham Lincoln on May 17, 1876, to engage in climactic battle with the Sioux. Nothing in the unit's experience of Indian warfare portended the mass of mounted warriors Chief Crazy Horse was mobilizing along the remote streams that fed the Yellowstone. No trooper—and, indeed, no general of the Western Command—could imagine that George Armstrong Custer would soon plunge the regiment into suicidal defeat, allow the Indians to demean the Army before the world and, in so doing, launch Captain Grant Marsh on the wildest, fastest steamboat voyage in American history.

Forty per cent of the 7th's troopers were raw recruits who had been brought in to replace "snowbirds" —men who had joined up to keep warm during the winter but who had deserted with the advent of spring. Its enlisted men had been driven hard, in consequence, and—worse yet—had been denied pay for two months at Fort Lincoln to prevent their drinking whiskey "to the further loss and detriment of discipline." They were not amused to discover that an Army paymaster was accompanying them during the first day's march, and was waiting to disburse the overdue cash as soon as they dismounted at their first temptationless bivouac. They had no means, furthermore, of grasping the full irony of this niggardly delay: a good deal of the money was to find

its way into a war fund maintained by Crazy Horse after his Sioux warriors collected it from the pockets of dead cavalrymen on the Little Bighorn.

Captain Marsh had arrived at Fort Lincoln 10 days after the regiment rode out. He tied up at the bank and loaded oats, bran, medical supplies, tents, tarpaulins and small-arms ammunition on which the 7th was to draw during its excursion into the wilds. General Phil Sheridan had asked Marsh to fulfill a special assignment: as master and pilot, to select the one steamer that could be expected—as Army supply boat, hospital ship, mobile command post and instrument of quick river crossings —to stay closest to the action during the summer's campaign. Marsh felt well prepared. No pilot in America understood the Yellowstone as well as he. No vessel, he felt, was better suited for it than the stern-wheeler *Far West*, a 190-foot upper-river boat he had picked, on being given his choice, from all the steamers operated by the Coulson Packet Company. But if Marsh was ready for the Rockies and the Sioux, he had given no thought at all to a more subtle but no less daunting adversary: George Custer's pretty wife, Libbie.

Knots of officers' wives approached the riverbank almost as soon as Marsh put his boat against the shore to begin loading. He asked them aboard, instructed his steward to give them as "dainty" a lunch as could be managed, excused himself, and went back to work. He was interrupted at noon; Mrs. Custer and the ladies, the steward informed him, would be desolated if the captain did not preside at the luncheon table. Marsh was busy; proper loading was crucial to a vessel bound for shallow water. But he broke off, went to his quarters to make himself presentable, and joined the women in *Far West*'s little cabin. Mrs. Custer seated herself on his right, and put Mrs. Algernon E. Smith, wife of one of her husband's lieutenants, on Marsh's left. Marsh began to enjoy himself; both women regarded him with ob-

Among the images sketched in pencil by artist William Cary during an 1874 voyage on *Far West* were these roustabouts and a heavy-caliber, lever-action carbine used by one of the boat's meat hunters.

203

vious admiration. He did not realize that he was a target of female machination until he rose to excuse himself at the end of the meal. The Mesdames Custer and Smith rose with him, drew him aside and offered him a dismaying confidence: they were going with him to join the 7th, if—and the demeanor of the colonel's lady suggested that this was a foregone conclusion—Captain Marsh was willing to take them.

Marsh had chosen *Far West* for the summer campaign because she would draw only 30 inches of water with the cargo he was presently loading; moreover, her minimal upper works and two powerful engines made her wonderfully handy in high winds. But he had wanted as few free riders as possible, too; *Far West* would accommodate no more than 30 cabin passengers. He indicated her cramped and spartan quarters with a wave of the hand; he was certain the ladies had not considered the danger and discomfort their request would involve. Mrs. Custer smiled patiently. Her husband had *authorized* her to join him, she said, *and* by traveling on this very boat. Marsh had no reason to doubt her. She had joined Custer on hair-brained excursions before. But—Custer or not—Marsh would not have them on his boat. He went on, with real embarrassment, to express regret. The ladies let him stammer a bit before turning, stiffly, to go ashore.

He put this awkwardness behind him the next morning. His deck hands cast off *Far West*'s lines; Marsh pulled her whistle cord and headed her upstream toward less disconcerting conflict. The boat had a good crew: two dependable engineers in George Foulk and John Hardy, a fine second pilot in Dave Campbell, and a deck and fireroom force of 30 hardy men. She took aboard a military guard—60 riflemen of the 6th Infantry —during a layover at Ford Buford. She also picked up Brigadier General Alfred H. Terry, whom she was to serve as a kind of landlocked flagship, and took him upstream to meet Colonel John Gibbon and a force of infantry that Gibbon was leading down river. A bracing sense of anticipation seized all aboard.

The Missouri River runs roughly east and west and, thus, roughly parallel to the Canadian border as it crosses western North Dakota and eastern Montana. The Yellowstone River enters the Big Muddy from the southwest at an angle of about 45 degrees near the bor-

Eight members of Fort Berthold's 70-man garrison meet in front of the commanding officer's quarters in 1865. Taken over from the American Fur Company in 1864, the ramshackle post was famed for an inexhaustible supply of whiskey delivered by steamer before it was deserted in 1867.

The newly completed sprawl of Fort Abraham Lincoln stretches along the Missouri, five miles below Bismarck. Constructed in 1873, the post was a major logistical center on the northern plains and was commanded by George Custer at the time of the Little Bighorn massacre in 1876.

der of these two states. Four lesser streams dangle below the Yellowstone (as one looks at the map) like pieces of twine hung from a loose jib stay. The mouths of these four streams—the Powder River, the Tongue River, Rosebud Creek and the Bighorn River, created natural points of rendezvous for the steamboat and the 7th's cavalrymen. She met the horse soldiers at the mouth of the Powder on June 7—and was governed by George Custer's tragic designs thereafter.

It was the assumption of the Army, and of General Terry who commanded all U.S. troops in the campaign, that the Sioux would try, as always, to scatter when attacked. The Army was in the process, thus, of moving troops into the Yellowstone country from three different directions, to force the elusive foe into conclusive battle. General George Crook was leading 1,500 men in a northwesterly direction up Wyoming's

Bozeman Trail. Colonel Gibbon's infantry was preparing to meet them by moving south along the Bighorn River; and Custer was ready to ride west toward their junction point to chop up any retreat the grand plan might engender. But Crazy Horse had the Napoleonic instinct for massive radial movement against separated peripheral enemies and did not await the outcome of all this maneuvering. He descended on Crook's Bozeman Trail column while it was still 100 miles from the Yellowstone, bloodied and halted it on the headwaters of Rosebud Creek and drew back to a position above the Little Bighorn to await new victims.

No word of this disaster reached the commanders on the Yellowstone, 100 miles away. But six companies of the 7th, which had been dispatched up the Powder on a scouting expedition, crossed a fresh trail the Sioux had churned up in their withdrawal, and rode back

down Rosebud Creek with the news. *Far West* headed farther up the Yellowstone, with Custer and his cavalry moving in parallel along the bank; and that night, moored at the 7th's bivouac near the Rosebud's mouth, she was the scene of a momentous council of war.

General Terry was able to deduce that Crazy Horse and his followers were holed up off to the south, somewhere between Rosebud Creek and the Bighorn's eastern tributary, the Little Bighorn River. Major Marcus Reno, who had been in command of the scouting force, was able to tell him that the Indian trail was extremely wide. But neither Terry nor Reno realized that they were talking about one of the greatest concentrations of Indians ever gathered on the continent: as many as 12,000 men, women and children, with from 1,500 to 2,500 warriors among them. And none of the men aboard *Far West* were aware that General Crook had

already been mauled and driven back into Wyoming.

Gibbon had come down the Missouri to join the meeting, but his column of infantry was still moving east down the Yellowstone and was not yet in position to be ferried across it for a march south toward the foe. Terry calculated—this being the night of June 21—that five more days would elapse before Gibbon could assist Crook and Custer in "enclosing" the Indians. It was nevertheless agreed that Custer should take his cavalrymen up the Rosebud the next day. His role was to be that of a bloodthirsty cat waiting outside a nest of mice. He was to pounce if the mice showed signs of straying, but to restrain himself if the prey—as Terry believed highly likely—stayed safely down their hole. Terry wanted Custer's cavalry ready for action after the main battle, to cut off a retreat of shattered Sioux into the Big Horn Mountains. Still, all this was theoretical and

Custer was given liberty by Terry to ignore these strictures if he "saw sufficient reason for departing from them." Gibbon did not leave it quite at that. "Now don't be greedy, Custer," he said, as the council broke up. "There are Indians enough for all. Wait for us."

Custer's tent had been erected on the bank only a few yards from the boat. He hurried ashore and began issuing orders to men who materialized out of the darkness. One of Gibbon's lieutenants, watching from the deck, guessed — as he wrote in his journal — that the infantry "had little hope of being in at the death. . . . Custer will undoubtedly exert himself to the utmost to win all the laurels." The horse soldiers themselves quickly came to the same conclusion. Custer had been urged to take three Gatling guns with his column, and Gibbon had offered to lend him four extra troops of cavalry. He had refused these encumbrances. He expected a long chase, and he now ordered his pack animals loaded with extra forage as well as 15 days' rations and 50 rounds of reserve ammunition for every trooper. He responded irritably when his commanders suggested that Reno's mules, worn out by their long scouting trip, would break down under such loads: "Well, gentlemen," he said, "you may carry what supplies you please, but you will be held responsible. We will follow until we catch them. You had better take extra salt; we may have to live on horse meat."

It was not a night for sleep aboard *Far West;* Grant Marsh was enmeshed in George Custer's compulsion for surrounding himself with members of his immediate family. A brother, Captain Thomas Custer, and the commander's brother-in-law, Lieutenant James Calhoun, were among the officers of the 7th. Custer had also managed to mount two civilian relatives in his wilderness cavalcade: his 17-year-old nephew Henry Armstrong ("Autie") Reed and his light-hearted youngest brother, Boston Custer.

Tom Custer and James Calhoun were among a restless throng of scouts, staff officers and cavalry commanders who drifted into *Far West's* cabin after midnight; they soon involved themselves — and Marsh — in a high-stakes poker game. Marsh was startled at the feckless betting that ensued. Rescued by duty, he went to unload *Far West's* stores before sunrise. But the cavalrymen left thousands of dollars in a heap on the table at dawn; an infantry captain, W. H. H. Crom-

208

The famed *Far West*, gangplank poised and firewood stacked, prepares to load freight for an upriver run. Chartered by the Army in 1876 for $360 a day, she served gallantly with the ill-fated Custer expedition and later carried the peace commissioners who treated with the Sioux.

well, had beaten Crazy Horse to their last nickel.

The incident left Marsh wondering whether the whole Custer family might not suffer some natural disinclination for caution. It also left him impelled to try talking Boston Custer out of riding away with them. *Far West* was the repository for the 7th's mail — hundreds of men scribbled letters to wives and families as the bright morning wore on — and young "Boss" was sitting in his cabin writing a note to his mother when Marsh tracked him down. Marsh leaned against the open door, warned the young man of the difficult riding that lay ahead of the 7th, asked him to remember his responsibility to his mother and urged him to stay aboard the boat until it resumed contact with the regiment.

Boss finally agreed. He sealed his letter, thanked Marsh for his hospitality and left to say goodbye to his brothers. Marsh, following, stopped at George Custer's tent to say goodbye himself. "Boss tells me he's going to stay with you," said the commander. "I'm glad of that. But I'm afraid he'll eat you out of house and home." Boss, however, was up on a horse when the regiment rode out of camp at noon and disappeared with Autie, Tom, Calhoun and the long lines of cavalrymen up the grassy valley of the Rosebud.

A sense of isolation claimed Marsh, his crew and the military guard of *Far West*. They had followed the 7th from the Powder to the Tongue and from the Tongue to Rosebud Creek, had moored beside their camps, had unloaded their stores, had eavesdropped on their councils but were now, suddenly, alone in a silent, sunlit and ironic wilderness.

Their sense of reverie was interrupted almost immediately. Three soldiers who had set off downstream in a skiff with the regiment's mail overturned within 50 feet of the steamer and were drowned. Marsh followed in *Far West's* yawl and spent hours probing with a boathook. The bodies were long gone downstream but he finally hauled up the missing mailbag and did not move the steamer until the letters, thus saved for the 7th's widows, were carefully dried in the sun.

The summer silence was broken again two days later when the boatmen ferried Gibbon's troops across the river and watched them vanish south toward Crazy Horse. The morning after that, a dispatch rider from Terry — who had ridden off south with Gibbon's column

— brought *Far West* orders to ascend the Bighorn itself as a means of maintaining the closest possible contact with the troops gone on ahead.

The Bighorn, like the Yellowstone, was in summer flood, but it presented Marsh — who was once more being asked to take a steamer where no steamer had ever penetrated before — with awesome difficulties. It was barely a hundred yards wide at its widest and was full of islands, bends and white water. The very narrowness of the river, however, allowed Marsh a means of attack that no vessel had ever assayed.

Far West boasted two steam-driven capstans, and — with soldiers and deck hands to haul from shore — he anchored cables on both banks and thus coaxed her slowly forward in midstream. The men spent most of the day sweating on land — Marsh seldom found stretches of navigable water longer than two or three hundred yards — and the steamer was forced to spar or warp repeatedly to maintain progress in the difficult water.

It was a hot day; its silence — rendered ominous by the smoke of innumerable Indian fires hanging above the southern horizon — seemed to press down on the boat and her laborers as the stream led them past steep cliffs and barren stretches of badland.

Marsh had been directed to reach the Little Bighorn — about 50 miles above the Yellowstone — unless the water became shallower than three feet. He reached it at noon on the 26th, his second day on the stream, thus coming within 11 miles of Custer's battleground at almost exactly the moment the 7th was launching its downhill approach to the waiting Indian hordes.

Far West's endeavors did not cease; Captain Stephen Baker, commander of the boat's infantry guard, insisted she had found the wrong tributary, and Marsh spent the rest of the day driving her an additional 15 miles upstream. At nightfall, however, he gravely told Baker a falsehood — that the water was now less than 36 inches in depth — and returned *Far West* to her original destination and tied her up, for safety, against an island in midstream. Captain Baker put riflemen around the boat to guard against any possible surprise. But the smoke of the Indian fires had vanished from the southern sky, and he assumed that Custer and Terry had attacked and that the Sioux were beaten and in flight.

The rest of the crew loafed in the bright sunlight. A few wandered across the island with fishing poles; pike

and channel catfish hung in the clear water that streamed over the Bighorn's gravel bottom and after a while Marsh, Engineer Foulk, Pilot Campbell and Captain Baker left the boat to try their luck as well. Foulk found himself staring at the willow thickets that bordered the stream's eastern bank; an Indian, he said—if any Indians were left to try—would have no trouble taking cover there to fire at the lot of them.

A naked, mounted tribesman burst instantly through the screen of bushes at which they were looking, jerked his lathered pony to a halt at the water's edge, and held up a carbine in the peace sign. They saw with relief that he wore the erect Crow scalp lock; and they recognized him, a few seconds later, as Curley, a scout who had ridden with Custer. They waved him forward and hurried toward the steamer as he pushed his horse across the stream. But Curley simply sank to his knees, once aboard the boat, and began rocking from side to side and bellowing as if in agony. Baker eventually produced a pencil and a piece of paper, demonstrated their use, and handed them to him. He threw himself flat on the deck, gripped the pencil in one fist, and drew a careful circle. He made a larger circle outside it and began jabbing dots into the space between them. "Sioux," he cried. "Sioux, Sioux, Sioux!" He twisted up to stare at them, and then, making dots within the inner circle, began yelling: "Absaroka! Absaroka!"

"By Scotts," said Marsh. "I know what *that* means. It means soldiers. That Englishman, Courtney, who runs the woodyard at the head of Drowned Man's Rapids told me so. Some Crows were there one time and he told me they were going to Camp Cooke to see the Absaroka." Absaroka was, in fact, the word—meaning The People—by which Crows defined themselves, but which, because they admired the Army for shooting up Sioux, Blackfeet and others of their ancient enemies, they generously used to describe U.S. soldiers as well.

"Absaroka!" cried Curley, leaping to his feet on hearing Marsh use the word. He poked his fingers at his chest and yelled: "Poof! Poof! Poof Absaroka!"

Baker was the first to understand the import of this pantomime. "We're whipped," he said. "That's what's the matter." The news seemed worse as they laboriously interviewed the Indian in sign language. He told them that he had escaped the battlefield on the Little Bighorn by pulling a blanket over his head (it was later

Officers and wives promenade while troopers crowd lower decks of two transports in the 1880s. Normally, a Missouri steamer would carry some 200 men. The photo, previously unpublished and printed from a damaged plate, was taken by Captain John Pitman, Fort Lincoln's ordnance officer.

Carrying survivors from the Little Bighorn, Grant Marsh in *Far West* raced 700 miles in 54 hours. "As fast as a railroad train in a narrow, winding stream," is how St. Paul's *Pioneer Press* described the feat.

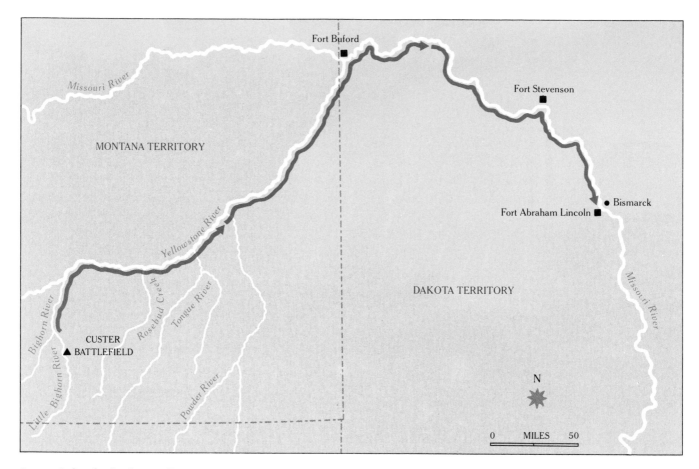

learned that he had actually run away before the fighting really began) and he seemed to believe that the entire regiment had been annihilated.

Far West's crew spent an uneasy night, and its trigger-happy sentries greeted one "Muggins" Taylor, a scout from Gibbon's column, with a wild fusillade when he rode up to the boat before dawn. Taylor was reeling with exhaustion after surviving a long, desperate chase by Sioux horsemen during the night. But he knew what had happened to the 7th: that Custer had violated the Western Command's best-laid plan of campaign and had attacked without waiting for Terry.

Taylor reported that Custer had divided his forces into three detachments and had died with one of them —five companies of cavalrymen he led in person. Also killed were Autie, Boss, Tom, Calhoun and Mark Kellogg—a reporter for the *Bismarck Tribune*. Elements of the other seven companies, under Major Reno and Captain Frederick Benteen, had survived 36 hours of fighting—though with many casualties—and the Indians had

finally pulled away. Though finding some relief in learning they were not about to be attacked, *Far West*'s crew soon received orders from Terry that gave them pause. Gibbon's infantry had found 59 wounded horse soldiers, of whom 52 were still alive; the steamer was to take these survivors—and news of the catastrophe—to Fort Abraham Lincoln with all possible dispatch.

Chilling words: Marsh could only wonder how he would be remembered if further harm came to men wounded in so tragic a battle. He prepared to receive the casualties by setting crew and military guard to cutting wild grass that grew luxuriantly in marshy patches along the river. They piled it 18 inches deep on open deck space aft of the boilers and stretched tarpaulins across it to create a vast, soft communal mattress. Medicine chests were hauled up from the steamer's hold. But exasperating—and pathetic—misadventures delayed delivery of the wounded men.

Pack mules grew unruly at the battlefield when they were harnessed to stretchers made of abandoned Sioux lodge poles. They tossed their helpless freight. Soldiers of Gibbon's force finally tried carrying the wounded down the Little Bighorn valley on hand-litters; but gave up at midnight—utterly exhausted—after covering less than five miles. The hapless survivors lay in the open the next day while more tractable mules were rounded up and new stretchers constructed. It was sundown before the caravan of invalids—each hoisted between two animals and guarded by four men—once more began its slow way down the valley. Then it rained. The procession was halted once more—this time by boggy land and pitch darkness—at midnight.

Marsh now intervened. He turned out his crew and set them to building bonfires along the three miles of river bottom that separated the stretcher column from its goal. The long line of mules and men emerged in firelight around the steamer at two in the morning; and crew, guard and attendant soldiers carried the wounded to the boat's makeshift hospital. With them came a haggard, bewhiskered Army physician, Dr. Henry R. Porter, who must, in retrospect, be considered the truest hero of the Battle of the Little Bighorn.

Porter had lived, though only by miracles, to be the only survivor of the 7th's three regimental surgeons; man after man had been hit and killed within inches of him. He had maintained a sardonic coolness when Major Reno led his men in a wild stampede to the barren knoll upon which they made their stand; and—having stayed behind with a dying soldier, and having ridden alone through a storm of Sioux fire to rejoin them—had walked among the wounded there as if oblivious of the arrows and bullets that hit one in three of all around him. Now, after wringing Marsh's hand, he looked to the wounded once again before surrendering to sleep in one of *Far West's* cabins.

One more refugee of battle was now led up to the steamer: a lurching, wounded sorrel stallion named Comanche; the beast had been ridden to Custer's fight by Captain Myles Keogh and was the only living creature to have survived it. Marsh took the horse aboard, ordered a grass-padded stall built for him aft, and—sorting through some of Gibbon's people who had followed the wounded down the valley—found a hysterical veterinary surgeon and hauled him aboard, too. "He was," the pilot said later, "the worst scared man I ever saw—the terror of Indians had entered his soul." Marsh bul-

lied him into dressing the horse's wounds. Comanche, thus attended, lived to become a symbol of heroism for the 7th, and was led—bridled, saddled, but riderless and draped in black—in all regimental parades until he died peacefully at the age of 28.

Successful steamboat pilots, and particularly those who lasted on the upper Missouri, seem to have been buoyed by some blend of optimism, self-confidence and serenity. Marsh was no exception. But he found himself, with the approach of sunrise, falling prey to a weakening sense of uncertainty—compounded from the sight of the wounded on his deck, from the realization of tragedy that was growing on all around him, and from a hard, professional understanding of the kind of water he would have to run before reaching the Missouri. It was not dissipated when General Terry rode up at dawn, disheveled and depressed, to rejoin the vessel.

Terry, a Connecticut lawyer who had become a professional soldier after service in the Civil War, was not a man for dramatics, but he called Marsh to his cabin after coming aboard and spoke with surprising emotion: "Captain, this is a bad river. You have the most precious cargo a boat ever carried. Every soldier here is the victim of a terrible blunder. A sad and terrible blunder. I wish to ask you to use all the skill you possess."

"I will give you my best," said Marsh. But his nerve failed him after he climbed to the pilothouse. *Far West* had to be turned from one narrow channel into another around the island against which she was moored, and had then to be headed into fast water downstream. The pilot—"I felt sick"—could not imagine bringing it off, although he had handled boats in hundreds of similar situations without a moment of conscious thought. Campbell, the second pilot, and the mate, Ben Thompson, had seated themselves on the bench at the rear of the wheelhouse. "Boys," Marsh said, turning to them, "I can't do it. I'll smash her up."

"Oh, no you won't," said Campbell. "Cool off a minute and you'll be all right."

Marsh leaned against the wheel and stared silently ahead. He ordered the steamer's lines to be cast off after a bit, rang up the engine room, turned the island—and began reacting, in a daze of concentration, to the kaleidoscopic succession of chutes, islands, rocks and rapids that were flung across his field of vision by the boat's startling speed in the narrow waterway. ◉

The 178-foot *Josephine,* a Missouri stern-wheeler converted for river-improvement work, dwarfs *Baby Josephine* beside her. The smaller boat

The chore of taming "Old Misery"

Engineers' insigne, dating from 1839, symbolizes early forts.

In the 1870s, as intensifying Indian warfare in the region of the upper Missouri made dependable delivery of Army supplies by steamboat more imperative than ever, the federal government finally felt compelled to reduce the river's perils to navigation.

The job of improving "Old Misery" —as it was ruefully known—was entrusted mainly to the Army's Corps of Engineers. The steamboats themselves played an important role, often serving as working platforms for labor crews, who either lived aboard when onshore accommodations were not available or in barracks-like scows that were towed behind the steamers.

The improvement program consisted not only of clearing the streambed of dead trees and other obstructions but also of altering sections of the river itself. Surveys conducted by the Corps of Engineers pinpointed the specific danger spots, among them rapids on the upper river through which safe passageways had to be blasted and stretches where bank erosion, especially in the flood season, sometimes choked steamboat channels with sediment overnight. (The clogging of the Missouri at Sioux

was used in water too shallow for her companion.

City was so bad in 1879 that wags told the story of a woman who attempted to commit suicide by jumping into the river, only to find herself stuck in two feet of mud.)

The Engineers relied on a number of techniques to keep the river open and to check bank erosion. One of the most effective was the building of "training structures" — dikes and piers angled into the river to divert the current away from an eroding shore line. These structures also increased the river's velocity, thus loosening sediment on the bottom and deepening the channel for steamboats.

A U.S. Engineers surveyor takes bearings on the Missouri around 1889.

Crews surveying a stretch of the Missouri near Fort Benton line up aboard their living quarters: canvas-roofed barges called quarterboats.

Entitled by rank to the best quarters, officers of the Corps of Engineers relax with their wives in *Josephine*'s spacious aftercabin.

Large quarterboats, floating barracks made of wood and equipped with bunks, could accommodate up to 100 men in relative comfort.

Maneuvering in shallow water close to the Missouri shore, *Baby Josephine* throws up a fine spray with her pint-sized paddle wheel.

Near a railroad bridge at Omaha in 1880, U.S. Engineers, supplied by steamboat, supervise the weaving of a huge retainer made of saplings and

designed to arrest cave-ins along the bank. Boulders anchored it in place.

It was axiomatic among pilots that every river had to be "learned" twice — going up and going down. Neither Marsh nor any other steamboatman had ever seen the Bighorn going down, and his every movement of the wheel — once he had cleared the first island — stemmed from split-second decisions that were based on instinct alone. It was sometimes possible, on larger streams, to briefly offset fast water by running paddle wheels in reverse; but the restricted Bighorn refused a pilot time for such a maneuver and, since a boat could not maintain steerageway without moving faster than the water going past her rudders, *Far West's* hurtling descent of rapids was almost more, at times, than her passengers could bear to watch.

Marsh covered 53 miles before the afternoon was spent, and tied up below the river's bank. Pilots and crew now found themselves immersed in anticlimax. Fourteen of *Far West's* wounded had recovered enough to be moved ashore. All but one of the rest — a man who shortly died — seemed to have passed the point of real danger. General Terry disembarked to make his headquarters at a riverside Army depot. He decided, though reluctantly, to hold the vessel there for two days in order to ferry Gibbon's weary infantrymen, now marching back from the battlefield, to sure safety on the north bank of the Yellowstone.

Western history has not, because of this pause, included Marsh's run down the Bighorn in the overall mileage that was covered in *Far West's* subsequent and astonishing race to Fort Lincoln. It is doubtful, nevertheless, that any other pilot ever covered such water at such speed. It is hard not to think, too — since men gain in élan from winning against odds — that Marsh, Campbell and the vessel's two engineers drove her more recklessly, once underway again, than might have been possible had they not discovered reserves of cunning and determination in themselves during the first, frightening hours of their voyage.

The Yellowstone was wider and less precipitous than the Bighorn, and *Far West's* crew had come to know it well. But it was a difficult, dangerous and reef-littered river, nevertheless; and Marsh — who was proud of his reputation as a pilot, proud of the responsibility with which the Army had entrusted him, and invigorated by the dramatic role in which he found himself — lengthened the odds that every steamer normally faced

Sioux Indians, with a few whites, crowd the upper decks of the Power Line packet *Helena* en route to the Indian agency at Standing Rock, below Bismarck, around 1880. Crushing Army pressure was forcing the Sioux onto reservations, though a number held out in Canada until 1881.

in negotiating it by resolving to run his vessel day and night until he reached Fort Lincoln and to crack on every possible pound of steam while doing so.

They set off at 5 p.m. on June 30. Sunlight lingered late, the sky stayed providentially clear, and dawn came early as *Far West* plunged downstream, with Marsh and Campbell standing alternate four-hour tricks at the wheel. But those who stared into the gloom as the boat swung through bends and down stretches of fast water found the short summer night the longest of their lives. An exhilarating excitement grew aboard the boat, for all that, as she churned on into the dazzling sunlight of morning — an excitement that was reflected (and more accurately, perhaps, than the 20th Century mind would guess) in the lurid prose *Far West* continued to inspire long after her trip was done.

"It was a strange land and an unknown river," wrote a correspondent for the St. Paul *Pioneer Press* in an article entitled: *A Lightning Steamboat Ride.* "She was running from a field of havoc to a station of mourners. What a cargo on that steamer! What news for the country! A steamboat moving as fast as a railway train in a narrow, winding stream is not a pleasure. Occasionally the bank would be touched and men would topple over like ten pins. It was a reminder of what the result would be if a snag was struck.

"*Far West* would take a shoot on this or that side of an island as the quick judgment of the pilot would dictate. Down the Yellowstone the stanch craft shot, and down that river sealed to pilots she made over twenty miles an hour. The bold captain was taking chances, but he scarcely thought of them. He was under flying orders. Lives were at stake. The engineer was instructed to keep up steam at the highest pitch. Once the gauge marked a pressure that turned his cool head and made every nerve in his powerful frame quiver. The crisis passed and *Far West* had escaped a fate more terrible than Custer's. The rate of speed was unrivaled in the annals of boating. It was a thrilling voyage!"

There was an Army depot at the mouth of the Powder. Its garrison, which had been lined up to fire a ceremonial volley (this being the Fourth of July) was dismissed as *Far West*'s whistle sounded upstream. Soldiers surged down to the bank when the steamboat tied up to take aboard personal equipment that officers of the 7th had discarded there on preparing to go into action. Indian scouts had come downriver with odd rumors of a defeat that the depot had found outlandish; the boat's crew confirmed them, steamed on and churned, finally, into the wide Missouri.

She paused at Fort Buford and again at Fort Stevenson. At both posts excited mobs of men leaped on board clamoring for news, were given the dismaying facts and pushed ashore again as Marsh waited impatiently to start his vessel on the last lap of her race to the telegraph office at Bismarck, immediately across the river from Fort Lincoln. General Terry — not a man to abandon protocol or to forget military formality — had given Marsh careful instructions as to the dressing of his steamer for her appearance at the 7th's home post: he was to raise a flag to half-mast and to drape the boat's jackstaff and derrick in black. These things were done as the afternoon of July 5 wore on. But it was 11 o'clock at night, darkness had fallen and the wharf at Bismarck was deserted when Marsh finally rang down FINISHED WITH ENGINES.

The silent town did not stay silent long. Gangs of men from the steamer hurried noisily up the empty streets — among them Marsh, Dr. Porter, and Terry's aide-de-camp, Captain E. W. Smith, who carried a bag full of messages, dispatches for Army headquarters in Chicago, and notes that had been found beside correspondent Mark Kellogg's body on the battlefield. Lamps were lighted and householders emerged, half-dressed, at the sound of voices shouting the impossible news. Marsh, Porter and Smith routed out C. A. Lounsberry, editor of the *Bismarck Tribune,* and hurried to the telegraph office with him and with a telegrapher named J. M. Carnahan. Lounsberry was a correspondent for the New York *Herald* and after asking a few startled questions he scribbled a bulletin and handed it to Carnahan for transmission:

"Bismarck, D. T., July 6, 1876: — General Custer attacked the Indians June 25, and he with every officer and man in five companies were killed. Reno with seven companies fought in entrenched positions three days. The *Bismarck Tribune*'s special correspondent was with the expedition and was killed."

Porter, Smith and Marsh began telling their stories to Lounsberry while Carnahan transmitted the notes that Kellogg had been jotting down until the day of the fight and that General Terry personally had salvaged from the pouch beside the correspondent's body. Carnahan then dispatched a long account of the battle written by one of Gibbon's commanders. Lounsberry went on interviewing and writing; Carnahan tapped out the hand-written copy on his telegraph key.

Editor and telegrapher stayed in their chairs for 22 hours, and they made Marsh and *Far West,* as well as Porter and the 7th's officers, familiar to millions; Carnahan sent 15,000 words (telegraph tolls cost the staggering sum of $3,000) in giving the *Herald* one of the greatest stories in U.S. history. But Marsh and his vessel had one more duty. He left the telegraph office after midnight with Captain Smith, recalled his crew and crossed the river to Fort Lincoln.

Wives of the 7th's soldiers and household troops at the fort had been experiencing premonitions of disaster for two days. The fort was headquarters for a detachment of Indian police—tribesmen who served as representatives of the government—and the whites there had gradually become aware that these men were in the grip of an intense, bated excitement. "There was whispering," as one witness wrote, "and rumors of a great battle. Those who watched them knew something unusual must have happened. But what? Fleet-footed warriors mounted on fleeter animals and aided, perhaps, by signals, had brought the news. But no white man knew. It was stifling." Now, at two in the morning, the post's officers were called to headquarters, given the news by Captain Smith and, just before sunrise, asked to break it to the regiment's wives and widows.

"I have heard the women tell of their intense excitement when they heard *Far West's* whistle blast as she approached Bismarck," Edward S. Godfrey, who served with Reno, said years later, "and how they waited and waited for tidings, each afraid to tell her anxieties, til near midnight when, with heavy hearts, almost with sobs, they separated and went to their homes. My wife told me how she tossed with restlessness until dawn when she was startled from a doze by a tap on her window, and instantly exclaimed: 'Is my husband killed?' She was answered by a voice choked with emotion: 'No, dear, your husband is safe, and Mrs. Moylan's husband is safe, but all the rest are dead.' "

Lieutenant C. L. Gurley of the 6th Infantry shared a harder task. "It fell to my lot to accompany Dr. J. V. D. Middleton, our post surgeon, to the quarters of Mrs. Custer. We started on our sad errand a little before 7 o'clock on that 6th of July morning. I went to the rear of the Custer house, woke up Maria, Mrs. Custer's housemaid and requested her to rap on Mrs. Custer's door, and to say to her that she and Mrs. Calhoun and Miss Reed were wanted in the parlor. But Mrs. Custer had been awakened by the footsteps in the hall. She called me by name and asked me the cause of my early visit. I made no reply but followed Dr. Middleton into the parlor. There we were almost immediately followed by the ladies of the household and there we told to them their first intimation of the awful result of the Battle of the Little Big Horn. Imagine the grief of those stricken women, their sobs, their flood of tears."

The morning was half-gone and the sun was hot on the river before the last of *Far West's* wounded men had been taken ashore and Marsh and his officers could sit down to consider the parameters of their own accomplishments. They had come a little more than 700 miles—from the mouth of the Bighorn to Bismarck—in 54 hours. They had averaged—and this included *Far West's* stops for wood as well as her delay at the Powder River and at the two forts—13 1/7 miles an hour over that distance. No vessel had gone that fast in all the years since Nicholas Roosevelt made his voyage to New Orleans.

But *Far West* represented something more than this ultimate triumph of steampower and human nerve. The course of history had already begun changing even as she tied up at Fort Lincoln, and both she and her crew were symbols of the past by the time their wounded soldiers had been taken ashore. The Sioux had sealed their own fate by their bloody victory over Custer. The Army was moved to extraordinary exertions in response, and within a year Indian resistance to white exploitation of the Rocky Mountain West was broken forever. The long, brave day of the Missouri's rivermen declined thereafter, for nothing now impeded railroad construction in the wilds, and the locomotive was the one predator the steamboat could not survive. *Far West's* voyage had brought an age to a stupendous climax; no American vessel ever approached her record and she remained the queen of speed when the steamboat had vanished—with her plume of smoke, her misted paddles and her mournful whistle—from the rivers of the West.

A brave alliance with the onrushing railroads

"Our great water route . . . is more than a match for the railroad, and from this day forward the importance of the Big Muddy as a commercial route will send forth its own praise by its thousands of steamers and cheap freight." This grandiose claim, voiced in the spring of 1870 in Yankton's *Union and Dakotaian* had a hollow ring and was in itself evidence that Missouri rivermen were on the defensive against the menace of the new and rapidly expanding form of transportation.

For more than a decade a state of uneasy cooperation had existed between the Missouri steamboat and the railroad, but by the 1870s this relationship was gradually turning into an all-out rivalry. Even then, so long as iron tracks merely touched the river at ports like Yankton and Bismarck, steamboaters could withstand the competition. They were still able to prosper on trade between ports and with upriver settlements not yet approached by rails. But as more and more tracks paralleled the river, the railroads drew away traffic at one port after another. With ever-increasing loss of passengers and cargo to the railroad's faster and more frequent service, the steamers were faced with a struggle for survival.

By 1887, when the first trains puffed into Fort Benton, the northernmost river port, the battle was virtually over. But even in defeat the vessels that had played a major role in opening the West continued to perform yeoman work on the river, particularly for the government on improvement projects. And a few were still threading the winding course of the Missouri as freight and passenger packets into the early years of this century — just as they had in the steamboat's Golden Age.

Steamboats line up at an Omaha dock in 1865 to unload supplies used in building the first stretch of the Union Pacific Railroad.

Before the Missouri was bridged at Bismarck in 1882, steamers were a vital link for railroads, at least in warm months. Here, in 1879, freight cars are hauled from a side-wheeler used by the Northern Pacific as a ferry between railheads at Bismark and Mandan, Dakota Territory.

During the winter, with the Missouri frozen solid, steamboat ferries were of no use to the Northern Pacific. But it made no difference to the inventive railroaders: they simply laid tracks on the ice and crossed the river on their own.

Outmatched by the railroad in the late 1880s, Missouri
steamboats still managed to score an occasional triumph.
Here a train, unable to cross the river via the bridge from
Bismarck to Mandan because tracks on the far side were
flooded, surrenders its passengers to a stern-wheeler ferry.

TEXT CREDITS

For full reference on specific page credits see bibliography.

Chapter 1: Particularly useful sources for information and quotes in this chapter are: Phil E. Chappell, "A History of the Missouri River," *Transactions of the Kansas State Historical Society 1905-1906,* Vol. IX; Hiram M. Chittenden, *Early Steamboat Navigation on the Missouri River: Life and Adventures of Joseph LaBarge,* Ross & Haines, Inc., 1962; William E. Lass, *A History of Steamboating on the Upper Missouri River,* University of Nebraska Press, 1962; W. J. McDonald, "The Missouri River and Its Victims," *Missouri Historical Review,* Vol. XXI, Jan. 1927, April 1927, July 1927; John Napton, "My Trip on the Imperial in 1867," *Contributions to the Historical Society of Montana,* Vol. VIII, 1917; William J. Petersen, ed. "The Log of the *Henry M. Shreve* to Fort Benton in 1869," *Mississippi Valley Historical Review,* March 1945. 30 — Samuel Hauser quotes from *Samuel T. Hauser letters in Samuel T. Hauser Papers,* The Beinecke Rare Book and Manuscript Library, Yale University, May 20, 1862. Chapter 2: Particularly useful sources for information and quotes: Henry M. Brackenridge, *A Journal of a Voyage up the River Missouri, Performed in 1811,* Coale & Maxwell, Pomery & Toy, 1816; Hiram Martin Chittenden, *The American Fur Trade of the Far West,* Vols. I & II, The Press of the Pioneers, 1935; Bernard De Voto, *The Course of Empire,* Houghton Mifflin, 1952; Richard Edward Oglesby, *Manuel Lisa and the Missouri Fur Trade,* University of Oklahoma Press, 1963. 70 — Brackenridge description of Lisa, Douglas, pp. 400-401; 72 — song, Vestal, p. 26; Lisa expresses indignation, Douglas, p. 382; 74-75 — Boller quotes, Richardson, ed. Chapter 3: Particularly useful sources of in-

formation and quotes: Hiram Martin Chittenden, *Early Steamboat Navigation on the Missouri River: Life and Adventures of Joseph LaBarge,* Ross & Haines, Inc., 1962; Joseph Mills Hanson, *The Conquest of the Missouri,* Holt, Rinehart & Winston, 1946; Louis C. Hunter, *Steamboats on the Western Rivers,* Octagon Books, 1969; W. J. McDonald, "The Missouri River and Its Victims," *Missouri Historical Review,* Vol. XXI, Jan. 1927, pp. 215-232; April 1927, pp. 455-480; July 1927, pp. 581-607; John H. Morrison, *History of American Steam Navigation,* Stephen Daye Press, 1958. Chapter 4: Particularly useful sources for information and quotes: Hiram Martin Chittenden, *History of Early Steamboat Navigation on the Missouri River: Life and Adventures of Joseph LaBarge,* Ross & Haines, Inc., 1962; Joseph Mills Hanson, *The Conquest of the Missouri,* Holt, Rinehart & Winston, 1946. Chapter 5: Particularly useful sources for information and quotes: John H. Charles, "Reminiscences of John H. Charles," *Proceedings of the Academy of Science and Letters of Sioux City, Iowa for 1905-1906;* Robert F. Karolevitz, *Yankton: A Pioneer Past,* North Plains Press, 1972; Ida Mae Rees, *Sioux City as a Steamboat Port — 1856-1873,* thesis, Dept. of History, University of South Dakota, 1967; 171-172 — Captain Able quote, Parker, pp. 244-251; 176-177 — Koch diary extracts, Koch; 180-181, 186 — Sarah Elizabeth Canfield diary extracts, pp. 190-220; 192 — female visitor on Yankton, *Dakota Panorama,* p. 211. Chapter 6: Particularly useful source for information and quotes: Joseph Mills Hanson, *The Conquest of the Missouri,* Holt, Rinehart & Winston, 1946.

PICTURE CREDITS

The sources for the illustrations in this book are shown below. Credits from left to right are separated by semicolons, from top to bottom by dashes.

Cover — *Lighter Relieving a Steamboat Aground,* George Caleb Bingham, copied by John Savage, courtesy Private Collection. 2 — *Missouri Roustabout at the Tiller of a Mackinaw Boat,* William Cary, copied by Oliver Willcox, courtesy The Thomas Gilcrease Institute of American History and Art, Tulsa, Oklahoma. 6,7 — Courtesy Kansas State Historical Society, Topeka. 8,9 — H. G. Klenze, courtesy Montana Historical Society. 10,11 — Courtesy Montana Historical Society. 12,13 — F. Jay Haynes, courtesy The Haynes Foundation. 14,15 — Courtesy Kansas State Historical Society, Topeka. 16 — Courtesy The State Historical Society of Missouri, Edwin H. Aehle Collection. 18,19 — Courtesy The Walters Art Gallery. 20,21 — Drawings and map by Rafael D. Palacios. 22,23 — *Northern Boundary Survey Under Major Twining,* William Cary, copied by Oliver Willcox, courtesy The Thomas Gilcrease Institute of American History and Art, Tulsa, Oklahoma. 25 — George Simons, courtesy Free Public Library, Council Bluffs, Iowa. 26,27 — Courtesy State Historical Society of North Dakota, Bismarck, N.D. 28 — Courtesy Montana Historical Society. 29 — From files of Missouri Historical Society, St. Louis. 30 — Sarony's, N.Y., courtesy Montana Historical Society. 33 — *Missouri Deck Hands on the Fontanelle,* William Cary, copied by Oliver Willcox, courtesy The Thomas Gilcrease Institute of American History and Art, Tulsa, Oklahoma. 34, 35 — H & R Studio, Inc., courtesy Paul C. Rohloff Collection, Chicago, except top far right and bottom row, courtesy Risvold Collection, Minneapolis. 36 through 39 — A. E. Mathews, courtesy Montana Historical Society. 40, 41 — Courtesy Montana Historical Society. 43 — Untitled sketch, William Cary, copied by Oliver Willcox, courtesy The Thomas Gilcrease In-

stitute of American History and Art, Tulsa, Oklahoma. 44,45 — Courtesy Rare Book Division, The New York Public Library, Astor, Lenox and Tilden Foundations. 46,47 — Paulus Leeser, courtesy Rare Book Division, The New York Public Library, Astor, Lenox and Tilden Foundations. 48 through 51 — Courtesy Rare Book Division, The New York Public Library, Astor, Lenox and Tilden Foundations. 52 — Courtesy Missouri Historical Society. 55 — Courtesy Rare Book Division, The New York Public Library, Astor, Lenox and Tilden Foundations. 56,57 — Courtesy Missouri Historical Society. 58 — Courtesy Rare Book Division, The New York Public Library, Astor, Lenox and Tilden Foundations. 61 — Courtesy Missouri Historical Society. 62 — Courtesy The New York Public Library, Astor, Lenox and Tilden Foundations. 65 — Courtesy Missouri Historical Society. 66 — Courtesy Risvold Collection, Minneapolis. 67 — Courtesy Missouri Historical Society. 68,69 — Courtesy Rare Book Division, The New York Public Library, Astor, Lenox and Tilden Foundations. 71 — Courtesy Department of Rare Books and Special Collections, Public Library of Cincinnati and Hamilton County. 72 — *Cree Chief Le Tout Pique and Fur Company Agents at Fort Union,* Rudolph Friedrich Kurz, copied by Oliver Willcox, courtesy The Thomas Gilcrease Institute of American History and Art, Tulsa, Oklahoma. 75 — Throbeck, courtesy State Historical Society of North Dakota, Bismarck, N.D. 76,77 — *The Wood Boat,* George Caleb Bingham, copied by John Savage, courtesy The St. Louis Art Museum. 78,79 — *Raftmen Playing Cards,* George Caleb Bingham, copied by John Savage, courtesy The St. Louis Art Museum. 80,81 — *Watching The Cargo,* George Caleb Bingham, courtesy The State Historical Society of Missouri. 82,83 — David F. Barry, courtesy Montana Historical Society. 84,85 — E. E. Henry, from the Collection of David R. Phillips. 86,87 — Courtesy Department of Rare Books and Special Collections, Public Library of Cincinnati and Hamilton County. 88 — John Savage, courtesy St. Louis Mercantile Library Association. 90,91 — Courtesy Missouri Historical Society. 93 — Courtesy Risvold Collection, Minneapolis. 94 — Courtesy Smithsonian Institution, Museum of History and Technology, Photo No. 72-7890. 96 through 99 — Drawings by John Fryant. 100 — Courtesy Risvold Collection, Minneapolis. 102,103 — Courtesy J. William Kisinger, Brownsville, Pa. 106,107 — Paulus Leeser, courtesy Rare Book Division, The New York Public Library, Astor, Lenox and Tilden Foundations. 108 — Figure I of U.S. Patent No. 913, by H. M. Shreve, September 12, 1838. 109 — Courtesy The State Historical Society of Missouri. 110 — Courtesy The New York Public Library, Astor, Lenox and Tilden Foundations. 112,113 — L. C. Cooper, courtesy State Historical Society of North Dakota, Bismarck, N.D. 114,115 — Courtesy Missouri Historical Society. 116,117 — Orlando S. Goff, courtesy State Historical Society of North Dakota, Bismarck, N.D. 118,119 — Courtesy St. Louis Public Library. 120,121 — Paulus Leeser, courtesy Rare Book Division, The New York Public Library, Astor, Lenox and Tilden Foundations. 122 — E. E. Henry, from the Collection of David R. Phillips. 124 — Courtesy Montana Historical Society. 125 — Courtesy Smithsonian Institution, National Anthropological Archives, Photo No. 2856-53. 127 — Courtesy Montana Historical Society. 128,129 — F. Jay Haynes, courtesy The Haynes Foundation. 132 — Courtesy Dorothy Blunt Hagen and Dr. James K. Blunt; courtesy The State Historical Society of Missouri. 133 — Courtesy Dorothy Blunt Hagen and Dr. James K. Blunt. 134 — Courtesy Dorothy Blunt Hagen and Dr. James K. Blunt; courtesy State Historical Society of North Dakota, Bismarck, N.D. 135 — Courtesy State Historical Society of North Dakota, Bismarck, N.D. 138,139 — Courtesy Oregon Historical Society. 141 — Courtesy The State Historical Society of Missouri. 142,143 — S. J. Morrow, courtesy State Historical Society of North Dakota, Bismarck, N.D. 144 — Courtesy Oregon Historical Society. 145 — Courtesy Risvold Collection, Minneapolis. 146,147 — Courtesy *The Waterways Journal*, St. Louis, Missouri. 149 — T. C. Power Collection, courtesy Montana Historical Society. 150 — Courtesy Dorothy Blunt Hagen and Dr. James K. Blunt. 152 through 157 — Oliver Willcox, courtesy The Thomas Gilcrease Institute of American History and Art, Tulsa, Oklahoma. 152,153 — *Buffalo Crossing the Missouri*, William Cary. 154,

155 — *The Fire Canoe*, William Cary. 156,157 — *Trading on the Upper Missouri*, William Cary. 158,159 — E. E. Henry, from the Collection of David R. Phillips. 160,161 — Al Lucke Collection, courtesy Montana Historical Society. 162,163 — Courtesy Montana Historical Society. 164,165 — Courtesy State Historical Society of North Dakota, Bismarck, N.D. 166,167 — Courtesy Montana Historical Society. 168 — Lee Corrigan, courtesy Shirley Coulson Walpole. 170 — Courtesy Smithsonian Institution, National Anthropological Archives, Photo No. 3545-A. 172 — Yankton County Historical Society's Dakota Territorial Museum. 174,175 — Tolman, courtesy Nebraska State Historical Society. 176,177 — Courtesy Nebraska State Historical Society. 178,179 — F. Jay Haynes, courtesy The Haynes Foundation. 181 — Mark Edgar Hopkins Hawkes, courtesy the B. Hay Collection. 182 — Courtesy State Historical Society of North Dakota, Bismarck, N.D. 183 — Thomas C. Power, courtesy Montana Historical Society — T. C. Power Collection, courtesy Montana Historical Society. 184 — Courtesy Montana Historical Society — F. Jay Haynes, courtesy The Haynes Foundation. 185 — F. Jay Haynes, courtesy The Haynes Foundation. 187 — Courtesy of the *Annals of Iowa*. 188 through 191 — Courtesy State Historical Society of North Dakota, Bismarck, N.D. 193 — F. Jay Haynes, courtesy The Haynes Foundation. 194 through 199 — Henry Beville, courtesy Library of Congress. 200,201 — F. Jay Haynes, courtesy The Haynes Foundation. 202 — *Roustabouts on the Steamer Far West*, William Cary, copied by Oliver Willcox, courtesy The Thomas Gilcrease Institute of American History and Art, Tulsa, Okla. 204 through 207 — Courtesy State Historical Society of North Dakota, Bismarck, N.D. 208,209 — Courtesy Montana Historical Society. 211 — F. Jay Haynes, courtesy State Historical Society of North Dakota, Bismarck, N.D. and The Haynes Foundation. 212,213 — John T. Pitman, © The James D. Horan Civil War and Western Americana Collection. 214 — Map by Nicholas Fasciano. 216,217 — Courtesy Montana Historical Society, except bottom left, courtesy U.S. Army Engineer Museum, Fort Belvoir, Virginia. 218,219 — Courtesy Montana Historical Society, except top left, courtesy National Archives. 220,221 — Courtesy National Archives. 222,223 — Orlando S. Goff, courtesy State Historical Society of North Dakota, Bismarck, N.D. 226,227 — Courtesy Union Pacific Railroad Historical Museum. 228,229 — F. Jay Haynes, courtesy State Historical Society of North Dakota, Bismarck, N.D. and The Haynes Foundation. 230,231 — F. Jay Haynes, courtesy The Haynes Foundation. 232,233 — David F. Barry, courtesy Dorothy Blunt Hagen and Dr. James K. Blunt.

ACKNOWLEDGMENTS

The editors wish to give special thanks to Dr. William E. Lass, Chairman, Department of History, Mankato State College, Mankato, Minnesota, for reading and commenting on portions of the book.

The editors also wish to thank: Yeatman Anderson III, Curator of Rare Books and Special Collections, The Public Library of Cincinnati and Hamilton County; W. R. Best, Director, Carolyn Bradshaw, Curator, Dan McPike, Senior Curator of Anthropology and Technology, The Thomas Gilcrease Institute of American History and Art, Tulsa, Oklahoma; Mildred Bradley, Assistant Librarian, Leavenworth Public Library, Leavenworth, Kansas; Dr. James Blunt, Bismarck, North Dakota; Herbert R. Collins, Assoc. Curator, Div. of Political History, Smithsonian Institution, Washington, D.C.; Maud Cole, Rare Book Room, The New York Public Library, New York City; Eugene Decker, Archivist, Kansas State Historical Society, Topeka, Kansas; William Diamond, Director, Sioux City Museum, Sioux City, Iowa; Richard H. Engeman, Photographs and Maps Librarian; Craig E. McCroskey, Assistant Librarian, Oregon Historical Society, Portland, Oregon; Janice Fleming, Librarian, Bonny Gardner, Library Technician, State Historical Society of South Dakota, Pierre, South Dakota; Tracy Forbes, Walters Art Gallery, Baltimore, Maryland; John Gardner, Assistant Curator, Mystic Seaport, Inc., Mystic, Connecticut; George German, Curator, Yankton Community Museum, Yankton, South Dakota; James Goodrich, Lynn Roberts, Alma Vaughan, The State Historical Society of Missouri, Columbia, Missouri; Mildred Goosman, Curator of Western Collections, Joslyn Art Museum, Omaha, Nebraska; John Hakola, Professor of History, University of Maine, Orono, Maine; Mrs. Fred Harrington, Librarian, Gail Guidry, Pictorial Curator, Missouri Historical Society, St. Louis, Missouri; Virginia Flanagan Harrison, Helena, Montana; Bryan Hay, San Diego, California; Mrs. Isabel M. Haynes, Bozeman, Montana; Martha Hilligoss, The St. Louis Public Library, St. Louis, Missouri; James D. Horan, Little Falls, New Jersey; Opal Jacobsen, Photo Librarian, Robert Pettit, Museum Curator, James Potter, State Archivist, Ann Reinert, Librarian, Nebraska State Historical Society, Lincoln, Nebraska; David Jarrett, New York City; Elizabeth Kirchner, The St. Louis Mercantile Library Association, St. Louis, Missouri; J. William Kisinger, Brownsville, Pennsylvania; Frederick S. Lightfoot, Huntington Station, New York; John Francis McDermott, St. Louis, Missouri; Harriett C. Meloy, Librarian, Brian Cockhill, Archivist, Lory Morrow, Photo Archivist, Rex Myers, Reference Librarian, Montana Historical Society, Helena, Montana; Joel Overholser, Editor, *The River Press*, Fort Benton, Montana; Norman Paulson, Curator, Frank Vyzralek, Archivist, State Historical Society of North Dakota, Bismarck, North Dakota; David R. Phillips, Chicago, Illinois; Thomas C. Power, Helena, Montana; John Reps, Professor of City and Regional Planning, Cornell University, Ithaca, New York; Jack Riley, Robert Wertenburger, U.S. Army Engineering Division/Missouri River, Omaha, Nebraska; Floyd E. Riswold, Minneapolis, Minnesota; Clements Robertson, Conservator, St. Louis Art Museum, St. Louis, Missouri; Paul Rohloff, Chicago, Illinois; Edwin C. Schafer, Barry Combs, Union Pacific Railroad Company, Omaha, Nebraska; Professor Morgan Sherwood, Department of History, University of California, Davis, California; Mildred Smock, Librarian, Free Public Library, Council Bluffs, Iowa; James Swift, Business Manager, *The Waterways Journal*, St. Louis, Missouri; Ellen Tobin, *Yankton Daily Press and Dakotan*, Yankton, South Dakota; Jane Tobin, Helena, Montana; Mrs. Shirley Walpole, Yankton, South Dakota; Captain Frederick Way, Jr., Sewickley, Pennsylvania.

BIBLIOGRAPHY

Abdill, George B., *Rails West*. Superior Publishing Company, 1960.

Abel, Annie Heloise, ed., *Tableau's Narrative of Loisel's Expedition to the Upper Missouri*. University of Oklahoma Press, 1939.

Annual Report of the Missouri River Commission, Government Printing Office, Washington, 1897.

American Heritage, The Editors of, *Trappers and Mountain Men*. American Heritage Publishing Co., 1961.

Athearn, Robert G., *Forts of the Upper Missouri*. University of Nevada Press, 1967.

Baker, I. P., *I. P. Baker Papers*. State Historical Society of South Dakota.

Baldwin, Leland D., *The Keelboat Age on Western Waters*. University of Pittsburgh Press, 1941.

Bates, Gibson, "Early Days in Siouxland." Sioux City Museum. Jan. 15, 1904.

Blair, Walter and Franklin J. Meine, *Half Horse Half Alligator, The Growth of The Mike Fink Legend*. The University of Chicago Press, 1956.

"Boat Blast Killed 200 Eighty-Six Years Ago," *The St. Joseph News-Press*, April 10, 1938.

Brackenridge, Henry Marie, *A Journal of a Voyage up the River Missouri, Performed in Eighteen Hundred and Eleven*. Coale & Maxwell, Pomery and Toy, 1816.

Bradbury, John, *Travels in the Interior of America*. Sherwood, Neely & Jones, London, 1819.

Brower, Hon. J. V., *The Missouri River and Its Utmost Source*. St. Paul, Minn., 1897.

Burton Historical Leaflet, Vol. VI, No. 4, March 1928.

Canfield, Sarah Elizabeth, "An Army Wife on the Upper Missouri," edited by Ray H. Mattison. *North Dakota Historical Quarterly*, Vol. 20, 1953.

Chappell, Phil E., "A History of the Missouri River." *Transactions of the Kansas State Historical Society 1905-1906*. Vol. IX.

Charles, John H., "Reminiscences of John H. Charles," *Proceedings of the Academy of Science and Letters of Sioux City, Iowa for 1905-06*.

Chittenden, Hiram Martin:

The American Fur Trade of The Far West, Vol. I and II, The Press of The Pioneers, Inc., 1935.

History of Early Steamboat Navigation on the Missouri River: Life and Adventures of Joseph La Barge. Ross & Haines, 1962.

Crouse, Nellis M., *La Vérendrye*. Fur Trader and Explorer. Cornell

University Press, 1956.

De Voto, Bernard, *The Course of Empire.* Houghton Mifflin, 1952.

Douglas, Walter S., "Manuel Lisa." *Missouri Historical Society Collections,* Vol. III, Nos. 3 and 4, 1911.

Donovan, Frank, *River Boats of America.* Thomas Y. Crowell Company, 1966.

Drago, Harry Sinclair, *The Steamboaters: From the Early Sidewheelers to the Big Packets.* Bramhall House, 1967.

Dunbar, Seymour, *A History of Travel in America.* Tudor Publishing Company, 1937.

Eifert, Virginia S., *Of Men and Rivers, Adventures and Discoveries Along American Waterways.* Dodd, Mead, 1966.

Fishbaugh, Charles Preston, *From Paddlewheels to Propellers.* Indiana Historical Society, 1970.

Forbes, R. B., "Steamboat Disasters." *North American Review.* 1880.

Gerber, Max E., "The Steamboat and the Indians of the Upper Missouri." *South Dakota History,* Vol. IV, No. 2, Spring 1974.

Graham, Colonel W. A., *The Custer Myth: A Source Book of Custeriana.* Bonanza Books, 1953.

Hanson, Joseph Mills, *The Conquest of the Missouri.* Holt, Rinehart & Winston, 1946.

Hauser, Samuel T., *Samuel T. Hauser Papers.* The Beinecke Rare Book and Manuscript Library, Yale University, June 1862.

Hereford, Robert A., *Old Man River, The Memories of Captain Louis Rosché,* Pioneer Steamboatman. The Caxton Printers Ltd., 1942.

History of Lafayette County, Mo. Missouri Historical Company, 1881.

Hunter, Louis C., *Steamboats on the Western Rivers: An Economic and Technological History.* Harvard University Press, 1949.

Jarrell, Myrtis, trans. and J. N. B. Hewitt, ed., *Journal of Rudolph Friederich Kurz.* University of Nebraska Press, 1970.

Jennewein, J. Leonard and Jane Boorman, editors, *Dakota Panorama.* Dakota Authors, Inc., 1973.

Johnson, Dorothy M., "Slow Boat to Benton." *Montana the Magazine of Western History,* Vol. XI, No. 1, Jan. 1961.

Karolevitz, Robert F., *Yankton: A Pioneer Past.* North Plains Press, 1972.

Kingsbury, George W., *History of Dakota Territory.* S. J. Clarke Publishing Company, 1915.

Koch, Peter, "Journal of Peter Koch— 1869 and 1870." *Historical Reprints,* State University of Montana, Missoula, 1929.

Lass, William E., *A History of Steamboating on the Upper Missouri River.* University of Nebraska Press, 1962.

Lloyd, James T., *Lloyd's Steamboat Directory.* James T. Lloyd & Co., 1856.

Mathews, A. E., *Pencil Sketches of Montana.* The author, 1868.

Mattison, Ray H., ed.:
   Henry A. Boller, Missouri River Fur Trader. Letters and Journal. The State Historical Society of North Dakota, 1966.
   "The Military Frontier on the Upper Missouri." *Nebraska History,* Vol. 37, September 1956.

McDonald, W. J., "The Missouri River and its Victims." *Missouri Historical Review,* Vol. XXI, Jan. 1927, pp. 215-242, April 1927, pp. 455-480, July 1927, pp. 581-607.

McEachran, D., *Notes of a Trip to Bow River.* The State Historical Society of North Dakota, 1881.

Morrison, John H., *History of American Steam Navigation.* Stephen Daye Press, 1958.

Napton, John, "My Trip on the Imperial in 1867." *Contributions to the Historical Society of Montana,* Vol. VIII, 1917.

Nichol, Ralph E., *Steamboat Navigation on the Missouri River with Special Reference to Yankton and Vicinity.* Thesis. Department of History, University of South Dakota, 1936.

O'Connor, Rose A., *Sioux City — A True Story of How It Grew.* Hoyt-Purcell, Sioux City, 1932.

Oglesby, Richard Edward, *Manuel Lisa and the Missouri Fur Trade.* University of Oklahoma Press, 1963.

"Old Lexington Residents Recall Sinking of Steamboat Saluda and Loss of Life that Occured," *Marshall Daily Democrat News,* May 2, 1932.

Parker, Theodore R., "William J. Kountz, Superintendent of River Transportation Under McClellan, 1861-62." *The Western Pennsylvania Historical Magazine,* Vol. 21, Dec. 1938.

Petersen, William J., ed., "The Log of the *Henry M. Shreve* to Fort Benton in 1869." *Mississippi Valley Historical Review,* March 1945.

Porter, Dr. H. R., "Thrilling Incidents in the Life of a Bismarck Physician, A Remarkable Steamboat Ride." *Plains Talk,* State Historical Society of North Dakota Newsletter, Vol. 2, No. 3, Fall 1972.

Power, T. C., *T. C. Power Papers,* Montana Historical Society.

Rees, Ida Mae, *Sioux City As A Steamboat Port 1856-1873.* Thesis. Department of History, University of South Dakota, 1967.

Richardson, Albert D., *Beyond the Mississippi.* American Publishing Company, 1867.

River Press, The, Fort Benton, Montana, June 16, 1937.

Rossi, Paul A. and David C. Hunt, *The Art of the Old West: From the Collection of the Gilcrease Institute.* Alfred A. Knopf, 1971.

"Steamboat Disasters." *North American Review,* Vol. 50, Jan. 1840.

Sunder, John E., *The Fur Trade on the Upper Missouri 1840-1865.* University of Oklahoma Press, 1965.

Taft, Robert, *Artists and Illustrators of the Old West.* Scribner's, 1953.

Thorp, Raymond W. and Robert Bunker, *Crow Killer.* The New American Library, Inc., 1969.

Tilden, Freeman, *Following the Frontier with F. Jay Haynes: Pioneer Photographer of the Old West.* Alfred A. Knopf, 1964.

Timmen, Fritz, *Blow for the Landing.* The Caxton Printers Ltd., 1973.

Utley, Robert M., *Custer Battlefield.* National Park Service, U.S. Dept. of the Interior, 1969.

Vestal, Stanley, *The Missouri.* University of Nebraska Press, 1964.

The Walters Art Gallery, *The West of Alfred Jacob Miller.* University of Oklahoma Press, 1951.

Way, Frederick, Jr., *Way's Directory of Western Rivers Packets.* F. Way, Jr., 1950.

Wayman, Norbury L., *Life on the River.* Crown Publishers, Inc., 1971.

Wiltsey, Norman B., *Brave Warriors.* The Caxton Printers Ltd., 1964.

Winship, George Parker, "The Coronado Expedition, 1540-1542," *Fourteenth Annual Report of the Bureau of Ethnology to the Secretary of the Smithsonian Institution, 1892-93.* Government Printing Office, Washington, 1896.

Winther, Oscar Osburn, *Transportation Frontier, Trans-Mississippi West 1865-1890.* Holt, Rinehart & Winston, 1964.

Wood, Charles R., *The Northern Pacific: Main Street of the Northwest.* Superior Publishing Company, 1968.